Marginalised Communities in Higher Education

Drawing on examples from nine countries across five continents, this book offers anyone interested in the future of higher education the opportunity to understand how communities become marginalised and how this impacts on their access to learning and their ability to thrive as students.

Focusing on groups that suffer directly through discriminatory practices or indirectly through distinct forms of sociocultural disadvantage, this book brings to light communities about which little has been written and where research efforts are in their relative infancy. Each chapter documents the experiences of a group and provides insights that have a wider reach and gives voice to those that are often unheard. The book concludes with a new conceptualisation of the social forces that lead to marginalisation in higher education.

This cutting-edge book is a must read for higher education researchers, policy makers and students interested in access to education, sociology of education, development studies and cultural studies.

Neil Harrison is an Associate Professor and Deputy Director of the Rees Centre at the University of Oxford, UK.

Graeme Atherton is Head of AccessHE and Director of the National Education Opportunities Network.

Society for Research into Higher Education Series

Series Editors:
Jennifer M. Case, Virginia Tech, USA
Jeroen Huisman, Ghent University, Belgium

This exciting new series aims to publish cutting edge research and discourse that reflects the rapidly changing world of higher education, examined in a global context. Encompassing topics of wide international relevance, the series includes every aspect of the international higher education research agenda, from strategic policy formulation and impact to pragmatic advice on best practice in the field.

Titles in the series:

The Education Ecology of Universities
Integrating Learning, Strategy and the Academy
Robert A. Ellis and Peter Goodyear

Designing Effective Feedback Processes in Higher Education
A Learning-Focused Approach
Naomi Winstone and David Carless

Reimagining the Higher Education Student
Constructing and Contesting Identities
Edited by Rachel Brooks and Sarah O'Shea

Exploring Diary Methods in Higher Education Research
Opportunities, Choices and Challenges
Edited by Xuemeng Cao and Emily F. Henderson

Marginalised Communities in Higher Education
Disadvantage, Mobility and Indigeneity
Edited by Neil Harrison and Graeme Atherton

For more information about this series, please visit: https://www.routledge.com/Research-into-Higher-Education/book-series/SRHE

Marginalised Communities in Higher Education

Disadvantage, Mobility and Indigeneity

Edited by Neil Harrison and Graeme Atherton

LONDON AND NEW YORK

First published 2021
by Routledge
2 Park Square, Milton Park, Abingdon, Oxon OX14 4RN

and by Routledge
605 Third Avenue, New York, NY 10158

Routledge is an imprint of the Taylor & Francis Group, an informa business

© 2021 selection and editorial matter, Neil Harrison and Graeme Atherton; individual chapters, the contributors

The right of Neil Harrison and Graeme Atherton to be identified as the authors of the editorial material, and of the authors for their individual chapters, has been asserted in accordance with sections 77 and 78 of the Copyright, Designs and Patents Act 1988.

All rights reserved. No part of this book may be reprinted or reproduced or utilised in any form or by any electronic, mechanical, or other means, now known or hereafter invented, including photocopying and recording, or in any information storage or retrieval system, without permission in writing from the publishers.

Trademark notice: *Product or corporate names may be trademarks or registered trademarks, and are used only for identification and explanation without intent to infringe.*

British Library Cataloguing-in-Publication Data
A catalogue record for this book is available from the British Library

Library of Congress Cataloging-in-Publication Data
Names: Harrison, Neil, editor. | Atherton, Graeme, editor.
Title: Marginalised communities in higher education : disadvantage, mobility and indigeneity / Edited by Neil Harrison and Graeme Atherton.
Identifiers: LCCN 2020053518 (print) | LCCN 2020053519 (ebook) | ISBN 9780367264550 (hardback) | ISBN 9780367264574 (paperback) | ISBN 9780429293399 (ebook)
Subjects: LCSH: Students with social disabilities--Education (Higher)--Cross-cultural studies. | Educational equalization. | Educational mobility. | Indigenous peoples--Education (Higher)
Classification: LCC LC4069.6 .M37 2021 (print) | LCC LC4069.6 (ebook) | DDC 379.2/6--dc23
LC record available at https://lccn.loc.gov/2020053518
LC ebook record available at https://lccn.loc.gov/2020053519

ISBN: 978-0-367-26455-0 (hbk)
ISBN: 978-0-367-26457-4 (pbk)
ISBN: 978-0-429-29339-9 (ebk)

Typeset in Galliard
by SPi Technologies India Pvt Ltd (Straive)

Contents

Series Editor's Introduction vii
List of contributors viii

1 Introduction: Marginalised communities in higher education 1
NEIL HARRISON AND GRAEME ATHERTON

SECTION I
Disadvantage 13

2 The journeys of care-experienced students in England and Scotland 15
NEIL HARRISON, LINDA O'NEILL AND GRAHAM CONNELLY

3 The collateral impact of post-prison supervision on college experiences in the United States 36
LINDSEY LIVINGSTON RUNELL

4 'More than just saving the government care costs': Re-presenting student carers' narratives in the United Kingdom 48
JACQUELINE PRIEGO-HERNÁNDEZ AND DEBBIE HOLLEY

5 Genderism and trans students in Hong Kong higher education 64
DIANA K. KWOK

6 The marginalisation of religious students in higher education in the United Kingdom 79
JACQUELINE STEVENSON

SECTION II
Mobility 95

7 Expectations, experiences and anticipated outcomes of supporting refugee students in Germany: Systems theoretical analysis of organizational semantics 97
JANA BERG

8 Irish Travellers and higher education 119
ANDREW LOXLEY AND FERGAL FINNEGAN

9 Sámi peoples' educational challenges in higher education and migration in Finland 139
PIGGA KESKITALO

10 Getting to university: Experiences of students from rural areas in South Africa 156
LISA LUCAS, KIBBIE NAIDOO AND SUE TIMMIS

SECTION III
Indigeneity 177

11 Improving higher education success for Australian Indigenous peoples: Examples of promising practice 179
KIM ROBERTSON, JAMES A. SMITH AND STEVEN LARKIN

12 The Orang Asli and higher education access in Malaysia: Realising the dream 202
GRAEME ATHERTON

13 Higher education and disadvantaged groups in India 216
N.V. VARGHESE

14 Concluding thoughts: Making meaning from diverse narratives 232
NEIL HARRISON AND GRAEME ATHERTON

Index 244

Series Editors' Introduction

This series, co-published by the Society for Research into Higher Education and Routledge Books, aims to provide, in an accessible manner, cutting-edge scholarly thinking and inquiry that reflects the rapidly changing world of higher education, examined in a global context.

Encompassing topics of wide international relevance, the series includes every aspect of the international higher education research agenda, from strategic policy formulation and impact to pragmatic advice on best practice in the field. Each book in the series aims to meet at least one of the principle aims of the Society: to advance knowledge, to enhance practice and to inform policy.

In this edited volume, Neil Harrison and Graeme Atherton address the theme of marginalised communities in higher education. The collective aim of the contributors has been to write about groups that have largely been absent from the literature on disadvantage and inequality in higher education. The chapters deal with a large variety of marginalised groups across a wide spectrum of national contexts, ranging from student carers, transgender students, students with religious beliefs, to students coming from rural and Indigenous communities. Importantly, the focus on marginalisation raises the question of who marginalises and how. In the final chapter, the editors offer food for thought for actions by policymakers and university managers to contribute to a more inclusive higher education.

Jennifer M. Case
Jeroen Huisman

Contributors

Graeme Atherton is Head of AccessHE and Director of the National Education Opportunities Network.

Jana Berg is a Researcher at the German Centre for Higher Education Research and Science Studies in Hannover.

Graham Connelly is an Honorary Senior Research Fellow at the Centre for Excellence for Children's Care and Protection (CELCIS) in the School of Social Work and Social Policy at the University of Strathclyde.

Fergal Finnegan is an Assistant Professor at the Department of Adult and Community Education at Maynooth University.

Neil Harrison is an Associate Professor and Deputy Director of the Rees Centre in the Department of Education at the University of Oxford.

Debbie Holley is the Professor of Learning Innovation in the Faculty of Health and Social Sciences at Bournemouth University.

Pigga Keskitalo holds academic posts at the University of Helsinki and the University of Lapland, and is also a Member of the Sámi Parliament.

Diana K. Kwok is an Associate Professor in the Department of Special Education and Counselling at the Education University of Hong Kong.

Steven Larkin is the Chief Executive Officer at the Batchelor Institute of Indigenous Tertiary Education.

Lindsey Livingston Runell is an Associate Professor in the Criminal Justice Department at Kutztown University of Pennsylvania.

Andrew Loxley is an Associate Professor in the School of Education at Trinity College Dublin.

Lisa Lucas is a Reader in Higher Education in the School of Education at the University of Bristol.

Kibbie Naidoo is Head of Professional Academic Staff Development at the University of Johannesburg.

Linda O'Neill is Education Lead at the Centre for Excellence for Children's Care and Protection (CELCIS) in the School of Social Work and Social Policy at the University of Strathclyde.

Jacqueline Priego-Hernández is a Senior Lecturer in Social Psychology at the University of Portsmouth.

Kim Robertson is the Senior Analyst, Indigenous Policies and Programs in the Office of Pro Vice-Chancellor Indigenous Leadership at Charles Darwin University.

James A. Smith is a Professor and a Father Frank Flynn Fellow at the Menzies School of Health Research.

Jacqueline Stevenson is a Professor of the Sociology of Education and the Director of the Lifelong Learning Centre at the University of Leeds.

Sue Timmis is a Reader in Higher Education in the School of Education at the University of Bristol.

N.V. Varghese is Vice Chancellor of the National University of Educational Planning and Administration, New Delhi.

Chapter 1

Introduction
Marginalised communities in higher education

Neil Harrison and Graeme Atherton

Internationally, concerns about differential access to, and contrasting experiences of, higher education have grown over the last 75 years. After the Second World War, higher education across the globe was typified by elite systems (Trow, 1973), where few members of society had the opportunity to attend by dint of the availability of places, qualification thresholds, and the direct and indirect costs of participation. Students were disproportionately men from the middle and upper classes, with little or no support to enable disadvantaged groups or individuals to participate. In many countries, higher education had been primarily a colonial pursuit with a small number of universities predominately serving the expatriate European community rather than indigenous peoples.

Perhaps the first chips in the wall came with post-war schemes like the so-called GI Bill in the United States (US) and Commonwealth Reconstruction Training Scheme in Australia that gave unprecedented educational opportunity to service veterans, including the right and means to attend higher education (Forsyth, 2015; Olson, 1973). Meanwhile, the exigencies of war had opened up new social and economic spaces for women and minority ethnic communities in many countries, leading to a rapidly-escalating demand for concomitant educational opportunities. Arguably, these threads of social change forced universities to think – perhaps for the first time – about how they might reconfigure themselves to accommodate new types of students with different needs, ambitions and experiences. Elsewhere, the retreat of colonial powers from the late 1940s onwards saw higher education opened up to previously excluded national and ethnic groups, albeit that access was still only available to a tiny proportion of the population within small and elite higher education sectors that often did not enjoy legitimacy in the eyes of local population (Jensen et al., 2016).

In most mid and higher income countries, the late 20th century was marked by a rapid growth in the provision of higher education places. In the United Kingdom (UK), for example, the proportion of young people participating rose from around 5% in the 1960s to 50% by the late 2010s, as well as opportunities opening up for older learners (Harrison, 2017; National Committee of Inquiry into Higher Education, 1997). Marginson (2016a) argues that this global phenomenon was driven in large part by growing social demand, especially from the burgeoning urban middle classes who valorised education as a means of maintaining or extending their socioeconomic status. However, this opening up of supply also provided new opportunities.

Widening access in the 21st century

Over the last twenty years, the political and academic spotlight has increasingly shifted to focus on which individuals and communities have access to higher education. This is partly due to concerns about international competitiveness in the 'knowledge age' and partly as a result of a wider emancipatory movements to address structural inequalities and expand educational opportunities to groups who have been deliberately excluded or whose ability to participate has been curtailed by legal constraints, personal circumstances or socioeconomic privilege (Marginson, 2016b).

In wealthier nations with mass systems of higher education, this attention has historically focused on common sites of inequality like social class, gender, ethnicity and disability, with a rich policy and practice landscape and a significant research literature (e.g. Bathmaker et al., 2016; Boliver, 2015; Brunner et al., 2006; Burke, 2012; Clancy and Goastellec, 2007; Koucký et al., 2010; Meyer et al., 2013; Reay et al., 2010; Waller et al., 2016). Intersectional studies have brought to light the ways in which these inequalities interact to mitigate or intensify disadvantages; this has, for example, led to concerns about the opportunities and experiences afforded to white working class boys in the UK (Atherton and Mazhari, 2019). Often due to the actions of charities and other social activists, attention has now started to turn to less-readily apparent groups who are subject to specific forms of disadvantage.

In low income nations, which tend to retain elite systems where higher education generally remains only available to a small proportion of the population, there are now attempts to expand higher education to include new social, ethnic and cultural groups (Chien et al., 2017; Salmi, 2018). However, continuing discrimination – direct or indirect – often means that these new opportunities are not equitably distributed, while the large-scale movement of people in response to global crises such as conflict and climate change is causing new strains on educational systems where people seek a better life through education in their adopted country (UNESCO, 2019).

Marginalisation – of whom and by whom?

The rationale behind this book is to explore new or re-emerging forms of disadvantage seeded by the processes of expansion and emancipation outlined above. Our aim has been to collate and present a collection of individual chapters that engage with groups that have generally been absent from the literature on disadvantage and inequality in higher education, drawn from different national contexts and distinct sets of circumstances.

While evocative, the term 'marginalisation' is slippery and we have used it somewhat reluctantly in framing this book. It brings to mind ideas about pushing to the edges of sociocultural spaces – people who are present, but peripheral and unrecognised. Marginalised students are in our universities, but they are unlike other students in key ways that compromise their opportunities to engage and thrive in the environment. Even alongside better known disadvantaged groups, marginalised communities may appear to policymakers, university staff and other students as out-of-step, displaced and even a distraction from the main business.

Messiou (2012) cites the United Nations Development Programme (1996, p. 1) in defining marginalisation as 'the state of being considered unimportant, undesirable, unworthy, insignificant and different resulting in inequity, unfairness, deprivation and enforced lack of access to mainstream power'. We will come on to question whether this might be too narrow, with some people more passively marginalised by collective indifference, uncaring bureaucratic systems or indirect exclusions from power that are *unenforced*, but nevertheless pervasive. Furthermore, Mowat (2015) argues that marginalisation is more than a state of being, but encompasses 'a sense that one does not belong and, in so doing, to feel that one is neither a valued member of a community and able to make a valuable contribution within that community nor able to access the range of services and/or opportunities open to others'. Messiou (2006, 2012) draws an interesting distinction between whether putatively marginalised learners feel that they are marginalised and whether this marginalisation is recognised by society at large.

As we will see, marginalisation is not a crude 'numbers game'. Some of the groups examined in the two chapters are indeed very small (e.g. transgender students in Hong Kong), but others are numerically large (e.g. rural students in South Africa) or even dominant (e.g. religious students in the UK). Social power does not come from weight of numbers alone and those who have power in some social fields may lack it in others. As Petrou et al. (2009) note, 'Societies often have the tendency to construct margins, considering those that are differentiated from the majority or the accepted normality to constitute a deviance.'

Similarly, the vectors for marginalisation that the chapters explore are varied. Direct forms of discrimination from mainstream society are readily apparent for some groups, but the marginalisation is more subtle in others, where traditional heritages, lifestyles and economic niches have been inexorably pushed to the fringes by the modern world (e.g. the Sami of Scandinavia or Traveller communities in Ireland). Some, like the indigenous peoples of Australia, continue to wrestle with the legacies of colonialism that saw them historically excluded from power and access to basic services like education, despite more recent efforts to provide legally protected rights.

Subtler still are those forms of marginalisation that are about time and space, where access to education is a constant balance between the constraints of family life (e.g. carers in the UK) or bureaucracy (e.g. parolees in the US). There are also examples of groups that have been marginalised suddenly or through their entry into new contexts, including those losing positions of relative power or prestige as a result of war or natural disasters (e.g. refugees in Germany).

There are therefore meaningful challenges in using the language of marginalisation in the way that we have done. Indeed, Messiou (2017) questions whether a focus on marginalised groups is appropriate, given that categorisations tend to obscure individual challenges, while the process of identifying and researching these groups may risk intensifying the stigmatisation or subjective marginalisation that they feel. Nevertheless, there is some consensus that there is considerable value in sensitive and ethical research. For example, Mowat (2015) argues that questions such as what it means to be marginalised and what people are marginalised from 'can only be fully addressed by looking at the experiences of individuals' – a starting point before starting an active dialogue where findings are shared between researcher and researched to add new insight and act as a stepping stone to practical action (Messiou, 2012).

It is in this spirit that we hope that this collection will contribute to this discourse within universities and with national policymakers. We have brought together what is currently known about twelve different communities of students in higher education whose stories are less commonly told and who experience varying forms of marginalisation in the hope that they will spark new conversations about these groups, as well as shedding light on the phenomenon of marginalisation more widely.

Marginalisation in higher education

As outlined above, there is a rich literature around disadvantage and inequalities in higher education. Some of this has focused on marginalised communities and their access to higher education, but very little has specifically been conceptualised in terms of marginalisation as a specific phenomenon or process by which those communities are excluded – nor on the links between these communities and others that are subject to similar processes. It is this space that this book aims to fill and we pause briefly to review the literature that does exist.

Based on their work in schools, Ainscow, Booth and Dyson (2006) view educational marginalisation as resulting from failures in ensuring the *presence*, *participation* and *achievement* of learners. In their study of indigenous Australians in higher education, Gale and Mills (2013) argue that it is insufficient to simply provide places for marginalised groups – policymakers and educators need to open up *spaces* where they are welcomed and valued. Walker and Mkwananzi (2015) note a similar challenge in South Africa, where the presence of Black students has risen rapidly with the reconfiguration of the higher education sector, but their ability to succeed remains compromised. Petrou et al. (2009) and Teranishi et al. (2015) highlight the pervasive and persistent link between socioeconomic disadvantage and marginalisation from education, the latter focusing on the situation of undocumented migrant students in the US who have no access to state support.

Gale and Mills (2013) focus on the centrality of learning to inclusion for marginalised groups, as the core function of higher education. They argue that pedagogy not only provides access to a curriculum, but also a means of signalling a wider intent and legitimacy to those groups. Similarly, Petrou et al. (2009) caution against well-intentioned initiatives predicated on students assimilating into alien educational forms, stressing that the role of educational renewal should be to identify divisive pedagogic practices and seek to remove them. On a more positive note, Mkwananzi and Mukwanbo (2019) highlight the potential role for online pedagogies in enabling the participation of vulnerable migrant students in South Africa.

Interestingly, Mowat (2015) asserts that for a group to be considered marginalised, there must be a sense of shared (perhaps even stereotypical) experience, but also a conceptualisation of an idealised state from which the group is excluded. Perhaps this begins to explain the lack of attention that such groups have received to date: there is no agreement about how a 'perfect' higher education system should look across time and space, with new forms waxing and waning in response to globalised market forces that also open up new forms of marginalisation (Balarin, 2011).

Structure of the book

In conceiving this book, we have eschewed chapters on higher-level sites of inequality such as gender, social class and disability. It is not that these topics are unimportant, but rather that these have received – and continue to receive – significant attention. Our desire has been to bring to light communities about which little has been written and where research efforts are in their relative infancy. As a result, some of the chapters are necessarily based around small-scale studies, high-level descriptions or analyses of research gaps.

As an organising principle, we have divided the chapters across three sections broadly representing different types of marginalised communities. Clearly these are not distinct and some of the chapters could have been placed in multiple sections, reflecting the multifaceted nature of the phenomenon.

The first section focuses on ***Disadvantage***. This takes in both direct forms of disadvantage caused by discrimination and stigmatisation, as well as more subtle forms of indirect disadvantage arising from a mismatch between students' lived lives and the bureaucratic milieu of higher education with its timetables, teaching spaces, policy documents and assessment deadlines. These forms of temporal, spatial and cultural dislocation from the mainstream student experience are perhaps less immediately obvious, but potentially no less marginalising. For some groups, the disadvantage relates to the legacy of their earlier lives, with higher education offering a sharp opportunity for transformational rebuilding – yet their likelihood of accessing it is low.

- In *Chapter 2*, Harrison, O'Neill and Connelly synthesise the findings from two studies of students in higher education in England and Scotland who spent some or all of their childhood in the care of the state. Children are generally taken into care due to neglect or abuse in the family home, which leads to profound impacts in terms of educational and social disruption, mental health and low expectations from adults – these can sometimes be further worsened by their experiences in care. Comprising around 1% of the student body, care-experienced adults have low higher education participation rates and high rates of early withdrawal. This chapter examines six underlying themes that contribute to these patterns, as well as outlining recent development in policy and practice.
- In *Chapter 3*, Runell focuses on individuals that are currently on parole following a period of incarceration in the prison system in the US. Drawing on narrative interviews, she explores their motivations for returning to education as part of a transformational process of rehabilitation, and particularly the practical difficulties associated with navigating between the mutually restrictive practices of the parole and higher education systems. The negative attitudes and low expectations of some parole officers is highlighted, along with the everyday struggles to achieve the necessary freedoms and support when their lives are heavily curtailed.
- In *Chapter 4*, Priego-Hernández and Holley shine a light on the lives of a potentially very large group of students whose experiences of higher education are often completely invisible. No official data are yet collected in the UK about students who have substantial caring responsibilities for family members – children, parents or others. Priego-Hernández and Holley report on the results of a photo elicitation study that explores the everyday compromises that student carers have to make and their very different experiences of engaging with university. The constraints on their time and finances, which are often unpredictable, as well as the impact on their own mental health, weigh heavily on their ability to engage successfully with higher education.
- In *Chapter 5*, Kwok brings together a series of studies into the lives of transgender students in Hong Kong. A very small group in absolute numbers, they are subject to extreme discrimination and stigmatisation in a society which is heavily influenced by both its Confucian heritage beliefs about family life and traditional Christian beliefs about gender

identity. While there has been significant progress in recent years in providing legal rights and protections for other minority groups such as the lesbian, gay and bisexual communities, transgender students continue to have realistic fears about their safety and their acceptance by higher education institutions and the wider student body. The chapter concludes with recommendations to policymakers and support professionals.
- In *Chapter 6*, Stevenson reflects on the potential marginalisation of a large student group that often has considerable presence in higher education and society more widely – namely, students with religious beliefs. Institutions in the UK are required to produce policy documents on religion and belief as part of government equality legislation. Drawing an analysis of twenty examples, Stevenson uses the capabilities approach to argue that the increasingly secular nature of higher education in the UK, coupled with a moral panic about Islamic radicalisation, is effectively curtailing religious students' lives, identities and freedom of expression, thereby pushing many to the margins of institutional life.

The second section focuses on **Mobility**. The chapters in this section have coalesced around the challenges that arise from movement – voluntary or involuntary, of recent origin or ancient roots. We are in a period of unprecedented human mobility, although the global Covid-19 pandemic that is ongoing at the time of writing (early 2020) demonstrates the fragility of our ability to move and the consequences of doing so. However, higher education is traditionally predicated on learning taking place in a fixed location, with embedded expectations of the sociocultural heritage of the students present. What happens when students are unable to access these locations or when they arrive with unfamiliar heritages? Technology, which often serves to erode ideas about the fixedness of higher education, can itself be a dimension of marginalisation for communities which have little access to the internet due to poverty or remoteness.

- In *Chapter 7*, Berg examines the response to a rapid increase in refugees among German higher education institutions in the late 2010s. Using the systems theoretical approach, she explores how the institutions have struggled to fit refugees into their longstanding student definitions and configuration of support systems. On the one hand, they are 'international', but not in the same sense as other internationally-mobile students who generally come from positions of relative privilege. On the other hand, they have additional challenges compared to other 'home' students – e.g. with language and acculturation into the German education system. Responses have therefore been *ad hoc* and precarious, with institutional leaders waiting to see what future government policy will bring before adjusting their organisational configurations further.
- In *Chapter 8*, Loxley and Finnegan place a forensic analysis of the access to higher education of the Irish Traveller community in the context of

the broader policy approach of the Irish government to widening access to higher education. Irish Travellers have a long established place in the history of the country, but it is only relatively recently that concerted work has been undertaken to understand the demographic and cultural nature of the community. Loxley and Finnegan point to the significant focus placed by policymakers in Ireland on widening access to higher education and specific attention placed on access for the Traveller community. However, progress has been slow and they argue that there is a real need for more work to understand the experiences of Travellers in higher (and compulsory) education in order to shape policy.

- In *Chapter 9*, Keskitalo provides an overview of the educational and linguistic history of the indigenous Sámi people of Scandinavia – a community with roots in traditional livelihoods such as hunting, fishing and reindeer herding. In particular, she charts the history of urban migration in Finland in order to seek out educational opportunities, often in the face of considerable social and linguistic discrimination and pressure to assimilate into the majority culture. While the Sámi community now benefits from targeted support programmes, tensions remain. Keskitalo's account is enlivened by narratives from contemporary Sámi who have migrated and their feelings of physical and cultural dislocation.
- In *Chapter 10*, Lucas, Naidoo and Timmins report on the findings of an extensive study of students drawn from the rural areas of South Africa, analysing co-created data from narrative interviews, group discussions and illustrative photographs from their lived lives. They focus on the unique ways in which rurality acts as a barrier to accessing higher education, including the unavailability of reliable information in schools and community norms that are hostile or dismissive. In particular, they discuss how contemporary higher education is inherently technocratic in its procedures, relying heavily on the internet to receive applications and process registrations, while many rural areas have little or no connectivity – and what is available is costly in the context of poorer communities.

The third section focuses on ***Indigeneity*** and the historical legacy of colonialism and internal repression that saw indigenous peoples excluded from access to higher education in their own lands. In some instances, these peoples were utterly excluded by racist laws that prevented them from participating. In others, the exclusion was educational and economic – that they did not have access to schooling that afforded them relevant entry qualifications or the financial wherewithal to fund study. In some cases, the peoples themselves had little interest in participating in learning and systems that were irrelevant to – or antagonistic towards – their own cultures. The twin trends of post-colonialism at the national level and the decolonisation of higher education itself are slowly opening up new spaces for indigenous peoples, although they generally remain woefully under-represented. These communities pose a particular challenge for policy and practice, requiring a balance between economic and educational development and their inherent threats to long-established and cherished ways of life.

- In *Chapter 11*, Robertson, Smith and Larkin consider the case of Aboriginal and Torres Strait Islander Australians who have long been historically excluded from higher education in Australia. Improving indigenous education outcomes is now a key focus of many national education policies but acknowledging the value of the voices of Aboriginal and Torres Strait Islander student, staff and researcher perspectives is still not embedded into what government and universities do. The chapter focuses on the experience of one university including interviews with indigenous students and staff to highlight enablers and barriers to access and success where indigenous students are concerned. It highlights how practical steps to foster ownership of the educational experience amongst indigenous students are key.
- In *Chapter 12*, Varghese examines inequalities in access, participation and success in one of the largest higher education systems in the world. Looking at India, Varghese describes in detail how the caste system in India shapes the lives of those from the lower caste groups. These groups who are classified as those from scheduled tribes and scheduled castes do benefit from a quota system for higher education admission which means there are places reserved in higher education for them. However, despite such a quota participation in higher education for scheduled tribes, participation from scheduled castes remains below the average for the country and as Varghese argues they are less likely to achieve their potential when they enter higher education. He argues that in order for those most marginalised groups in India to enter and succeed in higher education changes in institutional cultures will be required.
- In *Chapter 13*, Atherton discusses the relationship between the Orang Asli communities in Malaysia and higher education. The Orang Asli is a term used to describe a heterogeneous group of indigenous communities living in rural Malaysia. The majority of Orang Asli do not complete compulsory schooling and many live a subsistence but sustainable lifestyle. Those from the Orang Asli community only enter higher education in very small numbers. There are however attempts to address this by policymakers in Malaysia, but such attempts occur against the backdrop of a society where Orang Asli still face discrimination and a higher education system already divided on ethnic grounds between the broader indigenous Malay community and ethnic Chinese people. The chapter points to the potential for higher education in Malaysia to become more open to the Orang Asli and engage with them in order to re-balance their relationship with the education system.

Conclusion

We hope that these chapters will provide insight into a range of marginalised communities in higher education. They are clearly not intended to be exhaustive and there are many others that could have been included – in many cases, there is simply no research yet available, so we have necessarily been opportunistic in approaching authors. We believe that they shine a new light on the experiences of students who are often invisible or unconsidered, both in terms of the specific groups on which they focus and as part of a wider conceptual understanding of how communities can find themselves marginalised in diverse ways.

In the concluding chapter, we attempt to make meaning from these diverse accounts by focusing first on the individual constraints placed on the agency of members of marginalised communities – identifying parallels around whether, how, when and where they are able to participate in higher education. We then use these individual challenges to explore the processes by which marginalisation occurs in order to provide insights into possible solutions for policymakers, managers and practitioners.

References

Ainscow, M., T. Booth, and A. Dyson (2006) *Improving schools, developing inclusion.* London: Routledge.

Atherton, G. and T. Mazhari (2019) *Working class heroes: Understanding access to higher education for white students from lower socio-economic backgrounds.* London: London Higher.

Balarin, M. (2011) Global citizenship and marginalisation: contributions towards a political economy of global citizenship, *Globalisation, Societies and Education* 9(3–4): 355–366.

Bathmaker, A.-M., N. Ingram, J. Abrahams, A. Hoare, R. Waller and H. Bradley (2016) *Higher education, social class and social mobility: The degree generation.* London: Palgrave MacMillan.

Boliver, V. (2015) Exploring ethnic inequalities in admission to Russell Group universities, *Sociology* 50(2): 247–266.

Brunner, J., P. Santiago, C. García Gaudilla, J. Gerlach and L. Velho (2006) *Thematic review of tertiary education.* Paris: Organisation for Economic Co-operation and Development.

Burke, P.-J. (2012) *The right to higher education: Beyond widening participation.* Abingdon: Routledge.

Chien, C.-L., P. Montjouridès and H. van der Pol (2017) Global trends of access to and equity in postsecondary education, in A. Mountford-Zimdars and N. Harrison (eds.) *Access to higher education: theoretical perspectives and contemporary challenges* (pp. 3–32). Abingdon: Routledge.

Clancy, P. and G. Goastellec (2007) Exploring access and equity in higher education: Policy and performance in a comparative perspective, *Higher Education Quarterly* 61(2): 136–154.

Forsyth, H. (2015) Expanding higher education: institutional responses in Australia from the post-war era to the 1970s, *Paedagogica Historica: International Journal of the History of Education* 51(3): 365–380.

Gale, T. and C. Mills (2013) Creating spaces in higher education for marginalised Australians: Principles for socially Inclusive pedagogies, *Enhancing Learning in the Social Sciences* 5(2): 7–19.

Harrison, N. (2017) Patterns of participation in a period of change: Social trends in English higher education from 2000 to 2016, in R. Waller, N. Ingram and M. Ward (eds.) *Higher education and social inequalities: University admissions, experiences, and outcomes* (pp. 54–80). Abingdon: Routledge.

Jensen, S., H. Adriansen and L. Madsen (2016) Do 'African' universities exist? Setting the scene, in H. Adriansen, L. Madsen and S. Jensen (eds.) *Higher education and capacity building in Africa: The geography and power of knowledge under changing conditions* (pp. 12–28). Abingdon: Routledge.

Koucký, J., A. Bartušek and J. Kovařovic (2010) *Who gets a degree? Access to tertiary education in Europe 1950–2009*. Prague: Charles University.

Marginson, S. (2016a) High participation systems of higher education, *The Journal of Higher Education* 87(2): 243–271.

Marginson, S. (2016b) The worldwide trend to high participation higher education: Dynamics of social stratification in inclusive systems, *Higher Education* 72: 413–434.

Messiou, K. (2006) Understanding marginalisation in education: The voice of children, *European Journal of Psychology of Education* 21(3): 305–318.

Messiou, K. (2012) *Confronting marginalisation in education: A framework for promoting inclusion*. London: Routledge.

Messiou, K. (2017) Research in the field of inclusive education: Time for a rethink?, *International Journal of Inclusive Education* 21(2): 146–159.

Meyer, H., E. St. John, M. Chankseliani and L. Uribe (2013) *Fairness in access to higher education in a global perspective*. Rotterdam: Sense Publishers.

Mkwananzi, F. and P. Mukwanbo (2019) Widening participation in higher education for marginalised migrant youth through flexible teaching and learning mechanisms, *Widening Participation and Lifelong Learning* 21(2): 100–119.

Mowat, J. (2015) Towards a new conceptualisation of marginalisation, *European Educational Research Journal* 14(5): 454–476.

National Committee of Inquiry into Higher Education (1997) *Higher education in the learning society*. Norwich: HMSO.

Olson, K. (1973) The GI Bill and higher education: Surprise and success, *American Quarterly* 25(5): 596–610.

Petrou, A., P. Angelides and J. Leigh (2009) Beyond the difference: from the margins to inclusion, *International Journal of Inclusive Education* 13(5): 439–448.

Reay, D., G. Crozier and J. Clayton (2010) 'Fitting in' or 'standing out': Working-class students in UK higher education, *British Educational Research Journal* 36(1): 107–124.

Salmi, J. (2018) *All around the world: Higher education equity policies across the globe*. Indianapolis: Lumina Foundation.

Teranishi, R., C. Suárez-Orozco and M. Suárez-Orozco (2015) *In the shadows of the ivory tower: Undocumented undergraduates and the liminal state of immigration reform*. Los Angeles: University of California.

Trow, M. (1973) *Problems in the transition from elite to mass higher education.* Berkeley: Carnegie Commission on Higher Education.

United Nations Development Programme (1996) *Georgia human development report 1996: Glossary.* New York: United Nations.

United Nations Educational, Scientific and Cultural Organisation (2019) *Migration, displacement and education: Building bridges, not walls,* Paris: UNESCO.

Walker, M. and F. Mkwananzi (2015) Challenges in accessing higher education: A case study of marginalised young people in one South African informal settlement, *International Journal of Educational Development* 40: 40–49.

Waller, R., N. Ingram and M. Ward (eds.) (2016) *Higher education and social inequalities: University admissions, experiences, and outcomes.* Abingdon: Routledge.

Section I

Disadvantage

Chapter 2

The journeys of care-experienced students in England and Scotland

Neil Harrison, Linda O'Neill and Graham Connelly

Introduction

At any time, there are approaching 100,000 children in the care of the state in the United Kingdom (UK), including 70,000 in England and 15,000 in Scotland. For the majority, this occurs because they have been subject to neglect or abuse within their birth family. Their caring arrangements vary widely, but can include foster care, residential homes and kinship care within the extended family. The amount of time spent in care can also vary, from a single day to the whole of childhood. Local authorities, or health and social care trusts in Northern Ireland, have responsibilities for a child's welfare as the 'corporate parent'.[1]

Children who are in care at age 16 are deemed to be 'care leavers'. They receive ongoing support from their local authority for their transition towards adulthood; this varies between England and Scotland and we will come on to outline these differences.

There is also a wider group who were in care at some point in their childhood, but who left prior to 16 – usually by being reunited with their birth family. These are often referred to as being 'care-experienced', and they receive significantly less support, if any. The term, of fairly recent origin, has gained currency among adults who have themselves been in care at some time in their childhood. Its advantages include ownership by the community it seeks to describe and the fact that it acts as a collective term for people whose experiences are diverse. Its disadvantages include the lack of a precise legal definition which leaves some care-experienced people in eligible for support with strict entitlement criteria and invisible in official statistics.

This chapter engages with both care leavers and the wider care-experienced group as their childhood experiences are often similar, despite the different levels of support they subsequently receive. Despite the challenges they face, it is estimated that around 20–25% of care-experienced people participate in higher education at some point in their lives (Harrison, 2020). This is considerably lower than in the general population and, in particular, care-experienced students are more likely to attend later in life and make greater use of sub-degree and part-time forms of higher education.

This chapter synthesises the findings of two studies – one from Scotland (O'Neill et al., 2019) and one from England (Harrison, 2017) – that collectively capture stories from 440 care-experienced higher education students. It explores their particular challenges and examines these in relation to the contrasting policy frameworks between the two countries. The participants in the two studies span a wide range of ages, including those entering higher education at the earliest opportunity – around age seventeen (in Scotland) or eighteen (in England) – and those returning to education in their 20s, 30s or later.

Pathways through care

In the UK, there is a general assumption that the state should not interfere in children's upbringing, other than in the provision of compulsory education and routine health screening. This is a fine judgement because the state also has responsibility to ensure that children are cared for appropriately. The mechanisms by which the state intervenes are somewhat different between the constituent nations of the UK, although the pre-care circumstances precipitating intervention are broadly comparable, with a focus on avoiding abuse and neglect within families.

It is therefore difficult to typify journeys that are markedly individual with respect to the age of entering (and leaving) care, family circumstances, caring arrangements, quality of support, relationships with birth family and so on. For example, a child in family foster care for many years, and whose foster family continues to provide support into adulthood, has very different social and emotional circumstances to one whose care was characterised by several moves between birth family and different short-term placements. Rather, there are general interlocking themes that are common to most, but not necessarily all, care-experienced people.

Firstly, they are likely to have developed mental health difficulties as a result of their pre-care circumstances or subsequent experiences of care. Figures from both England and Scotland (Department for Education and Skills [DfES], 2007; Meltzer et al., 2004; Smith, 2017) suggest that approaching half of all children in care have a diagnosable condition including post-traumatic stress disorder, chronic depression and social anxiety. Others may have developed issues of behavioural self-regulation, building relationships with others or substance misuse. For many, these issues persist into adulthood.

Secondly, most will have experienced significant educational disruption. Pre-care circumstances may include significant amounts of missed schooling, while frequent placement moves – perhaps at short notice and without preparation – often also mean changing schools. The mental health issues outlined above can also lead to difficulties in engaging positively with school, even in the absence of missed time or moves. Children in care are also disproportionately likely to undergo fixed-term exclusions (Department for Education [DfE], 2019).

Thirdly, many will have few or no trusted adult relationships, having a history of abusive, fractured or otherwise problematic interactions with family members, teachers, social workers and others. This limits exposure to adults who could support educational engagement and access to information and guidance about adulthood – e.g. independent living or potential career pathways.

Analysis of national datasets has demonstrated how these experiences interact to exert a strong influence on educational pathways. Using English data, Sebba et al. (2015) documented the strong differences between children in care and other young people, with a particular focus on the disruption caused by placement and school moves, in contrast to long-term placements that were seen to have a protective effect. This is echoed by data from the Scottish Government (2019) which show that the qualification levels achieved by children continuously in care are typically higher than for those in care for part of the year, indicating the protection conferred by stability and conversely the educationally damaging effects of disrupted home life.

Pathways into higher education

Progression to higher education now typifies early adulthood transition, with the majority of young people in both Scotland and England participating by the age of 21 (Universities and Colleges Admissions Service, 2019). Very low participation rates for care-experienced young people, therefore, are a mark of severe inequality. For example, only around 6% of care leavers in England enter higher education at 18, rising to 12% by 23 (Harrison, 2017). However, as noted above, care-experienced people often return to higher education later in life, once their personal circumstances have made it possible for them to accumulate the required qualifications (see Brady and Gilligan, 2019 for this phenomenon in the Irish context).

Research interest in participation in higher education among those with care experience was pioneered by Sonia Jackson and colleagues in the 'By Degrees' project which tracked three successive cohorts of 50 care leavers for three years, two years and one year respectively (Jackson, Ajayi and Quigley, 2005). This research concluded that while the majority of participants were academically successful, students nevertheless faced challenges distinct from those of other students or heightened because of their experience of care. Among the challenges reported were financial difficulties, access to year-round accommodation and academic difficulties attributable to disrupted schooling.

Another landmark contribution to understanding was the 'YiPPEE' project, a five-country (England, Denmark, Hungary, Spain and Sweden) study of the post-compulsory educational pathways of care-experienced young people holding some educational qualifications (Jackson and Cameron, 2011). The researchers noted that instability in early life experiences was often reflected in their student experience, in a pattern they described as 'yo-yo transitions' – where young people repeatedly enrolled and dropped out of different courses. They found continuity in enabling factors for post-compulsory education, including 'stability of placement and schooling, being placed with carers who gave priority to education, feeling that there was someone who really cared about them and their achievements and having sufficient financial support and suitable accommodation to pursue their educational objectives' (p. 9).

Driscoll (2013), Lewis et al. (2015) and Cotton, Nash and Kneale (2017) also emphasise the importance of supportive relationships for care-experienced students, especially where this helps to mitigate low academic confidence or facilitate integration into the higher education community. In particular, Cotton, Nash and Kneale (2014) stress the transition into higher education as a key point of stress for care-experienced students, with new challenges to navigate – usually in the absence of the family 'safety net' enjoyed by others.

English policy context

While care-experienced students have always been present in higher education, significant policy concern only arose in the mid-2000s, driven jointly by general concerns about children's life outcomes (Department for Children, Schools and Families, 2003) and efforts to widen access to higher education for disadvantaged groups (DfES, 2003; Higher Education Funding Council for England, 2008). This concern culminated – via Green (DfES, 2006) and White (DfES, 2007) Papers – in the Children and Young Persons Act 2008 which was intended to improve the educational outcomes for children in care and smooth their progression into higher education; they were subsequently acknowledged as a target group for outreach efforts by higher education institutions (Department for Business, Innovation and Skills, 2014).

Various initiatives have cascaded from this policy attention, sustained by successive governments over the last ten years. For example, local authorities now have a statutory obligation to have a 'virtual school head' whose role it is to monitor educational outcomes for children in care, provide additional academic support and advocate on behalf of the child with other professionals (Berridge et al., 2009). Access to support after the age of 16 has also been strengthened, including access to a personal adviser until the age of 25 and extending young people's right to remain with foster carers – by mutual consent – while in education (Munro et al., 2012).

More broadly, however, local authorities have significant discretion over what they provide to care leavers. This has historically spawned individual and informal arrangements leading to inequalities. As a result, local authorities have recently become obliged to publish their 'local offer' to ensure parity among care leavers, including the help available for those moving into higher education (National Leaving Care Benchmarking Forum, 2019).

While this will lead to greater consistency within local authorities, a 'postcode lottery' remains whereby young people in different areas might receive very different packages of support for higher education. This might typically comprise a cash bursary, help with housing costs (pre-existing or student accommodation), a laptop computer, assistance with travel and access to advice and guidance.

English students are also able to take out a loan to cover their tuition fees (a key difference to Scotland, where no fees are charged) and living costs, with income-contingent repayments after graduation. In addition, higher education institutions are obliged to offer bursaries to care leavers to help with living costs, varying from a few hundred to several thousand pounds annually and funded from tuition fee income. Nearly all institutions also now offer year-round accommodation reflecting that care leavers often have nowhere to go during holidays.

More recently, the government has taken an increasingly directive role in requiring institutions to place more emphasis on supporting care leavers, publishing a set of 'principles' (DfE, 2018) for high-quality academic and pastoral support, while encouraging institutions to sign the Care Leaver Covenant – a public commitment enshrining their provision. Meanwhile, the Office for Fair Access[2] (2017) issued guidance on best practice in outreach and retention activities.

The overarching picture is therefore one where support for care leavers in higher education is improving rapidly, but where the specific package received by individuals can vary widely depending on their local authority and higher education institution. The difference in value can amount to thousands of pounds per year, which may or may not reflect differences in need between students.

Care-experienced students who do not meet the legal definition of care leaver do not generally have access to this support, even if they were in care at sixteen or spent many years in care. The picture is mixed among higher education institutions, with some electing to extend their support to all care-experienced students and others defaulting to care leavers only. Overall, care-experienced students who are not care leavers are generally much less well supported and may effectively be treated like the general student population, despite the manifest disadvantages and disruptions of their childhood.

Scottish policy context

The Children and Young People (Scotland) Act 2014 amended wording in earlier statute that unfortunately linked entitlement to aftercare support with the minimum age for leaving school (previously 16); any young person who ceases to be looked after by a local authority on or after their 16th birthday is now eligible for aftercare services. These services may include support to obtain accommodation, employment and/or education and financial support. The Act also extended the opportunity for care leavers to request

Table 2.1 Scottish domiciled entrants with care experience

	University				College	
	First degree		Sub-degree		Higher education	
	Full-time	Part-time	Full-time	Part-time	Full-time	Part-time
2017–18	255	45	40	25	265	25
2016–17	170	40	35	20	165	30
2015–16	160	30	25	20	140	20
2014–15	170	30	25	15	40	5
2013–14	145	30	25	10	20	5

aftercare support up to and including the age of 25, rather than the previous age limit of 18. In 2017–18 there were 6,109 young people eligible to receive aftercare services, 3,817 of which were receiving them.

The Scottish Funding Council (SFC) is responsible for funding Scotland's 19 universities and 26 colleges. Table 2.1 above shows the numbers of 'Scottish domiciled' students declaring care experience (i.e. omitting students whose care experience was not in Scotland) on entry to a programme of study over a five year period (SFC, 2019). As can be seen, there is a marked increase over time, especially in further education colleges, although this may be due in some part to improvements in capturing data.

The main policy driver for supporting care-experienced students in Scotland is a set of recommendations for widening participation in further and higher education arrived at by a commission chaired by Dame Ruth Silver. In its report, *A Blueprint for Fairness* (Commission on Widening Access, 2016), the Commission called for a non-repayable bursary for care-experienced students to replace maintenance loans and the entitlement to a university place for students who meet the minimum entry requirements.

These recommendations have been implemented, though it will be some years before their impact can be evaluated. A bursary of £7,625 per annum for higher education was introduced in 2017–18 for care-experienced students aged under 26, but raised to £8,100 in 2018–19 following a review of student support recommending that all students in further and higher education should have a guaranteed minimum income at this level (Gadhia, 2017). In September 2019, the Scottish Government announced that, from 2020–21, the age cap on the bursary would be removed making all care-experienced students eligible.

The Commission on Widening Access's recommendation of a guaranteed university place presented complexities because higher education institutions are autonomous; nevertheless, in July 2019, Universities Scotland (the representative body for universities) announced that agreement had been reached to implement the guarantee from 2019–20.

In addition, the SFC (2015) published a National Ambition for Care Experienced Students – 'by 2021–22 there is no difference between the outcomes of care experienced students compared to their peers' – and some strategic activities:

- Collecting, analysing and reporting statistics from colleges and universities on enrolments and progress of students who self-declare care experience;
- Requiring colleges and universities to demonstrate their commitment to care experienced students through 'outcome agreements' (this is broadly comparable to the role of the Office for Students in England);
- Supporting colleges and universities as they develop responses to their new legal responsibilities as 'corporate parents' under the Children and Young People (Scotland) Act 2014;
- Providing financial support information and details of contacts for care-experienced applicants to Scottish colleges and universities; and
- Establishing a Care Experienced Governance Group (including care-experienced students) to provide advice and oversee work aimed at realising the National Ambition.

The two studies

The first of the two studies was undertaken in England in late 2016 and early 2017 as an exploratory element of a wider project on care-experienced students commissioned by the National Network for the Education of Care Leavers (Harrison, 2017). An online survey was distributed via universities' student services and/or outreach departments, as well through social media; resource constraints prevented engagement with colleges offering higher education programmes.[3] The anonymised survey collected quantitative and qualitative data through yes/no questions, rating scales and free text responses. A total of 212 usable responses were received.

The Scottish study (O'Neill et al., 2019) was commissioned by the SFC and undertaken in late 2018 and early 2019. It used the English survey as a starting point, adapted for the policy context, and targeted students in both universities and colleges. A total of 228 usable responses was received: 137 from universities and 91 from colleges.[4]

One of the challenges in researching this field is that neither the true numbers of care-experienced students nor their demographic profile is well understood (Harrison, 2020). Given the relative size of the two countries, the Scottish sample derived a stronger response rate than the English one, in part due to the exploratory nature of the latter and greater resourcing for the former. As estimates, the English study may represent around 3% of care-experienced students, with the Scottish study achieving around 15%. Table 2.2 shows the demographic breakdown of the two samples; while not necessarily representative, it is clear they have captured significant diversity.

Table 2.2 Demographic profile of Scottish and English samples (%)

		English study	Scottish study	
		University	University	College
Gender	Female	68	81	68
	Male	29	17	31
	Non-binary	1	2	1
	Prefer not to say	1	0	0
Ethnicity	White	65	88	90
	Black	12	3	3
	Asian	3	3	2
	Mixed, other and unknown	21	6	4
Age	Under 18	–	2	18
	18 or 19	–	22	28
	20 to 25	–	42	35
	26 to 29	–	10	7
	30 or over	–	25	13
Disability	Disabled	15	51	43
	Not disabled	81	41	53
	Prefer not to say/not known	4	8	4
Level	Foundation/first year	41	38	72
	Second year	24	22	28
	Third year or later	29	31	0
	Postgraduate	7	11	0
Mode	Full time	–	88	91
	Part time	–	12	9
Housing	Family (birth or foster)	12	11	43
	Own home	36	59	43
	Student housing	52	24	8
	Other housing	–	6	7

Notes: (i) dashes denote that this question/category was not used in the English study, (ii) the disability question was phrased differently between the studies, the Scottish question being more expansive.

Both studies used a similar approach to analysis. The free text responses were analysed using a thematic approach of close reading, coding, combination of related codes, rereading and review until confidence was reached that the emerging macro themes were meaningful and accurately represented the data. The quantitative data were analysed using simple statistical tests (chi-square, t, Mann-Whitney and Kruskal-Wallis) to look for patterns in responses, either by demographic variables or between the responses to different questions; a 5% significance level was used.

Overall, there was considerable positivity from the respondents about their experiences of higher education to date, with the majority reporting that they were doing well – 71% in the English study and 74% in the Scottish study. However, many had considered withdrawing from their course at some point, including 55% of the Scottish respondents and 57% of their English counterparts. It was therefore clear that many of the students had experienced strong challenges along the way, even if they were feeling more positive about their lives when they completed the survey.

In the remainder of this chapter, we present the six main thematic areas that students highlighted with respect to these challenges. In particular, they provide insight into the ways in which their experiences of higher education differ from students without a history of care.

Transitions – managed and unmanaged

Entry into higher education represents a major transition for all students, but this was particularly keenly felt by care-experienced students in both studies. It was a time of vulnerability, where they were expected to manage significant changes, often on their own and in the absence of strong support networks. Indeed, a lack of easy access to support in difficult times can be particularly challenging for care-experienced students:

> It was more so the assumption that all students had support at home. Being a parent with no family for support was a huge challenge for childcare. I had to be proactive in seeking out supports. They were not offered or readily available. Staff did not seem to have understanding or empathy on the whole.
>
> (Scottish university student)

> I think I found the whole process difficult as I felt so alone and it became really obvious that I didn't have any family or anyone who cared about me. Everyone else had their parents there who helped them unpack, bought them food and checked in on them.
>
> (English university student)

In Scotland, 24% of respondents reported difficulties with transition – the equivalent figure in England was 19%. Importantly, in both studies, transition difficulties were significant predictors for later thoughts about withdrawing from higher education. In the Scottish study, which had a greater focus on transition, difficulties were found to be more marked among men, white students, students with disabilities and those at university (as opposed to college), the latter perhaps reflecting the need to move away to attend. Only a minority reported getting support with their higher education applications and these tended to be those who had progressed directly from school or college and who had been advised by staff.

The Scottish study also asked whether students had declared their care status to their institution when applying (as is actively encouraged) and found that nearly all (95%) had. However, a much lower proportion (59%) reported having been contacted by college or university staff as a result of declaring their care status and students' experiences of this contact were markedly variable; notably, students with disabilities and other complex needs were more likely to report negative outcomes from declaring their care history. Others, however, found the process immensely positive:

> Everyone had been so nice to me and understanding about my situation. For example, they understand that some days I don't feel the best so work with me to make me feel better.
>
> (Scottish college student)

A notable element of the English study was the highly variable support provided by the student's local authority – this was less marked in the Scottish study. While some readily recognised that social workers, personal advisers and others had smoothed their transition to the best of their ability, this was sometimes compromised by professionals' own lack of knowledge of higher education systems:

> The help I did get was very supporting but it felt like it was something that no one had dealt with before which made me anxious about getting my application right and on time to start the course.
>
> (English university student)

However, other students used the language of conflict or disappointment to describe their relationship with their local authority, where they had to fight for their entitlements or to ensure that paperwork was filed correctly:

> The transition was a stressful period and communication and arrangements still had not been confirmed up until the second month of uni.
>
> (English university student)

The role of support services and trusted individuals

Colleges and universities increasingly recognise the need to offer students a holistic range of support which goes further than offering purely additional academic support and guidance. Financial advice, support for students with disabilities, careers guidance and wellbeing/counselling services are ubiquitous in both Scotland and England; some institutions also offer coaching/mentoring programmes and advice and support in relation to equality and diversity issues.

Care-experienced students in both countries were extensive users of these services. For example, 26% of Scottish students and 29% of English students had sought financial advice, 28% of Scottish and 30% of English students had attended wellbeing/counselling services, and 29% of Scottish and 24% of English students had sought support from disability advice services. The Scottish study also found that students at both college and university who had been contacted by staff after declaring their care status tended to make more use of wellbeing/counselling services.

An increasing trend observed in both countries was the appointment of a staff member with designated responsibility for supporting care-experienced students, either as their sole job or combined with other duties. These were particularly strongly valued where they existed and a strong factor in ensuring student retention and success:

> I have received a support worker who is helping me to ensure I keep up with my work and deadlines.
>
> (English university student)

This highlights the importance of the relational approach to providing support and both studies emphasised the need for a consistent, trusted contact who is knowledgeable, seeks to understand individual needs and provides appropriate and timely support across a range of issues. This can be in stark contrast with the absence of trusted figures elsewhere in the student's life, especially for younger students.

Particularly useful was help with navigating and troubleshooting complex institutional procedures, which care-experienced students were more likely to encounter due to their multiple and overlapping needs. This could also involve a role in advocacy on the student's behalf with other staff:

> If it was not for the additional support from the Care Experienced Co-ordinator, I would have left university before achieving my goals. He managed to negotiate a repeat year when academic staff wanted me to just do exams only - which I would not have coped with.
>
> (Scottish university student)

Both studies found that students felt more included and thought they had more chance of success when they had strong supportive relationships, with trusted staff members acting as conduits to accessing other services within institutions. Students were more likely to seek help from these services when they had experienced a proactive and welcoming approach from their institution.

Financial support and financial management

Responses from students about financial support and managing finances highlight the complexity of this area and show how financial issues impact more widely on the student experience. As outlined above, there are significant differences in the packages available to English and Scottish students. Nevertheless, there were interesting similarities in the experiences reported by the two sets of students.

For example, 50% of students in the English study reported that they were coping well with their finances compared to 59% of Scottish respondents. In the Scottish study, analysis revealed a distinction between 'coping' and being 'comfortable'; whilst the majority reported coping, the qualitative data indicate that for many students this was only the case due to strict budgeting and financial management skills that they had to develop:

> There is no fall back or bank of mum and dad, so you learn to ensure you have enough to get by on or life will be more difficult.
> (Scottish university student)

Financial considerations influenced students who had considered leaving their course. In the Scottish study, 73% of respondents who had reported not coping financially had also considered leaving their course. In the English study, 15% of students who had considered leaving their course cited financial difficulties as the main reason for doing so. Caution should be used in drawing causal relationships between struggling financially and withdrawal from study because of the interrelationship finances have with other aspects of a student's life such as accommodation and mental health. The responses in these studies suggest that meeting basic financial commitments creates a significant amount of stress, anxiety and disruption for care-experienced students.

Students in both studies said that sometimes their financial difficulties are not due to the amount of money received, but about their skills and abilities in managing money and navigating complex financial and administrative systems without support. Reported difficulties included the assumption of a 'parental contribution' in calculating entitlements, delays in receiving loan, grant or bursary instalments and problems opening bank accounts related to proof of identity. They also described receiving little or no financial education for a variety of reasons including disrupted education, placement moves or leaving care at a young age:

> My budgeting skills are horrendous. I can't budget at all. I was never taught how to budget in care or growing up. So, I really don't know the concept of money and trying to explain this to people is difficult as they don't understand.
> (Scottish college student)

The financial difficulties described are not unique to care-experienced students, but what is arguably unique to these students, and perhaps estranged[5] students, is the complexity of their family and living circumstances, which can compound financial difficulties:

> The money itself is enough for me, but I have a daughter with my girlfriend and I help support her but don't get any help money wise towards this as my daughter doesn't live at my house. My girlfriend has had a lot of problems with the job centre not paying her properly and it's left her struggling to get by unless I help and that puts us both in a really bad situation with money.
> (Scottish college student)

Because financially it is difficult to be a student in a private rented home, while raising a family and being pregnant.

(English university student)

Housing: availability, appropriateness and security

Care-experienced students starting higher education live in very varied accommodation. Older students are likely to have their own house or flat, especially if they have a family of their own. Students in the process of leaving care may have been in foster homes, residential care or independent living (potentially a flat or a room in a hostel), while others may be living with birth or extended family. A small number of all ages will have previously been homeless or in custodial settings.

Entering higher education involves change of living arrangements for many care-experienced students, with some wanting to maintain existing accommodation while adjusting to their new student identity, while others will wish to move on – either to a new area or new housing. This can create novel – and potentially unanticipated – concerns about finding a deposit on rent and providing references.

Perhaps the most common concern, especially among younger students, was having somewhere to live in the summer months when it is generally assumed that students will 'go home'. Most universities now provide some form of guaranteed year-round housing, on request, and this was highly valued:

> I was offered (eventually) full term accommodation that was invaluable because it provided me with a sense of security and one less thing I worry about, so I could focus on my studies. Financially it helped significantly.
>
> (Scottish university student)

However, some did not have accommodation or care-experienced students were unaware of it:

> My primary difficulty was a lack of support in between term times as I did not have a place to live. If I did not have girlfriend at the time I wouldn't have known where to stay.
>
> (English university student)

> It would be nice to have the option to stay longer on student accommodation. I don't really have a stable solution to accommodation over the summer.
>
> (Scottish university student)

Others did avail themselves of what was offered, but it turned out not to be quite as expected. Moves are often required because institutions use residences for conferences or summer schools; such moves can disorient the student and evoke memories of repeated house moves while in care:

> [Name of University] told me they could give me a place in halls all year round but didn't mention that my placement would be made up of short stays in different halls over summer - I had to move 5 times. Most of these moves, I had to be out of my accommodation by 10am but I couldn't get keys to the next flat until 12pm. I had nobody to help me do all of this, my mental health deteriorated, and nobody seemed to care.
>
> (Scottish university student)

Other respondents were more concerned by the nature of the accommodation that was available during term-time. They were keenly aware of the potentially uncomfortable challenges that university might present and sought to find housing that suited them with varying degrees of success:

> From first contact I stressed the importance of a quieter, more relaxed place to live. Being vulnerable as a recovering drug addict I was keen to not be at the centre of student parties etc. For over two years I lived in the noisiest part of the city, in a halls that was constantly partying. If I was less experienced and less stable in my recovery I would have been in real danger.
>
> (English university student)

> I did not take university accommodation as I have a dog which are not permitted. If I did not have my dog, then I would struggle with my mental health. He is part of my journey and family.
>
> (Scottish university student)

One group that particularly struggled with appropriate housing was students who were parents, but who needed to relocate for higher education. Many universities appear unable to offer family-friendly accommodation, while securing a home in the private rented sector could be challenging due to discrimination against benefit recipients and the need for rent deposits and guarantors, and references; this latter issue was not confined to student parents.

Many care leavers were reliant on their local authority to cover their rent costs, either in their original housing or new student accommodation, and some experienced difficulties due to slow payments or an apparent change in policy:

> I was told my accommodation would always be paid for, and then at [the] last minute the [local authority] changed their mind, which made things difficult.
>
> (English university student)

> My rent was also supposed to be paid by my council, but councils never pay on time. The university kept sending threatening letters and phoning me asking for payment despite me explaining constantly.
>
> (Scottish university student)

The relationships between housing and other elements of the student experience were apparent in both studies. In the English study, students in their own homes were significantly less likely to feel supported by their university, to take part in social activities and to feel part of the university community. In the Scottish study, 45% of respondents reported having accommodation difficulties, including 18% who had to move home unexpectedly during their studies; this latter group had a significantly more negative appraisal of their experiences to date. As such, accommodation issues can be a key risk factor of care-experienced students.

Disability, mental health and emotional wellbeing

English care-experienced students are roughly twice as likely to consider themselves disabled as other students (Harrison, 2020); there are no figures currently available for Scotland, but there is no reason to suspect that this would be radically different. Indeed, as shown in Table 2.2, nearly half of the respondents to the Scottish survey identified as being disabled.

One important element of this phenomenon is that care-experienced students are, by dint of their childhood experiences of abuse, neglect or other forms of trauma, considerably more likely to have mental health difficulties. Both surveys included respondents with a wide range of conditions, ranging from relatively mild anxiety and depression through to post-traumatic stress disorder. Physical health challenges were also frequently mentioned, notably including chronic conditions such as fibromyalgia and those relating to early life experiences (e.g. foetal alcohol syndrome).

In particular, students referred to the legacy of their childhood trauma impacting directly or indirectly on their ability to study successfully. Disabled students in both surveys were significantly more likely to have considered leaving higher education than their peers. Many felt that the stresses of studying at university were exacerbating – and exacerbated by – their health issues, making it difficult to concentrate and thrive in the new environment:

> I have continuously questioned if the hard work is worth it as it can get very emotionally stressful. I have stayed on because I refuse to struggle for the rest of my life.
>
> (English university student)

> My mental health and financial circumstances have suffered greatly due to university pressures and expectations. I would like to take a year out next year but worry I won't go back to finish my final year.
>
> (Scottish university student)

The impact of stress was particularly marked where it coincided with financial or housing concerns or parenthood. For some, these feelings of not being able to cope were temporary, perhaps due to good support, but others felt that they were not able to access the professional services that they needed, leading to a sense of frustration or despair:

> I have once [thought about leaving] because of my health, I have a quite serious health conditions which mean I have to sometimes be off and began to feel like I was really falling behind but managed to sort it and am quite happy now.
>
> (Scottish college student)

> I found that not having a GP surgery specifically for students with mental health issues or a health professional on site has been difficult, as I really struggle with post-traumatic stress.
>
> (English university student)

> Because sometimes I don't feel good enough and I feel lonely and struggle with mental health, and I have no money and I feel like my life will not go anywhere anyway.
>
> (English university student)

Beyond these students was a wider group who were struggling to fit into the higher education community and whose emotional wellbeing was diminished as a result. They lacked familial support and had difficulties making friends. This could be because they lived in their own homes rather than in student housing or because of anxieties about meeting new people and a fear of being stigmatised:

> I feel very left out of the community and overwhelmed with no one to talk to. Didn't drop out because I literally have nowhere else to go.
>
> (English university student)

> It has been a very isolating experience, particularly since I have no one to go home to during the holidays. I've been grappling my mental health and my finances which has been impacting my studies, causing me to repeat a year.
>
> (Scottish university student)

This social isolation and exclusion left many students feeling vulnerable and at risk of leaving their course. The potential transformational effect of having a close friendship network on students' ability to succeed is illustrated in the following comment:

> Struggled to fit in during first year – didn't make friends and felt very alone. By the end of second semester I had managed to find strong friends, which transformed the whole university experience for me.
>
> (English university student)

Academic challenges and adaptation

The final theme we have chosen to highlight concerns academic life. Most care-experienced students have had disrupted education due to absences resulting from their personal circumstances, including changes in school. One consequence is that they may have gaps in their foundational knowledge, even of the subjects that they are pursuing in higher education, or a low level of confidence in their abilities. Only 60% in the English survey and 63% in the Scottish survey expressed confidence, leaving a long tail of those unclear or negative about whether they had the potential to succeed; 'imposter syndrome', as one Scottish participant put it. These narratives emerged in the quotes from participants too:

> I didn't attend school regularly and not at all from the age of 13. I did 1 year's access course to get on to my degree, so I feel my academic abilities are limited.
> (English university student)

> It was hard as lecturers presume you know everything and not always the case.
> (English university student)

But the surveys also uncovered accounts of resilience and overcoming initial difficulties, either through one's own efforts or the intervention of key staff:

> I found the amount of work slightly overwhelming at first, which knocked my confidence a lot when other students found it "easy". I chose to remain because I didn't want to let myself down, I knew I was more than capable! I worked hard and improved my grades a lot and feel I am on track to get at least 60%+.
> (English university student)

> I have thought about leaving because I failed two modules in first year and I am currently resitting them. I chose to remain because I have had a lot of bumps in the road over the years so I didn't want to just give up on this one.
> (English university student)

Students on courses related to their previous life experiences, such as social work and nursing, reflected on the particular challenges of studying an area that was close-to-home and where the content could be 'triggering':

> I study social work and I found it very emotionally, physically and mentally challenging. It brought a lot of memories back from my childhood and time in care and it felt quite isolating at times.
> (Scottish university student)

> There was a tutorial on adult and child protection. In our groups we had to rate the types and acts of abuse from worst to the unthinkable. I was looking at the paper thinking all of these things have happened to me. It was hard to hear the discussions in class. We also had to feedback as a class where the discussion went on to how these people may act in later life and I thought "I am sitting here" as many of them were negative.
> (Scottish university student)

Discussion and conclusion

The findings from these two studies raise important considerations for leaders, practitioners and policymakers in thinking about how care-experienced students experience the journey into and through post-school education.

The policy contexts in England and Scotland are quite different. It could be argued that Scotland's policies in relation to support for care-experienced students are more inclusive, enabling and far-reaching. A generous national bursary scheme, guaranteed provision of support up to the 26th birthday and the integration of the wider care-experienced group (rather than just those formally classed as care leavers) are all examples of policy drivers that can mitigate the adverse circumstances that care-experienced students can encounter whilst accessing and attending higher education.

Conversely, support in England is heavily devolved to individual local authorities and higher education institutions, leading to much greater individual variability in support. In some instances, students in England may receive more support than in Scotland (e.g. by accumulating loans, grants and bursaries from multiple sources), but there are also more opportunities for students to fall through the gaps due to under-developed or poorly administered systems at local level. The key role of the local authority was particularly important in the English study, with students reporting highly variable policies and practices.

Comparing the findings of both studies suggests that despite the steps that have been taken in policy and practice, care-experienced students continue to face similar barriers in accessing, sustaining and positively experiencing higher education, regardless of where they study. Respondents in both surveys identified challenges in transition to university, applying for and managing finances, precarious housing, academic work and complexities associated with disabilities and mental health; interestingly, these remain broadly consistent with those identified fifteen years ago by Jackson et al. (2005), as well as with several more recent studies (Ellis and Johnston, 2019; Hauari, Hollingworth and Cameron, 2019; Stevenson et al., 2020). These are areas of difficulty which any student might experience at some point in their academic career, but the findings suggest that for care-experienced students it is the intersectionality of these significant factors, alongside feelings of isolation or being unsupported, which exacerbates the difficulties.

In particular, older students had a tendency to bring complex constellations of need with them into higher education. While it remains impossible to construct a 'typical' care-experienced student, those entering later in life are more likely to be parents or have long-term partners, to have complex housing situations, to require help with benefit entitlements, to have non-traditional educational pathways and so on. There is a danger that the policy and practice, improving rapidly in both countries, leaves these students behind – yet, the legacy of childhood trauma and disruption persists.

Findings from both studies strongly indicate that having a trusted, consistent and supportive staff member within higher education institutions, who can be relied upon for personalised and timely support, is a core component in success and feelings of inclusion and confidence for all care-experienced students. Strong relationships, in addition to an enabling and inclusive policy context which enhances wellbeing and upholds rights, are vital components for positively influencing how students experience university and, subsequently, achieve and attain whilst there. Such staff members are also key in ensuring parity of experience between students, through advocacy within and outside the institution.

While somewhat outside the scope of this chapter, the studies also highlighted the need for a broader approach to supporting care-experienced students into higher education. Much of the recent campaigning work has focused on seeking improvements in the supports provided by colleges and universities, but equally important is the encouragement of teachers, social workers, carers and employers. Many care-experienced adults have described childhoods characterised by an assumption that they would not be going to post-school education – or even being actively discouraged. Many respondents in our studies reported using alternative pathways to education later in life, but access to these is likely to be unfairly distributed.

The overall picture is of an improving situation in both England and Scotland. There have been enabling policy changes in both countries and higher education institutions have improved awareness of the support needs of care-experienced applicants and students. Research in both countries suggests that there is still too much variability in the support provided, especially in England, and particularly in responding to precarity and continuing mental health difficulties.

Notes

1 A term widely used in the UK to denote a collective responsibility among organisations for the promotion of wellbeing for children in care and care leavers.
2 The regulator for universities' commitments to disadvantaged students and now known as the Office for Students.
3 Higher education courses delivered in further education colleges constitute a much higher proportion of the total students in Scotland (around 40%) than England (around 10%).

4 The Scottish study also surveyed care-experienced students taking further education courses, but these results have been removed to facilitate a direct comparison.
5 Younger students who lack the support of a family network.

References

Berridge, D., L. Henry, S. Jackson, and D. Turney (2009) *Looked after and learning: An evaluation of the virtual school head for looked after children local authority pilots.* London: Department for Children, Schools and Families.

Brady, E. and R. Gilligan (2019) Exploring diversity in the educational pathways of care-experienced adults: Findings from a life course study of education and care. *Children and Youth Services Review* 104: 104379.

Commission on Widening Access (2016) *A blueprint for fairness: The final report of the Commission on Widening Access.* Edinburgh: Scottish Government.

Cotton, D., T. Nash, and P. Kneale (2014) The experience of care leavers in UK higher education, *Widening Participation and Lifelong Learning* 16(3): 5–21.

Cotton, D., T. Nash and P. Kneale (2017) Supporting the retention of non-traditional students in Higher Education using a resilience framework, *European Educational Research Journal* 16(1): 62–79.

Department for Business, Innovation and Skills (2014) *National strategy for access and student success.* London: Department for Business, Innovation and Skills.

Department for Children, Schools and Families (2003) *Every child matters.* Norwich: The Stationery Office.

Department for Education (2018) *Principles to guide higher education providers on improving care leavers access and participation in HE.* London: Department for Education.

Department for Education (2019) *Timpson review of school exclusion.* London: Department for Education.

Department for Education and Skills (2003) *The future of higher education.* Norwich: The Stationery Office.

Department for Education and Skills (2006) *Care matters: Transforming the lives of children and young people in care.* Norwich: The Stationery Office.

Department for Education and Skills (2007) *Care matters: Time for change.* Norwich: The Stationery Office.

Driscoll, J. (2013) Supporting care leavers to fulfil their educational aspirations: Resilience, relationships and resistance to help, *Children and Society* 27(2): 139–149.

Ellis, K. and C. Johnston (2019) *Pathways to university from care: Findings report one.* Sheffield: University of Sheffield.

Gadhia, J.-A. (2017) *A new social contract for students: Fairness, parity and clarity.* Edinburgh Scottish Government.

Harrison, N. (2017) *Moving on up: Care leavers and care-experienced students' pathways into and through higher education.* Winchester: National Network for the Education of Care Leavers.

Harrison, N. (2020) Patterns of participation in higher education for care-experienced students in England: Why has there not been more progress? *Studies in Higher Education* 45(9): 1986–2000.

Hauari, H., K. Hollingworth and C. Cameron (2019) *Getting it right for care experienced students in higher education.* London: University College London.

Higher Education Funding Council for England (2008) *Guidance for Aimhigher partnerships: Updated for the 2008–2011 programme*. Bristol: HEFCE.

Jackson, S., S. Ajayi, and M. Quigley (2005) *Going to university from care*. London: Institute of Education.

Jackson, S. and C. Cameron (2011) *Final report of the YiPPEE project – young people from a public care background: Pathways to further and higher education in five European countries*. London: Thomas Coram Research Unit.

Lewis, E., E. Williams, P. Lewis, and D. Allison (2015) Success 4Life: An aspirational programme for looked after children, *Widening Participation and Lifelong Learning* 17(4): 116–127.

Meltzer, H., D. Lader, T. Corbin, R. Goodman and T. Ford (2004) *The mental health of young people looked after by local authorities in Scotland*. London: The Stationery Office.

Munro, E., C. Lushey, National Care Advisory Service, D. Maskell-Graham, and H. Ward, with L. Holmes (2012) *Evaluation of the Staying Put: 18 Plus family placement programme: Final report*. London: Department for Education.

National Leaving Care Benchmarking Forum (2019) *Care leaver local offer: Guide and key messages*. London: National Leaving Care Benchmarking Forum.

Office for Fair Access (2017) *Topic briefing: Care leavers*. Bristol: OFFA.

O'Neill, L., N. Harrison, N. Fowler and G. Connelly (2019) *'Being a student with care experience is very daunting': Findings from a survey of care experienced students in Scottish colleges and universities*. Glasgow: CELCIS.

Scottish Funding Council (2015) *National ambition for care-experienced students*. Edinburgh: Scottish Funding Council.

Scottish Funding Council (2019) *Report on widening access 2017–18*. Edinburgh: Scottish Funding Council.

Scottish Government (2019) *Education outcomes of looked after children 2017–2018*. Edinburgh: Scottish Government.

Sebba, J., D. Berridge, N. Luke, J. Fletcher, K. Bell, S. Strand, S. Thomas, I. Sinclair, and A. O'Higgins (2015) *The educational progress of looked after children in England: Linking care and educational data*. Oxford/Bristol: Rees Centre and University of Bristol.

Smith, N. (2017) *Neglected minds: A report on mental health support for young people leaving care*. Ilford: Barnardo's.

Stephenson, J., Z. Baker, N. Harrison, B. Bland, S. Jones Devitt, A. Donnelly, N. Pickering and L. Austen (2020) *Positive impact: what factors affect access, retention and graduate outcomes for university students with a background of care or family estrangement?* Bristol: Unite Foundation.

Universities and Colleges Admissions Service (2019) *End of cycle report 2019*. Cheltenham: UCAS.

Chapter 3

The collateral impact of post-prison supervision on college experiences in the United States

Lindsey Livingston Runell

Introduction

In the United States, eligible incarcerated persons are released from prison on parole, which requires compliance with designated stipulations and liberty restrictions. They are assigned to parole officers who utilize wide discretion in managing their everyday movements in community settings. Parole is considered a privilege reserved for individuals who have demonstrated progress toward crime avoidance during incarceration. Participation in carceral college and work programs are known indicators of offender reform and in turn eligibility for early release under community supervision (Scott, 2016; Sokoloff and Schenck-Fontaine, 2017). Parolees who continue involvement in postsecondary education are still within the correctional system and therefore subject to freedom restrictions which might conflict with class attendance, employment and participation in extracurricular campus events.

The manner in which parole officers weigh college participation in setting the terms and conditions of community sentences is an unexplored topic (Blasko et al., 2015; Chamberlain et al., 2018). What is the collateral impact of post-prison supervision on parolees, their college experiences and perceptions of fairness about community corrections? (see Blasko and Taxman, 2018; Dowden and Andrews, 2004; Taxman, 2002, 2008). Procedural justice is a concept used to explore ways that interactions between citizens and law enforcers can influence motivation for rule compliance (Tyler, 2006). The basic premise is that if people perceive applicable criminal justice processes as fair, they will be more inclined to respect those practices and in turn the people who administer them. Neutrality and transparent communications are essential components to legitimate governmental authority (Jackson et al., 2010; Tyler, 2010). The focus is not on the outcome but instead whether encounters with rule enforcers are viewed as fair (Johnson et al., 2014; Reisig and Mesko, 2009).

Most procedural justice studies examine police-citizen encounters during stops and questioning along with any relevant contextual factors that contribute to police searches, arrests and use of force decisions in those circumstances (Blasko and Taxman, 2018; Bradford, 2014; Klockars, 1972; Nix et al., 2015;

Sunshine and Tyler, 2003). The findings reveal that people are more inclined to follow police orders when they feel respected and able to voice any related questions or concerns. That concept has also been applied in correctional institution contexts to understand perceptions of power legitimacy that incarcerated persons have toward individuals who supervise their carceral movements. Prison officials who execute their authority in a procedurally just manner, are better positioned to maintain order and control crime among persons confined to those environments in effective and efficient ways (Beijersbergen et al., 2015; Beijersbergen et al., 2016; Reisig and Mesko, 2009). Ultimately, procedural justice in institutional settings can inspire law abidance among individuals during and after incarceration, which has important implications for how formerly imprisoned individuals respond to police surveillance and community supervision.

Early release from prison on parole is an opportunity to complete a criminal sentence in non-carceral settings, subject to certain guidelines and liberty restrictions. Persons who leave imprisonment under those conditions must demonstrate employment progress and other efforts indicative of re-entry and desistance from crime (Blomberg et al., 2012; Nally et al., 2014; Rakis, 2005). Participation in college classes during or after imprisonment can also help facilitate successful transitions from prison (Baranger et al., 2018; Duwe and Clark, 2014). There are federal sources of financial aid that incarcerated persons can access to fund their postsecondary carceral education (Castro et al., 2018; Korte, 2016). Programs, such as the one discussed in this chapter, create avenues for those students to complete their higher education at four-year colleges after release from prison. Yet, there remains scant knowledge about whether and to what extent community corrections officers are willing to adjust their terms and conditions of supervision to accommodate or at least support individuals who are taking college classes (Potts and Bierlein Palmer, 2014).

The management of offenders in non-institutional settings is largely guided by criminal offense history and severity, but there is some allowance for individualized treatment (Seiter, 2002). While formerly incarcerated persons share a criminal background in common, they have divergent needs with respect to varying levels of academic and professional achievement, family responsibilities, housing and job attainment, among other circumstances that necessitate case-by-case determinations (Uggen and Stewart, 2014). This chapter explores the unintended consequences of community supervision on college participation and also the implications for offenders, corrections officers and society in general.

Under community supervision and in college

In recent years, there has been increased support for the creation and expansion of opportunities for incarcerated and formerly incarcerated persons to pursue a higher education given that college educated ex-prisoners are more likely to have smoother re-entry experiences, obtain gainful employment and avoid crime (Bozick et al., 2018; Escobar et al., 2013; Gorgol and Sponsler, 2011). Community corrections officers can even consider post-prison college participation in deciding whether to employ curfew restrictions, scheduled, impromptu meetings or other methods in managing citizens who return to society from prison (Glaser, 1985; Lipsky, 1980). Little is known about the nature and scope of such discretionary power and how it might impact college and work study involvement among individuals who are subject to it (Scott-Hayward, 2011).

The rationale behind community sanctions is clear, that some formerly incarcerated persons need to be monitored because their criminal histories indicate a need for extended correctional treatment and support with adjusting to life after imprisonment (Rudes, 2012). Yet, there are collateral consequences to being under such close surveillance which might contravene efforts made in furtherance of re-entry, especially for formerly incarcerated college students who need the freedom and flexibility to attend classes, study, work and experience campus culture (Klingele, 2013). Taking college classes after incarceration is an experience in itself that can prove both challenging and time consuming given that ex-prisoners are exceptional non-traditional students (Potts and Bierlein Palmer, 2014; Strayhorn et al., 2013).

Formerly incarcerated college students in particular need exposure to and immersion in campus-wide academic and social activities to better facilitate their transitions from prison to community environments (Walters, 2018). In most cases, there is a noticeable age difference between them and their college 'peers' who began pursuing postsecondary education directly after high school graduation. There are accompanying insecurities surmounted by struggles to assimilate into higher learning subcultures that are distinct from and at odds with place of origin/residence characteristics especially those criminogenic in nature (Runell, 2017). Ex-prisoner college students can reconcile divergent contextual influences by spending more time on campus, engaged in activities both in and out of classroom settings (Livingston and Miller, 2014). But correctional supervision creates conditional liberties that might infringe on efforts to achieve that goal. There is a gap in research on what best practices corrections officials should use to monitor parolee college students in ways that align with both public safety interests and re-entry goals. There is evidence that perceptions of fairness are central to that inquiry (Blasko et al., 2015; Bonta et al., 2008; Taxman, 2002).

Data and methods

This qualitative data was collected from June through July 2015 as part of a follow-up study to one completed in 2011 and it included information shared by seventeen of the original 34 research participants. The interviewees were ex-prisoners and also members of a program that affords incarcerated persons the opportunity to complete carceral college courses and continue their postsecondary education at 'State College', a four-year institution, after release from prison. The program director shared updated phone numbers and email addresses for almost all of the 34 original study participants. At that time, there was no contact information on file for three of them: two were re-incarcerated and one was murdered.

The 31 sample members to this second-round study received phone calls and emails that detailed the focus, nature and purpose of the follow-up questionnaire. A total of seventeen respondents agreed to share their stories of hardship and success in navigating college, parole and job markets since 2011. Either phone or face-to-face meetings were arranged on or near State College campus, whichever was the most convenient to the individual participant. The other fourteen individuals contacted were either unresponsive to phone and email messages or declined a second interview stating time constraints related to employment and familial responsibilities.

This chapter is based on 2015 data collected from second interviews with seventeen ex-prisoners who through their acceptance into a higher education program for incarcerated individuals were able to pursue, and in some cases complete a four-year degree at State College. The respondents were between 30 and 35 years of age and mostly males, with the exception of two women[1]. They willingly disclosed their racial identities for demographic purposes and responded as follows: Egyptian (1), Chinese (1), White (2), Hispanic (1), Multi-racial (3) and Black (9). Their audio-recorded conversations were anonymized and open reflections on developments, consistencies and life-course events related to college/program involvement, employment, re-entry and community supervision (where applicable) that had transpired since 2011.

The interviews began with a simple, open-ended question inviting participants to share their experiences adjusting to life outside of prison and the role of their higher education involvement in those processes. These conversations then turned to employment as nearly half of the interviewees graduated from State College within the four years since the initial study and were working, pursing internships or advanced degrees. The research participants, including those who were current State College students spoke about their career aspirations, barriers posed by criminal stigmas and ways that being in college offers opportunities to help offset such challenges to finding gainful employment. Related to that inquiry was the topic of community sanctions as some individuals revealed, without any prompting, parole conditions that interfered with college participation, work and other efforts to engage in productive routines after incarceration.

The respondents were directly asked to reveal or further explain any conditions on their freedom imposed through parole or probation sentences. All but two were released from prison under community supervision and remained subject to related liberty restrictions while attending State University[2]. The fifteen individuals placed on a parole or probation status(es) disclosed their sentence terms and ways those circumstances framed and were framed by their college involvement. Among them, six were no longer on parole at the time of this study, but they too remembered having to construct their postsecondary educational or employment activities around limitations posed by community supervision requirements. The nine returning citizens assigned to parole officers shared present accounts of how those aspects of their lives overlapped.

Inductive techniques were used to analyze the transcribed data and identify emergent themes such as procedural justice issues related to parole supervision. As mentioned, the interview questionnaire consisted of specific inquiries into conditional release statuses and stipulations. An organic part of those collected responses included expressed attitudes and beliefs about the fairness of time, place and movement restrictions that were described as discretionary in nature. Research participants connected those feelings to community supervision conditions and how such rules shaped levels of engagement in college classes, work performance and participation in campus events. The data were re-read and coded to confirm and further develop that procedural justice storyline. Perceived efficacy of parole requirements such as unplanned mandatory meetings, spontaneous appearances by parole officers and curfews influenced motivation and willingness to comply with such terms. The length of parolee-parole officer relationships was also identified as an important factor in evaluating the value of being subject to close surveillance across home, college and work contexts.

This research contributes to scarce information on procedural justice issues experienced by formerly incarcerated college students on parole. However, the impact is limited because the results cannot be generalized beyond the study sample members, six of whom gave retrospective accounts which involves telescoping and possible inaccurate recall. There is some risk of selection bias because all seventeen research participants were ex-prisoners and college-educated, but these very attributes enhance knowledge about the role of community supervision in post-prison college participation and re-entry progress.

Discussion

The study data show that being on parole is a direct consequence of crime involvement and incarceration, yet it is a conditional status which can stymie efforts to move past those histories. All of the research participants completed college coursework during and after incarceration and for some, part of that higher education experience coincided with a parole status. Only two of the seventeen individuals interviewed served their entire sentences while imprisoned and were not subject to any liberty restrictions upon release. The others were paroled and expressed both relief and frustration over the extent to which their assigned officer(s) treated post-incarceration college involvement as a salient factor in setting community supervision conditions.

This research confirms that parole agents have legitimate authority to make discretionary decisions about how to control and manage the movements of offenders on their caseload. In that regard, the research participants shared experiences that were in large part influenced by officer management style and reciprocal parole-parolee interactions. This presented some challenges for Farley and other interviewees who were required to switch parole officers after moving or for other unexplained reasons. Farley analogized the rationale behind it: 'when you move to a different county, you have to transfer to that county […] it's kind of like a gym membership. If I sign up [for a gym] in Piscataway […] but I keep going to the one in Trenton eventually they gonna tell me "look you have to transfer your membership to Trenton"'. Three years had passed since Farley completed a three-year parole sentence. Speaking from personal experience, he believed time is key to building trustful relationships with parole officers because 'once they [parole officers] see you're involved in something, they know you don't have as much time to be doing nonsense'.

Mike, a parolee at the time had to change parole agents 'for some reason' and based on his positive experiences with the original one, had a similar 'mindset like I've been in school for three years, I've never had any issues […] I have a track record'. He had the 'same parole officer for three years who treated him 'like a human being' and respected that he 'was going to school, working, having a family, creating another family'. Mike explained how that all changed after his assignment to a different parole officer whom he described as 'by the book' and unwilling to factor academic and employment successes into supervision considerations. He was even told by that person: 'you're not a normal citizen, you're on parole'. That remark deeply frustrated Mike because after serving a ten-year prison sentence for armed robbery he was trying hard to prove capable of reform by progressing in work and college.

The research participants released from prison on parole were required to show proof of their involvement in productive routine activities like work or college classes but some parole officers preferred participation in one activity over the other. For instance, Geoff who was enrolled at State University finished a relatively short parole sentence of 'six or seven months' and during that time felt pressured to solely focus his re-entry efforts on employment. As he put it, 'they [parole] didn't want me going to school. Like they were so hard-nosed about working but I'm trying to do this and this and they're like "work and give us your money"'. Geoff completed parole but was on probation for accruing $5,000 in fines, which remained in arrears for some time due to a series of post-incarceration events. He became homeless during his junior year at State College, received a technical probation violation for not having an address on record and had to serve a brief jail sentence as a result. Once released, he was able to continue college and satisfy almost all of his debt. Geoff's history might have influenced his treatment on parole, but nevertheless he expressed the following feelings over it: 'now I have proved myself to be a productive member of society. I have not caught any new cases, I haven't pissed dirty ever'.

Even though he and the other research participants continued their higher education post-prison and most also had jobs, such progress did not necessarily contribute to more favorable parole experiences. Rather, they were subject to varied levels of community supervision, and attributed such treatment to differences in officer discretion and dynamics of parolee-parole officer relationships. Consistency also mattered because program members whose parole assignments never changed perceived their parole officers as facilitators in their post-release transitions.

Jaeger was on the same parole officer's caseload for the entire three years of his sentence. During that time, he performed well in college, maintained a tutoring job and planned to further his education with an advanced degree in physical sciences. As Jaeger recalled, that parole officer 'was very supporting of me [...] of getting this situation [post-incarceration college enrollment]'. He thought parole officers 'usually see you as a scumbag' so he felt lucky not to have been perceived that way and believed that contributed to him 'staying clean, staying out of trouble'.

Similarly, Tarik considered his experience on parole to be atypical and described his parole officer as someone who was 'impressed from the door [...] and kind of didn't really hassle' him especially after seeing his work and class schedules. He was even permitted to circumvent a stipulated curfew by simply calling his parole officer to say: 'I'm on campus, I'll be home later'. Tarik greatly appreciated that flexibility which allowed him the time needed to successfully balance college classes, a work study position and a coveted internship in his field of study.

Other parolee interviewees believed their college enrollment and employment were not considered sufficient indicators of trustworthiness. As Victor put it, his parole agent was initially very skeptical, 'really not believing that I went to college and that I was actually out here trying to better myself'. Everton recalled a similar experience and believed it was 'unwarranted' and an interference with reintegration efforts. Similar to Tarik, he would often remain on campus into the evening, to participate in collegiate activities but was reprimanded for doing so. Everton recalled one night in particular when he arrived home around 12:30am or 1:00am after finishing classes, attending a student board meeting and library study group. His parole officer had been there and left a note asking Everton to call him. Everton obliged, left a message and was back on campus the next day when he received a return call from his parole officer demanding an impromptu face-to-face meeting. He remembered the following exchange: 'I answered the phone in class so he could hear me walking out [...] I go into the hallway and he's like "I need you to come home" and I'm like, "I don't know if you just heard but I'm in class right now" and he's like "I need you to come home [...] right now"'. Once there, Everton reminded his parole officer that there was no stipulated curfew, but the response was: 'it doesn't matter, you're not supposed to be out that late'.

The study findings also revealed similar complications that arise when parole officers expect employed parolees to meet them on days and times that conflict with regular business hours. Peter, in an attempt to develop a good rapport with his new parole officer, communicated that he has a 'real professional job' at State College which requires him to be on the campus 'at certain times'. That parole agent replied by saying that meeting with her 'takes priority over [his] work' which ultimately meant that he had to sacrifice part of his work day in order to accommodate a home visit. Peter further explained that after several missed opportunities for a meeting, due to no fault of his own, he 'actually took a half a day [...] called out sick to go back there [home] to meet with her [the parole officer] who was there for like 2 minutes and left'. He 'was getting angry' over such inexplicable inconveniences and expressed: 'what do you [the parole officer] want me to do? It's just like I've done everything right ... I've never gotten in trouble, no infractions. I graduated from college in three years with honors, what else could I possibly do to show that I'm on the right track?'

Research participants expected parole officers to allow them time and leeway to complete college and work responsibilities given that involvement in legitimate, routine activities such as these is indicative of parole and re-entry progress. But some of them were assigned to parole officers who monitored their movements so closely that it was sometimes difficult for them to concentrate on those activities. Mike perceived his second parole assignment as impacting his life in similar ways. The person told him 'if you're not home by 10 o'clock, send me a text or phone call where you're at'. Mike never had a curfew during the three years prior on parole and thought it would be challenging to effectively balance academic, employment and familial responsibilities within a condensed time frame. He lamented 'I'm not home by 10 o'clock. I can try to make it home by 12 o'clock'. Mike believed that restriction was unnecessary so he asked the parole officer: 'why would I have to do this? I'm in school, I work [and] I got this [work] award.' The parole officer answered with 'I'm your officer, that's what I need you to do.' Mike recalled that conversation and stated: 'I don't respect the rules that he [the parole officer] gives'.

Everton too did not understand why his parole officer imposed curfew and pleaded with him: 'I'm doing everything, I'm working, going to school, getting good grades. I'm doing everything you want me to do. What else do you want me to do?' but to no avail. That condition remained but Everton 'still didn't come home at night' if he 'was out doing something'. This study was narrowly focused on the experiences of parolees who were part of a higher education program and through that connection had the opportunity to take college classes post-incarceration. The findings have widespread implications for policy development in the areas of re-entry, post-carceral college participation and community corrections. The college student parolee participants shared real-life challenges and successes navigating higher education pursuits in correctional contexts. This data can help guide transparent and respectful interactions between individuals leaving prison and those responsible for supervising their post-incarceration transitions, which also serves societal interests in procedural fairness.

Conclusion

It is well-known that ex-prisoners who are employed and college educated possess a greater potential to successfully sustain themselves through legal means. Yet some of the parolee research participants were subject to curfew and meeting requirements that contravened their efforts to fulfill work and college related functions. They perceived such conditions as senseless and unfair given their demonstrated abilities to implement and adhere to personal, academic and professional schedules that facilitated engagement in constructive activities. The interviewees felt disregarded by parole agents who continually imposed time and place constraints without any explanations.

This research offers guidance for parole officers to consider parolees' college enrollment, degree completion and employment in implementing supervision requirements given the established benefits of pursuing such endeavors. The application of community sanctions is based in large part on criminal history and offense severity, but parole officers can also account for personal, social and economic factors in determining how to supervise each specific individual on their caseload. Perhaps the use of such discretion can be developed through training opportunities designed to promote balanced, clear and effective communications between parolees and their assigned agents. The study findings support this, as some of the participants became upset by parole officers who were unresponsive to their inquiries about mandatory procedures which were described as a hindrance to their college and work routines. They viewed such interactions as lacking transparency, which made them feel disrespected and hardly motivated to follow conditional release terms and conditions.

The findings expand on prior research that highlights the role of postcarceral college and work involvement in promoting smooth assimilations to life after prison. Parolees who pursue a higher education are not only more likely to avoid crime but are also typically motivated to make concerted reentry efforts. Both are basic intended purposes of community supervision sentences. This study can be used to drive the creation of incentivized parole systems where individuals under community supervision who demonstrate college success, advancement and degree attainment earn certain privileges and freedoms such as less stringent curfew times. The associated benefits should be relative to what is perceived and communicated by college student parolees as fair to help serve procedural justice interests. The implementation of programs like this might even inspire higher education endeavors among ex-prisoners who are hesitant to take on college responsibilities while on parole.

This research raises awareness about how parole officers can best support parolees in their higher education endeavors through engagement in balanced communications and utilization of carefully planned supervision tactics which account for individual needs and circumstances. The data were collected from half of the original research participants and cannot be generalized beyond that sample but nonetheless shed light on real challenges parolees face in trying to reconcile their liberty restrictions with college and work schedules. There are practical and far-reaching implications for parole officers who have the discretion to execute community supervision in ways that serve both public safety re-entry goals. Future research should explore the experiences of other ex-prisoner college student cohorts and include the perspective of parole officers who managed them.

Notes

1 Kerri and Deb were the only two female research participants. Deb served her entire sentence in prison and was never on parole. Kerri completed a three-month community sentence that involved 'intense supervision', which made her an outlier. She expressed suicidal ideations and was consequently placed on house arrest and required to meet with her parole officer on a daily basis after release from prison.
2 Deb and Sam were the two exceptions. They both 'maxed out,' each serving the respective maximum imposed sentence during incarceration.

References

Baranger, J., D. Rousseau, M. Mastrorilli and J. Matesanz (2018) Doing time wisely: The social and personal benefits of higher education in prison, *The Prison Journal* 98(4): 490–513.

Beijersbergen, K., A. Dirkzwager, V. Eichelsheim, P. Van der Laan and P. Nieuwbeerta (2015) Procedural justice, anger, and prisoners' misconduct: A longitudinal study, *Criminal Justice and Behavior* 42(2): 196–218.

Beijersbergen, K., A. Dirkzwager and P. Nieuwbeerta, P. (2016) Reoffending after release: Does procedural justice during imprisonment matter? *Criminal Justice and Behavior* 43(1): 63–82.

Blasko, B., P. Friedmann, A. Rhodes and F. Taxman (2015) The parolee-parole officer relationship as a mediator of criminal justice outcomes, *Criminal Justice and Behavior* 42(7): 722–740.

Blasko, B. and F. Taxman (2018) Are supervision practices procedurally fair? Development and predictive utility of a procedural justice measure for use in community corrections settings, *Criminal Justice and Behavior* 45(3): 402–420.

Blomberg, T., W. Bales and A. Piquero (2012) Is educational achievement a turning point for incarcerated delinquents across race and sex? *Journal of Youth and Adolescence* 41(2): 202–221.

Bonta, J., T. Rugge, T. Scott, G. Bourgon and A. Yessine (2008) Exploring the black box of community supervision, *Journal of Offender Rehabilitation* 47(3): 248–270.

Bozick, R., J. Steele, L. Davis and S. Turner (2018) Does providing inmates with education improve postrelease outcomes? A meta-analysis of correctional education programs in the United States, *Journal of Experimental Criminology* 14: 1–40.

Bradford, B. (2014) Policing and social identity: Procedural justice, inclusion and cooperation between police and public, *Policing and Society* 24(1): 22–43.

Castro, E., R. Hunter, T. Hardison and V. Johnson-Ojeda (2018) The landscape of postsecondary education in prison and the influence of Second Chance Pell: An analysis of transferability, credit-bearing status, and accreditation, *The Prison Journal* 98(4): 405–426.

Chamberlain, A., M. Gricius, D. Wallace, D. Borjas and V. Ware (2018) Parolee-parole officer rapport: Does it impact recidivism? *International Journal of Offender Therapy and Comparative Criminology* 62(11): 3581–3602.

Dowden, C. and D. Andrews (2004) The importance of staff practice in delivering effective correctional treatment: A meta-analytic review of core correctional practice, *International Journal of Offender Therapy and Comparative Criminology*, 48(2): 203–214.

Duwe, G. and V. Clark (2014) The effects of prison-based educational programming on recidivism and employment, *The Prison Journal* 94(4): 454–478.

Escobar, E.-K., T. Jordan and E. Lohrasbi (2013) Redefining lives: Post-secondary education for currently and formerly incarcerated individuals, *The Vermont Connection*: 34(1): 5.

Glaser, D. (1985) Who gets probation and parole: Case study versus actuarial decision making, *Crime & Delinquency* 31(3), 367–378.

Gorgol, L. and B. Sponsler (2011) *Unlocking potential: Results of a national survey of postsecondary education in state prisons*. Washington: Institute for Higher Education Policy.

Jackson, J., T. Tyler, B. Bradford, D. Taylor and M. Shiner (2010) Legitimacy and procedural justice in prisons, *Prison Service Journal* 191: 4–10.

Johnson, D., E. Maguire and J. Kuhns (2014) Public perceptions of the legitimacy of the law and legal authorities: Evidence from the Caribbean, *Law & Society Review* 48(4): 947–978.

Klingele, C. (2013) Rethinking the use of community supervision, *The Journal of Criminal Law and Criminology* 103(4): 1015–1069.

Klockars, C. (1972). A theory of probation supervision, *The Journal of Criminal Law, Criminology, and Police Science* 63(4): 550–557.

Korte, G. (2016) Pell grants for prisoners: Obama to give inmates a second chance at college, *USA Today*, https://www.usatoday.com/story/news/politics/2016/06/24/pell-grants-prisoners-obama-give-inmates-second-chance-college/86312598

Lipsky, M. (1980) *Street level bureaucrats*. New York: Russell Sage Foundation.

Livingston, L. and J. Miller (2014) Inequalities of race, class, and place and their impact on postincarceration higher education, *Race and Justice* 4(3): 212–245.

Nally, J., S. Lockwood, T. Ho and K. Knutson (2014) Post-release recidivism and employment among different types of released offenders: A 5-year follow-up study in the United States, *International Journal of Criminal Justice Sciences* 9(1): 16–34.

Nix, J., S. Wolfe, J. Rojek and R. Kaminski (2015) Trust in the police: The influence of procedural justice and perceived collective efficacy, *Crime & Delinquency* 61(4): 610–640.

Potts, K. and L. Bierlein Palmer (2014) Voices of parolees attending community college: Helping individuals and society, *Community College Review* 42(4): 267–282.

Rakis, J. (2005) Improving the employment rate of ex-prisoners under parole, *Federal Probation* 69(1): 7–12.

Reisig, M. and G. Mesko (2009) Procedural justice, legitimacy, and prisoner misconduct, *Psychology, Crime & Law* 15(1): 41–59.

Rudes, D. (2012) Getting technical: Parole officers' continued use of technical violations under California's parole reform agenda, *Journal of Crime and Justice* 35(2): 249–268.

Runell, L. (2017) Identifying desistance pathways in a higher education program for formerly incarcerated individuals, *International Journal of Offender Therapy and Comparative Criminology* 61(8): 894–918.

Scott-Hayward, C. (2011) The failure of parole: Rethinking the role of the state in reentry, *New Mexico Law Review* 41: 421–467.

Scott, K. (2016) Corrections and education: The relationship between education and recidivism, *Journal of Intercultural Disciplines* 15: 147–169.

Seiter, R. (2002) Prisoner reentry and the role of parole officers, *Federal Probation* 66(3): 50–54.

Sokoloff, N. and A. Schenck-Fontaine (2017) College programs in prison and upon reentry for men and women: A literature review, *Contemporary Justice Review* 20(1): 95–114.

Strayhorn, T., R. Johnson and B. Barrett (2013) Investigating the college adjustment and transition experiences of formerly incarcerated Black male collegians at predominantly White institutions, *Spectrum: A Journal on Black Men* 2(1): 73–98.

Sunshine, J. and T. Tyler (2003) The role of procedural justice and legitimacy in shaping public support for policing, *Law & Society Review* 37(3): 513–548.

Taxman, F. (2002) Supervision-exploring the dimensions of effectiveness, *Federal Probation* 66(1): 14–27.

Taxman, F. (2008) No illusion: Offender and organizational change in Maryland's proactive community supervision model, *Criminology & Public Policy* 7(2): 275–302.

Tyler, T. (2006) *Why people obey the law*. Princeton: Princeton University Press.

Tyler, T. (2010) Legitimacy in corrections: Policy implications, *Criminology & Public Policy* 9(1): 127–134.

Uggen, C. and R. Stewart (2014) Piling on: Collateral consequences and community supervision, *Minnesota Law Review* 99: 1871–1912.

Walters, G. (2018) College as a turning point: Crime deceleration as a function of college attendance and improved cognitive control, *Emerging Adulthood* 6(5): 336–346.

Chapter 4

'More than just saving the government care costs'

Re-presenting student carers' narratives in the United Kingdom

Jacqueline Priego-Hernández and Debbie Holley

> Most people going into uni with disabled parents aren't just low income households but they're low income households with no savings or very little to their name, so every little help is not just appreciated but it goes towards getting these people back into the economy more than just saving the government care costs
>
> (Research participant, workshop discussion)

The research reported in this chapter draws on narratives of care from university students, generated through biographic and photography-based methods. These narratives give us insights into the lives of student carers, an under-researched, often resource-challenged and marginalised population. The opening quote exemplifies how articulate and acutely aware student carers can be about their position within the interlocking structural systems of inequality in which they are embedded. This chapter documents their resourcefulness, while analysing their stories through the conceptual lenses of intersectionality and transitions.

Care and student carers in the UK context

In the United Kingdom (UK), the rights of carers were recognised for the first time in the law, alongside provisions for those they care for, through the Care Act 2014. This piece of legislation promotes the wellbeing of carers, including 'participation in work, education, training or recreation'. However, as a matter of statutory policy, Carer's Allowance recipients 'must not be in full-time education, and must not have earnings of more than £128 per week after deductions' (Powell et al., 2020, p. 5). This restriction renders the phrase 'student carer' a contradiction, as officially students are not recognised as carers (or at least not recognised to the point of being entitled to Carer's Allowance). Furthermore, while there are means-tested financial support allowances that student carers could potentially access (e.g. Adult Dependants' Grant of £3,094 in the 2020/21 academic year), these are not aimed to carers specifically but to undergraduates in general.

The UK's Department of Health and Social Care (2018, p. 7) considers that a carer is 'anyone who spends time looking after or helping a friend, family member or neighbour who, because of their health and care needs, would find it difficult to cope without this help regardless of age or whether they identify as a carer'. Despite this established definition, data regarding care are variable, complicating policy development and implementation. While the 2011 Census found that 5.8 million people (10.3% of the population) in England and Wales provide unpaid care (Office for National Statistics, 2013), the Family Resources Survey reported 5.4 and 4.5 million of informal carers in the UK in 2016/17 and 2017/18, respectively (Department for Work and Pensions [DWP], 2019). Data are patchier for student carers, with the National Union of Students (2013) estimating that they account for between 3% and 6% of the student population in the UK, and the Family Resources Survey finding that they constituted around 3% of the total of carers in 2017/18 (DWP, 2019).

More than a decade ago, Alsop et al. (2008) noted the minor role of care in the widening participation policy agenda, calling for a 'higher education "care culture"' (p. 623). In recognition of the growing evidence regarding student carers' struggles, from 2018 the UK's Universities and Colleges Admissions Service (UCAS) included new questions in the postgraduate application process allowing candidates to self-identify as carers, with plans to do so for undergraduates in the future. UCAS also offers information to prospective university students with caring responsibilities, highlighting that 'many universities and colleges have initiatives or support programmes in place to help students with care responsibilities' (UCAS, n.d.). In the UK, however, there are no official policy provisions in terms of caring responsibility needs of university students: academic, financial and emotional support for student carers remain at the discretion of individual higher education institutions.

Research involving participants in their dual role as students and carers is scant. Early studies included healthcare students in caring roles, focusing mainly on the manifold challenges, concerns and negative impact on their studies, underscoring the need for targeted support (Hussain et al., 2011; Kirton et al., 2012). Recent research with student samples mirrors this focus on the adverse effects of caring, with one study revealing that frequency of face-to-face contact with a cared for friend, housemate or partner with mental health issues predicted negative consequences of caregiving for university students in caring roles (Byrom, 2017). On these grounds, it is hardly surprising that 29% of the young adult carers survey respondents who had been to college or university reported dropping out due to their caring responsibilities, in a study commissioned by the Carers Trust (Sempik and Becker, 2014, p. 3).

More recent, fine-textured studies with student carers and a focus on meaning-making are also considering negotiation of barriers (Kettell, 2020) and student carers' resilience and ability to cope (Jones, 2018). It is to this emerging body of literature that this chapter seeks to contribute, challenging the deficit model in care research whereby care is tacitly presented as a burden and services as assistance (Milne and Larkin, 2015, p. 9), and following trends in international young carers research that problematises straightforward associations between caring and negative outcomes (Skovdal, 2011).

Theoretical underpinnings

Intersectionality

Quantitative research has offered evidence of the detrimental effects of multiple disadvantages on adults' mental and physical health, and functional limitations (Grollman, 2014). This research has also shown that a focus on a single disadvantage (in this case, that of carer status while in higher education), misses potential concomitant disadvantages that are interlocked and in fluid relationship with care – social divisions including gender, age, race/ethnicity, social class, (dis)ability and political orientation both shape and are shaped by the experience of caring. For instance, feminist researchers have discussed the gendered dimension of care, underscoring the reproduction of structural gender-based expectations (Barnes, 2012; Tronto, 2013). While gender is central as a social division, a number of multifaceted salient identities of carers, only one of which is gender, intertwine and unfold through caring interactions. Another important example of these salient identities for caring is age. Care researchers (Larkin et al., 2019, p. 62) highlight that, taken as a single salient characteristic, a sizable amount of research has been conducted including young carers, despite the fact that they account for only 3% of all carers in the UK. Instead of an exclusive focus on age, the importance of a 'life-course' approach to care is now acknowledged, suggesting that age interacts with other (potentially disadvantaging) characteristics such as gender to provide a different care experience and wellbeing consequences (Hamilton and Cass, 2017, p. 80) and that care evolves over time (Bowlby et al., 2010, p. 46, cited in Milne and Larkin, 2015, p. 8).

Against this backdrop, recent care research has called for the use of an intersectionality lens to analyse particular groups of carers, to account for the complexity of caring and of these groups (Hankivsky, 2014; Larkin et al., 2019, p. 61). The present chapter responds to these calls by following Collins and Bilge's (2016) approach to intersectionality, acknowledging that 'people's lives and the organization of power in a given society are better understood as being shaped not by a single axis of social division, be it race or gender or class, but by many axes that work together and influence each other' (p. 2). Using intersectionality as an analytical tool, we seek to identify forms of resistance by highlighting how student carers are not just passive receivers of oppression and inequality, but active agents and respondents to these processes (Rosenthal, 2016).

Transitions

The conceptual tool of transitions is widely used in higher education as well as in developmental psychology and the social sciences, with O'Donnell et al. (2016) identifying definitions that go from movement from one institutional context to another and life-defining events or milestones to more fluid conceptualisations in terms of constant change across the lifespan. Sociocultural accounts of transitions understand them as 'becoming' (Gale and Parker, 2014) and as processes used to reduce the uncertainty brought about by ruptures in a taken-for-granted life structure (Zittoun, 2007). In this way, transitions are seen as non-linear, flexible and fluid series of movements through life, with opportunities for meaning-making, identity-positioning and the generation of coherent (if fragmented) narratives in seeking life pathways in continuous renegotiation.

Transitions offer a powerful lens to explore the life experiences of students with caring responsibilities. First, transitions account for the manifold pathways through which students may find themselves caring at different points in their lives, with care organically becoming part of their personal narrative. Second, this concept affords the acknowledgement of meaning-making and identity-positioning when student carers fulfil the simultaneous demands between the family home, higher education and social care services, in relation to their multiple and overlapping roles. Third, transitions convey the continuous, porous and potentially unintentional navigation between spaces, events, self-conceptualisations, aspirations and challenges of caring while studying.

Research methods

This project is a participatory study, drawing on Freire's (1974/2007) work on education for critical consciousness, whereby the full engagement of research participants and work *with* them is pursued. In engaging student carers, we acknowledge care as relational. Our focus is, however, on the carers as students, for it is our contention that their stories, in the form of words and images, offer a glimpse into the *carer-person-cared-for* relationship in a fine-textured, policy-relevant way.

Institutional ethical approval was obtained and, recognising the 'hard to reach' nature of the student carer population, a purposive sampling strategy sought to maximise heterogeneity in terms of gender, young/mature, cross-faculty, beneficiaries and non-beneficiaries of an institutional bursary. Seven students from a large university in Southwest England were included in the wider study; all gave their informed consent to take part in the study. Here we focus on two of these participants, using their narratives as case studies to maximise contrast in terms of intersectionality and transitions.

Data collection followed a threefold step:

a) *Photodiaries over a month.* Participants were asked to take 'a picture a day' that best represented their daily experiences. The project provided digital cameras, and sent weekly reminders via email and text messages. Using a photodiary aimed to address 'the "snapshot" nature that characterises much of the research [which] tends to present care as a static process fixed in time and space' (Milne and Larkin, 2015, p. 9).

b) *Photo-elicited biographical narrative interviews.* These focused on biographical elicitation (distant past), the university experience and caring responsibilities vis-à-vis studies. The final stage of the interview was photo-elicited: interviewees were asked to go through each photo, describe it and explain the reasons for taking it.
c) *Participatory workshop.* This activity sought to garner the views of participants as a group in terms of their experiences with support within the university and beyond. It also served as a preliminary participatory analysis exercise. All seven participants took part in the first two steps, with four participants joining the workshop.

In exploring the data for this chapter, we focus on student carers as storytelling agents, on their agency in the narrative action, and on their everyday experiences that respond to multiple and intersecting sources of marginalisation. We consider narrative is a social, cognitive and emotional process to make sense of our experiences and articulate experiential knowledge (Bruner, 1990; McAdams, 1993). Drawing on biographic methods (Holley and Oliver, 2011), we adopt a narrative reconstruction approach that takes interviews and photographic accounts as a coherent unit of analysis, aiming to show how narratives are produced in context (Squire et al., 2014). In re-presenting these stories, we relate individual accounts to wider social and structural narratives around caring vis-à-vis higher education.

Narratives of care intersecting with higher education

Sydney came to the UK from Southeast Asia as an infant, with her mum and maternal grandmother. They have lived together since, and were all present when the interview was conducted. Sydney lost her father before being born and narrated mixed memories from her childhood, with experiences of being an interpreter for her grandmother and enjoying the dividends of her mother's job. However, she also recounted 'low level bullying' at school and how even now 'occasionally I'll walk down the street and I'll get someone doing the slanty eyes going [racial slur]'. Despite obtaining good GCSE results, Sydney attained lower than predicted A-level grades, which she related to attendance problems and depression. She also recalled having panic attacks at school and being prescribed anxiolytic medication around this time. Turning eighteen was important for her, she acknowledges, as school was over and she could now represent her mother more fully at an institutional level and avoid 'bilingual problems'. Being an adult, she was now able to 'take over some bills' directly.

Finances have influenced Sydney's education: after Year 9 she moved from a fee-paying school to what she describes as a 'voluntary contribution' institution, when her family's financial circumstances changed due to her mother's deteriorating health. She was in 'the final year to get the £3K fees' and this weighted into her decision about starting university immediately after school. She only had sporadic jobs, as her mother wanted her to focus on her studies and go to university.

With brief interjections from her mother, during the interview Sydney recounted many examples of how she progressively became a carer for her grandmother, before caring for her mother as well. She reminisced her first caring responsibilities: 'Taking Grandma to the hospital, taking Grandma to the GP, to the dentist, the cancer stuff [...] I had to take her to her radiotherapy appointments'. This coincided with the time in which to make the decision to go to university. While Sydney acknowledges that she chose a specific university because the course 'was the first on the search results [...] it had the best outcomes', she also stated that there was 'almost a silent agreement that "oh, you need to come back and get things taken care of"'. She took the train back home from university 'at weekends, but then the weekends became longer'. Despite these responsibilities, Sydney acknowledged she 'can't be listed officially as a carer [...] Mum's listed officially as a carer for Grandma, even though Mum has her own issues'.

About her academic experience, Sydney narrated:

> It was good during the first year and second year because I had a friend like me who was there, but then when I had to repeat the year, they'd gone on placement [...] the second half hasn't been that great [...] The academic advisors during my first year weren't great [...] when I came to them with "oh, I have these mental health things" [...] you know men, they're very awkward [...] when I came back for the second year, after I had to repeat, I think I went to additional learning support [...] they diagnosed me with dyspraxia.

Sydney's mental health problems are inextricably related to her university and caring experience, having had to repeat her second year due to 'mitigating circumstances'. She explained how she has used some strategies gained from cognitive behavioural therapy, but also how providing evidence repeatedly is taxing: 'when I came back to start the final year the administrator didn't know [about my diagnosis], and then I had to submit letters and submit the things again [...] the programme administrators aren't too understanding'. Finally, 'having to deal with stuff at home and then having to sort out the course and stuff, until in the end it got overwhelming and I just suspended it'. Before going back home, however, Sydney received one important act of support from university staff: '[social services] came in the beginning mostly because my academic advisor wrote some letter to my MP[1] [...] they knew they were sending me back here, they wanted me to have some sort of support [...] our priority moved to the top of the pile'.

Sydney's placement year seemed to serve as a bridge between the world of work, university life, and caring for her relatives, insofar as it allowed her to gain experience, receive an income to support her family and apply her course: 'During my placement I was doing okay, we were coping, we were getting enough money to get by but when the financial stuff stopped because I went back to uni, that's when it became difficult [...] because at the time my mum had to stop [work] because her hands were getting worse'. Being a student carer comes at a cost at different levels: 'I'm suspended from the Union at the moment until I go back but there are some things I can't claim that other carers would be able to claim, because I am a student [...] Carer's Allowance'.

All of Sydney's images in her photodiary express a domestic environment in which actions to care for her relatives are foregrounded. The sharing of activities in her family was also present in the process of completing the photodiary, as Sydney's mother joined her in taking a number of photographs. Sydney verbally expressed that,

> right now I have nothing, I have not a lot going on, I just need to take care of people and go to the support worker and sort out bills and that's my life [...] Every day is the same, carer comes, gives Grandma a bath, at some point she has her food, at some point Mum goes out, we go out, it's the same routine.

These intimate images corroborate her present as a carer: her suspended university studies were not in the picture.

'Oh, that's just my grandma's carer alarm thing so if she falls over it will I think that day it kept going off, yes 'cause I think the phone alarm went off and it kept going off so no one got any sleep [...] it like fills the whole house when it goes off'.

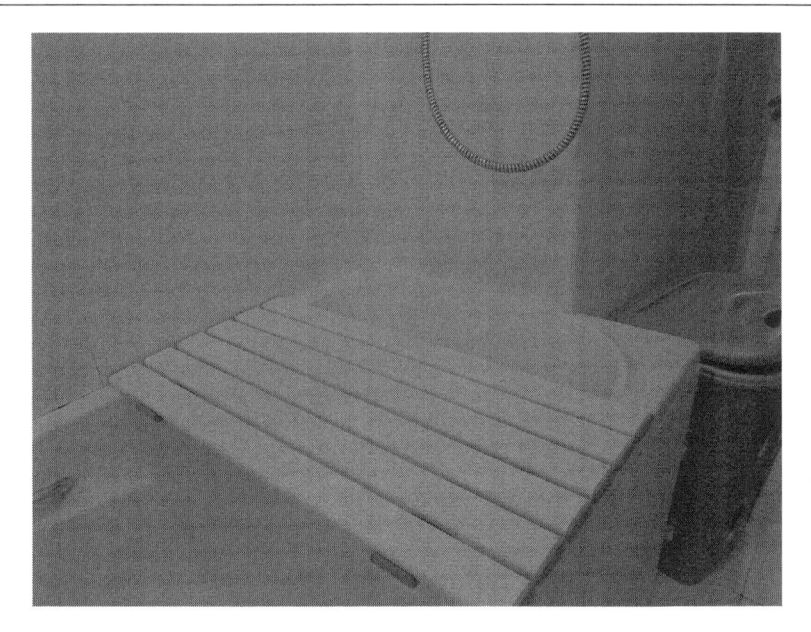

'Grandma's bath board at the time to show that she needs equipment and just the change in equipment because before she was using a shower stool, which was wobbly and creaky but then the occupational therapist came and they put that in instead'.

'And then the food. Grandma only eats [Southeast Asian] food so she has to have her food specially prepared [laughs]'.

At the time of the study Sydney had been at home for months, dedicated exclusively to caring, and was not planning to go back to university the following academic year, as a surgical procedure for her mother was scheduled during term-time. About her future, she hopes 'actually finishing uni at some point maybe, because my course is only four years and I've taken so long'.

Joseph started university in his thirties and was in the last year of undergraduate studies when the interview took place in the university premises. When asked about his background, he narrated:

> a lot of things in my life have led me to this particular path [...] I was born in [City] [...] I didn't seem to develop normally [...] I just plodded along [...] My mum and dad, separated, divorced when I was about five [...] I had a brother a couple of years younger than me [...] I went to secondary school and probably for them six years it's probably like one of those chapters I'd like to forget [...] my grades were very poor [...] they found out I was slow [...] finances were very difficult so you know I just stuck with this school and at sixteen I left.

Despite recounting having travelled to more than 50 countries in his twenties, Joseph felt he was 'up and down like that, zigzag, zigzag, and relationship after relationship and kind of dead-end job to dead-end job, and kind of sleep-walking from late twenties to thirty'.

When he was 29, Joseph recalled, 'I just had absolutely no direction in my life' but wanted to 'make something of myself' and, after travelling to Australia on a working holiday visa, he came back to the UK to pursue a number of qualifications with the financial support of his mother. At this point, he decided to pursue a university access course at a nearby college. Joseph recounted applying to 'loads' of courses in universities in different parts of the UK, but was accepted only by the university in the city where he lives. He was offered a university bursary, which was supplemented by a £5,000 compensation award for injuries after being the victim of knife crime.

Joseph's role as carer has been intermittent, and intensified during his university studies. He narrated:

> I remember as an early child I used to wake up my mum every day [...] I shouldn't have really had that role as a kid of making her dinner, doing the dishes, making cups of tea, making sure my mum woke up [...] I see that this was taking on care responsibilities at an early age [...] it was just put upon me, and my mum got ill, I mean we are going back eighteen years ago [...] and she hasn't worked since [...] My mum had a subarachnoid haemorrhage [...] it started like the first week I started the second year so it took about a year for her to be out of the woods and it has been a bit of a nuisance.

Joseph's father was absent during most of Joseph's childhood. Joseph, in turn, changed his name to reflect the distance between them. After they renewed contact, his father had a stroke and found himself homeless. For a year, Joseph assisted his father with accommodation, he 'kept going back and forth to [City] doing all these appointments […] then I've gotta start working on my assignment and then be back at college in the morning'. At this point, Joseph offered for his father to be brought to the city where he lives:

> I thought about, "we could live together, he could get like housing benefit, I could be his main carer whilst doing my studies", but I knew that would be counterproductive because he wouldn't get better, he has got this learned helplessness, so I don't want to be a live-in carer […] He was asked to leave […] his shared accommodation. I thought "aw, this is all I need when I am at university".

Joseph saw his caring role as a barrier to attaining higher marks: 'In many respects I wish my dad hadn't come down, I hadn't been caring you know I wish I'd actually been uncaring like I did years ago […] because caring for him here has had a strain on my life, an impact on my studies, which is unfair'. Furthermore, Joseph also felt that his efforts were not reciprocated with his father's appreciation, which is compounded by his father's dementia:

> I tried to cut my visits because emotionally it's too much […] I want the relationship to be fairly equal and […] you feel there's, you know, no light at the end of the tunnel […] this place that I want him to go, I used to take him to the Alzheimer's Club, and then I had to change my lessons at uni on a Monday so I couldn't go, so he never went.

Despite acknowledging that he 'never told people about my problems so I've been completely alone, I didn't know what kind of help there was out there', Joseph has been 'registered with this [County] carers resource centre and had little bits of pickings'. Being a carer gives Joseph the recognition he does not obtain from his father. For example, at university he has been able to access hardship bursaries and a carers' bursary: 'it's just really great, not just financially but just for [University] to give that recognition, that we recognise that there are a handful of students who deserve that little extra help'.

Joseph was prolific with his photo-taking, producing more than 100 pictures. He classified them into a number of categories: 'caring' for his father; 'uni' ('visiting the library, my desk at home, that kind of thing'); 'leisure' ('myself going out getting a coffee'); 'home', with domestic scenes; 'wellbeing' ('went to the doctors a couple of times'); 'achievement' documenting everyday life gains ('I have done various piles of ironing'); and 'stress', with the most photographs ('waiting at bus stops, doing lots of heavy shopping, going for walks because I am stressed'). While numerous, Joseph's photographs document his interactions with a reduced number of networks, including the university, health and social care services, and his immediate family, as illustrated below.

'This was father's day, with me and my brother taking my dad out and it was meant to be a nice day, and he just had what we call the strops, he didn't want to be there. We done it all for him, got him drinks, a little bite to eat, and he just wanted to go home.'

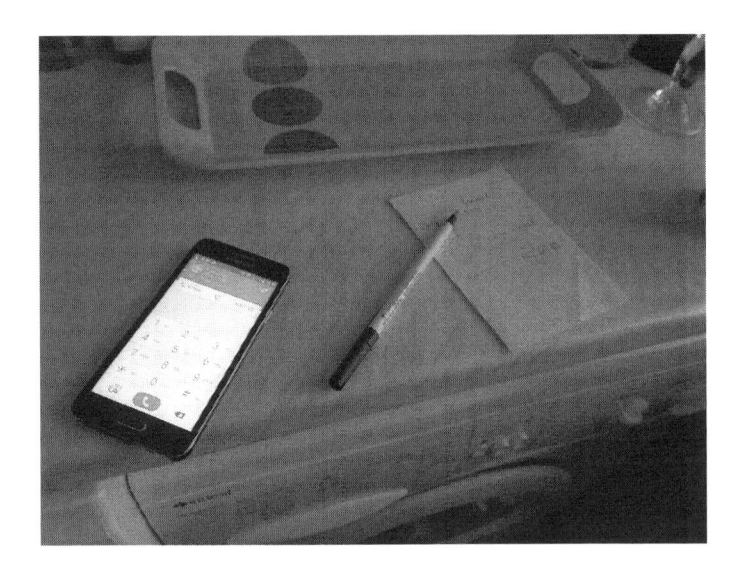

'More than just saving the government care costs' 59

'This was like a kind of like a work call. This was to do with the carer's thing, I do that quite a lot. You know, get a message, pen and paper, this was about the day centre and then I was quite stressed about it.'

'This is like my little domain, this is my section of books, so they look really neat there but certainly when I leave, whenever I leave uni at some point, I will really miss that.'

For his future, Joseph would like to 'look at a career and have a partner, maybe have children [...] I'm worried though, particularly with my mum, when I finish uni, I'll go back to how it was, get into old habits and start seeing them all the time, coz uni's been a wonderful, you know, my excuse, to distance yourself'.

Discussion

The narratives presented here display fluid, involuntary and sometimes painful life transitions, all brought together by caring vis-à-vis the university experience. Mirroring research into caring, these narratives demonstrate that entering into care is non-linear (McGarry, 2008, p. 83, cited in Milne and Larkin, 2015, p. 8; Hamilton and Cass, 2017). This study contributes students carers' narratives as they evince their increasingly transitioning in and out of caring responsibilities, from home-based to distance caring, from resigned responsibility to undesired duties, with the different demands of caring and university studies evolving in parallel.

Caring intersects with manifold social divisions in terms of age, gender, ethnicity, social class and disability. Sydney's and Joseph's narratives show a sharp contrast in terms of age and the transition into higher education: while the former followed the mainstream route into university, the latter is a mature student with a complex pathway into his degree, including a course transfer after one year. At the same time, while both life stories have been influenced by caring responsibilities before their university studies, it is during their journey as students that these responsibilities deepen and their roles are shaken and renegotiated. Similarly, gendered expectations are subtly played out, as one could assign typical feminine and masculine roles to Sydney and Joseph's physical positioning in relation to caring – she stays at home with her family, while he manages to keep separated from those he cares for. However, this is complicated by *how* their stories were told: both Sydney and Joseph expressed assertiveness, resourcefulness and political engagement, which until recently would have been associated with a specific gender.

The two student carers' ethnicity needs to be understood in the context of social class and disability. As a white male, ethnicity is absent from Joseph's narratives, but not his acute awareness of financial difficulties throughout his life and what he perceives as the significance of higher education for social mobility. In contrast, Sydney's narrative is charged with the experience of racial discrimination. Her experience is in turn shaped by migration, the fact that three generations of women with varying degrees of English proficiency and acculturation live together and mutually support each other, and their fluctuating financial situation. Finally, disability is an analytical layer that permeates all other categories: both student carers report special educational needs, albeit experienced in different manners. While Joseph heard from an early age that he was 'slow', affecting his self-esteem, the onset of Sydney's mental health conditions took place in her adolescence, with the consequence of disturbing an otherwise notable academic performance.

The fluid transitions between education and care show simultaneity, with liminal spaces filled by ambiguity about the present and uncertainty about the future, both of which depend on the relationship and needs of those student carers care for. The apparently seamless move between different spaces, such as the family home and university, and responsibilities, highlight the need for support in fulfiling those responsibilities and effectively occupying those spaces. While for some student carers it may be the case that 'turning points' or 'life-changing events' are identifiable, these narratives reveal continuous ruptures and adjustments in which student carers reposition their values, priorities and expectations. It is during those moments of identity repositioning that support is needed and when universities could offer assistance that makes a remarkable difference.

Three policy recommendations have emerged from this research. First, due to the multi-layered and fluid nature of caring, the intersection between different social divisions and the dual responsibilities of simultaneously being a student and a carer should be acknowledged. An intersectional analysis of student carers' experiences reveals how different characteristics such as age, gender and disability work concertedly to shape these experiences. They intertwine as a coherent whole that can only be understood in context, rather than as factors to be addressed in isolation. Second, it is necessary but not sufficient to offer the opportunity of self-identification at the point of application for a university place. As documented in this chapter, transitions are non-linear and caring responsibilities can appear or heighten at any point of the university journey. Mechanisms should be put in place to allow disclosure and support for students who become carers before and during their studies and, importantly, while they have suspended their studies. Third, tailored support for student carers is needed as a matter of policy, not only driven by individual university contributions and criteria. While this may mean restricting the definition of student carers, institutionalising support for this population would entail foregrounding their presence and recognising that they are doing more, much more, than just saving the government care costs.

Note

1 Member of Parliament.

References

Alsop, R., S. Gonzalez-Arnal and M. Kilkey (2008) The widening participation agenda: The marginal place of care, *Gender and Education* 20: 623–637.

Barnes, M. (2012) *Care in everyday life: An ethic of care in practice.* Bristol: Policy Press.

Bowlby, S., L. McKie, S. Gregory and I. Macpherson (2010) *Interdependency and care over the life course.* Abingdon: Routledge.

Bruner, J. (1990) *Acts of meaning.* Cambridge/London: Harvard University Press.

Byrom, N. (2017) Supporting a friend, housemate or partner with mental health difficulties: The student experience, *Early Intervention in Psychiatry* 31: 202–207.

Collins, P. and S. Bilge (2016) *Intersectionality.* Cambridge: Polity.

Department of Health and Social Care (2018) *Carers action plan 2018–2020: Supporting carers today.* London: Department of Health and Social Care.

Department for Work and Pensions (2019) *Family resources survey: Financial year 2017/18 – carers data tables.* London: Department of Work and Pensions.

Freire, P. (1974/2007) *Education for critical consciousness.* London: Continuum.

Gale, T. and S. Parker (2014) Navigating change: A typology of student transition in higher education, *Studies in Higher Education* 39(5): 734–753.

Grollman, E. (2014). Multiple disadvantaged statuses and health: The role of multiple forms of discrimination, *Journal of Health and Social Behavior* 55(1): 3–19.

Hamilton, M. and B. Cass (2017) Capturing the centrality of age and life-course stage in the provision of unpaid care, *Journal of Sociology* 53(1): 79–93.

Hankivsky, O. (2014). Rethinking care ethics: On the promise and potential of an intersectional analysis, *American Political Science Review* 108(2): 252–264.

Holley, D. and M. Oliver (2011) Negotiating the digital divide, in R. Land and S. Bayne (eds.) *Digital difference: Educational futures rethinking theory and practice* (pp. 101–113). Rotterdam: Sense Publishers.

Hussain, Z., V. Pickering, D. Percy, J. Crane and J. Bogg (2011) An analysis of the experiences of radiography and radiotherapy students who are carers at one UK university, *Radiography* 17(1): 49–54.

Jones, L. (2018) Exploring the resilience and identity of young carers in higher education: A thematic analysis. Unpublished undergraduate dissertation, Manchester Metropolitan University.

Kettell, L. (2020) Young adult carers in higher education: The motivations, barriers and challenges involved – A UK study, *Journal of Further and Higher Education* 44(1): 100–112.

Kirton, J., K. Richardson, B. Jack and A. Jinks (2012) A study identifying the difficulties healthcare students have in their role as a healthcare student when they are also an informal carer, *Nurse Education Today* 32(6): 641–646.

Larkin, M., M. Henwood and A. Milne (2019) Carer-related research and knowledge: Findings from a scoping review, *Health and Social Care in the Community* 27(1): 55–67.

McAdams, D. (1993) *The stories we live by: Personal myths and the making of the self.* New York/London: The Guilford Press.

McGarry, J. (2008) Defining roles, relationships, boundaries and participation between elderly people and nurses within the home: An ethnographic study, *Health and Social Care in the Community* 17(1): 83–91.

Milne, A. and M. Larkin (2015) Knowledge generation about care-giving in the UK: A critical review of research paradigms, *Health and Social Care in the Community* 23(1): 4–13.

National Union of Students (2013) *Learning with care: Experiences of student careers in the UK.* London: National Union of Students.

O'Donnell, V., M. Kean and G. Stevens (2016) *Student transition in higher education: Concepts, theories and practices.* York: Higher Education Academy.

Office for National Statistics (2013) *2011 Census analysis: Unpaid care in England and Wales, 2011, and comparison with 2001*. London: Office for National Statistics.

Powell, A., B. Francis-Devine, D. Foster, D. Thurley, N. Roberts, P. Loft, R. Harker, R. McInnes, S. Danechi, S. Kennedy and T. Powell (2020) *Carers (Briefing Paper Number 7756)*. London: House of Commons Library.

Rosenthal, L. (2016) Incorporating intersectionality into psychology: An opportunity to promote social justice and equity, *The American Psychologist* 71(6): 474–485.

Sempik, J., and S. Becker (2014) *Young adult carers and employment*. London/Nottingham: Carers Trust and University of Nottingham.

Skovdal, M. (2011) Agency, resilience and the psychosocial well-being of caregiving children: Experiences from western Kenya, in E. Ommering, S. Evers and C. Notermans (eds.) *Not just a victim: The child as catalyst and witness of contemporary Africa* (pp. 247–268). Leiden: Brill.

Squire, C., M. Davis, C. Esin, M. Andrews, B. Harrison, H. Lars-Christer and M. Hydén (2014) *What is narrative research?* London: Bloomsbury.

Tronto, J. (2013) *Caring democracy: Markets, equality, and justice*. New York/London: New York University Press.

Universities and Colleges Admissions Service (n.d.) *Students with caring responsibilities* [online], https://www.ucas.com/undergraduate/applying-university/individual-needs/students-caring-responsibilities.

Zittoun, T. (2007) Symbolic resources and responsibility in transitions, *Young* 15(2): 193–211.

Chapter 5

Genderism and trans students in Hong Kong higher education

Diana K. Kwok

Introduction

Students attending universities or colleges come from diverse groups, including racial, ethnic, ability status, sexual orientation, gender and intersex identities. Institutions of higher education may encounter challenges in acknowledging the needs of diverse groups of students. Particularly, these institutions could possibly have difficulties in understanding transgender students' needs. In the education literature, transgender students often face intolerant/negative attitudes, prejudice and discrimination against them in society (Beemyn, 2016; Wernick et al., 2014). Transgender or, to use a more inclusive term, 'trans' students in this chapter are defined as those students who 'do not identify with or normatively enact the gender assigned to them at birth' (Wernick et al., 2014, p. 927). Scholars in the field of trans prejudice often adopt the concept of genderism to conceptualize prejudice, discriminatory and intolerant attitudes against trans people. For instance, Hill and Willoughby (2005) perceived genderism as 'an ideology that reinforces the negative evaluation of gender non-conformity or an incongruence between sex and gender' (p. 534).

In the literature, trans students in an education context, particularly from higher education institutions, are observed to face tremendous barriers, which affect their mental health (Goldberg et al., 2018; Messman and Leslie, 2019). Institutional barriers faced by college and university students are now a growing concern in an international context (Beemyn, 2016; Bilodeau, 2005; Case et al., 2012; Catalano, 2015; Donatone and Rachlin, 2013; Effrig et al., 2011; Messman and Leslie, 2019; Goldberg et al., 2018; Goldberg and Kuvalanka, 2018; Grant et al., 2011; Nicolazzo, 2016a, 2016b; Pryor, 2015; Seelman, 2014a, 2014b, 2016; Woodford et al., 2017). Campus and institutional support appears to be small-scale or even non-existent, especially in the Asian Chinese cultural context (Goldberg et al., 2018; Suen, 2015). For example, in a study with 27,000 trans individuals, Goldberg (2018) revealed the following results: '24% of respondents who were out as or perceived as trans in college reported being verbally, physically, or sexually harassed at that time', and '16% of those who experienced harassment left college because of the harassment' (p. 2). Literature also found that discrimination and prejudiced experiences of trans students may increase higher mental health risks (gender minority stress), particularly in the areas of sexual health, gender-based violence and substance abuse. Affirmative and appropriate campus counseling service may act as an important source of support (Messman and Leslie, 2019) for the students.

Despite the potential involvement of trans students in college mental health or counseling services, the literature to date on college trans students is very limited. Most studies include trans groups with lesbian, gay and bisexual students without addressing trans students as a unique group (Dugan et al., 2012); no trans people are typically found within studies of Chinese societies. Publication of this chapter will help to fill this knowledge gap. By increasing this knowledge and understanding, universities and colleges would enhance their frontline practice for better position. This chapter aims to provide terms and discuss trans identity development and to highlight the prejudice experienced by trans students in higher education institutions based on a synthesis of international studies. Research results from two Hong Kong studies on trans prejudice projects will be highlighted and recommendations for college counselors on supporting trans students in Hong Kong sociocultural context will be made.

Literature review

Language and terms

Conceptualizations of the term 'transgender' have been evolving continually in the past ten years in education and psychology literature, from binary conceptions of male and female (e.g. male vs. female and trans man vs. trans woman) to the notion that gender identities can go beyond binary definitions and fall 'along a continuum' (Dugan et al., 2012, p. 720). Although trans communities are working hard to have a collectively shared language (Beemyn, 2003; Carter, 2000), trans (a more recent language to embrace broader and diversities of trans communities) or transgender has become an inclusive concept to embrace individuals with diverse gender expressions or/and gender identities going beyond binary assumptions (American Psychological Association [APA], 2011; Wernick et al., 2014) and individuals whose sex at birth differs from their subjective identification (Bilodeau, 2005). For example, transgender as defined by APA (2011) is 'an umbrella term for persons whose gender identity, gender expression, or behavior does not conform to that typically associated with the sex to which they were assigned at birth' (p. 1). In this chapter I follow Carabez et al. (2015) who use the term trans as an umbrella concept to include 'non-cisgender variations that encompass the entire spectrum, including transgender, transitioned, transsexual, trans man, trans woman and other terms' (p. 3307).

Trans people have been described as a derogatory term, 'yan yiu', in Hong Kong Chinese society, which refers to a 'human monster' and connoting 'freak' or 'person changed against nature'. This insulting term reflects stigmatization and social disapproval in Chinese culture (Winter and King, 2010). Trans communities have become more visible in recent years and are more public about advocating their equal opportunities rights, due to the rise of human rights awareness among the general public, as well as among the sexual and gender diversity communities in Hong Kong. An umbrella term 'kwa-sing-bit' (跨性別), meaning 'across gender boundaries' has emerged to represent diverse trans identities within Hong Kong society. Scholars have suggested that obstacles due to genderism in higher education institutions are likely to negatively impact trans individuals' mental health and study outcomes, while affirmative and accommodated supports from higher education institutions can foster trans students' resilience (Messman and Leslie, 2019). College mental health practitioners, such as campus counselors, student affairs officers, and health center practitioners, with their professional training to respect diversity and to support students from diverse groups, are expected to play their professional roles to support and to affirm trans students' gender identities and expressions (Messman and Leslie, 2019).

Trans identity development, campus context and trans students

Trans students usually have experienced a unique process of identity development during their social or gender transitioning. Identity development, or 'coming out', can be a painful and difficult process for trans persons. They go through a period of transitioning in the coming out process, during which trans persons change their gender expression and gender presentation to match their preferred gender. According to Korell and Lorah (2007), trans students often feel betrayed by their bodies during puberty, particularly when undergoing the development of secondary sex characteristics, such as the deepening of voice, development of breasts, presence of pubic and facial hair, etc. They feel that their gender identity and their bodies are not consistent. Feeling uncomfortable over their gender dysphoria and different from their peers in the developmental stage, trans students may experience an intense feeling of loss, isolation and exclusion in their daily lives, which often leads to mental health difficulties. Some trans students experience 'intense feelings of urgency to openly express their transgender identity, especially if they have been suppressing their transgender identity since early childhood or adolescence' (Korell and Lorah, 2007, p. 275). In the university/college campus, as binary sex/gender systems are often adopted in university rules and regulations, as well as reinforced in the campus facilities (restrooms, recreational clubs, etc.), trans students may not feel safe to come out during their social or medical transition. As a result, they have to mask their transition and only reveal their trans status when necessary. Schools, as institutions in our society, assume that students should fit into the binary gender norms (female and male) based on students' assigned sex at birth. At the same time, coming out as a trans student in the university or college classroom challenges these binary institutions but also places significant gender minority stress on trans students to present their gender 'correctly and appropriately'. The students' campus experience can be very difficult and uncomfortable when their gender expressions and/or identities do not fall within the norms of the female or male gender binary. Trans students, including those with binary (e.g. trans man or trans woman) and non-binary (e.g. gender queer or bi-gender) trans identities are thus excluded and marginalized because these students contest the traditionally defined sex and gender system within the campus. At the same time, as trans students are members of marginalized minority groups, they are likely to experience more socially based mental health risks, gender-based bullying and/or harassment than their cisgender counterparts (Beemyn et al., 2005; Goldberg et al., 2018; Grant et al., 2011; Messman and Leslie, 2019).

Genderism has been conceptualized by researchers as a code of dogma that encourages discriminatory attitudes to trans and other gender variant individuals (Hill and Willoughby, 2005). Those who hold this dogma 'believe that people who do not conform to sociocultural expectations of gender are pathological' (p. 534). Genderism, as similar to heterosexism, is considered as a 'source of social oppression and psychological shame, such that it can be imposed on a person, but also that a person may internalize these beliefs' (p. 534). Aligned with the definitions and conceptions of genderism by Hill and Willoughby (2005), concepts and ideas from the literatures related to the gender minority stress model may be useful for us to understand the effect of genderism on trans students. This model proposes that when trans students encounter gender-based discrimination and prejudice, they may have additional stress, and their mental health will be affected, with internalized psychological shame (Testa et al., 2017). According to Testa et al. (2017), trans individuals, as members of a minority group, may experience additional stress (socially-based) due to discrimination toward their minority/trans identity. These socially-based stressors are as follows: 1) 'gender-based discrimination', 2) 'gender-based rejection', 3) 'identity non-affirmation' and 4) 'gender-based victimization' (Testa et al., 2017, p. 126). Researchers found trans individuals may suffer from minority stress when they observed signs of genderism manifested on campus institutional practices or environment (Wernick et al., 2014).

Trans students in colleges and universities

There are rising global concerns about trans student experiences in higher education. Klugman (2014) revealed that over half of his participants reported negative experiences, such as overt hostility and violence, as well as microaggressions. He noted that even faculty and staff could be miseducated and insensitive. Studies have found that trans students encountered more bullying and harassment experiences than their cisgender, lesbian and gay peers. In another study, Dugan et al. (2012) found that trans informants experience higher rates of discrimination and have lower scores on self-perceived cognitive skills. The National Transgender Discrimination Survey in the United States (US) found that among 6,500 trans college informants, around one-third of the informants revealed negative treatment by students, teachers and staff. Among the informants, trans women from ethnic minority communities were particularly likely to experience those barriers (Goldberg, 2018, p. 2). Besides harassment from teachers and peers at the individual level, scholars suggested that harassment targeting trans students in higher education institutions are likely to be maintained or perpetuated through institutional practices, such as a non-inclusive campus climate and policies at the institutional level (Goldberg, 2018). Typical examples are segregated student hostels/accommodation, campus restrooms, and recreation facilities based on a binary definition of sex. Trans students were excluded from campus participation or exposed to discomfort, invisibility, and even harassment, thus causing additional stress (Seelman, 2014a). Likewise, other studies found that trans students, if they decided to come out and to seek space to express their trans identities, also encountered extreme difficulty following or obeying the culturally prescribed gender codes, rules, or norms, such as dress, pronouns, hairstyle and appearance. In exploring trans college students' experiences, Seelman (2016) found that a higher risk for suicidality was associated with being denied access to campus facilities, such as gender-appropriate housing and restrooms. Thus, we observed from the above literature, genderism is manifested in higher education in various aspects, from the individual level (attitudes of students, educators, and administrators) to the institutional level, such as setting up of binary system of policies, to facilities, housing and classroom practices. The accumulated experiences of invisibility, discrimination, bullying or harassment may induce socially-based minority stress for them (Hendricks and Testa, 2012; Marine et al., 2017).

Besides discussing the negative impacts of genderism and gender minority stress on trans college students, other studies have focused on suggestions for making campus climates more welcoming for trans students. In a recent study of over 500 trans college students, Goldberg et al. (2018) found a better sense of belonging was associated with the existence of trans-inclusive campus/institutional supports and policies. In their study, what trans students appreciated most were non-discrimination policies that respect gender identity, trans-inclusive restrooms, and the campus record policy that allows trans students to change their names during their social transition. In the face of rising global concern over support to trans students facing difficulties in higher education institutes and related gender minority stress, the prevailing genderism in the social context of Hong Kong is silent in the discussion, in both public and academic domains. In the following sections, the cultural forces regarding attitudes to trans people in Hong Kong and themes on the experiences of Chinese trans college students will be highlighted.

Cultural forces in Hong Kong

Formerly a British colony, Hong Kong, as a Special Administrative Region of the People's Republic of China, is now a cosmopolitan city with a blend of Western and Chinese cultures. Around 95% of Hong Kong residents are ethnic Chinese. Around 43% of the Chinese residents participate in religious and cultural activities, for example, Taoism, Buddhism, Confucianism and Christianity. In a multicultural city influenced by both its Chinese culture and the British colonial days, it is inevitable that cultural forces stemming from Confucianism and Christian religious values, together, impact upon manifestations of genderism and anti-trans prejudice (Chan, 2013; Hong Kong Christian Institute, 2006; Kwok, 2015, 2016, 2019a, 2019b; Kwok et al., 2013; Kwok and Wu, 2015; Ng and Ma, 2006; Winter and King, 2010).

In the Chinese collectivist context, the most profound foundation of social institution is the family, and 'filial piety' (or 'xiao') is a strongly emphasized theme. According to Yu and colleagues, this traditional Chinese saying reflected this principle: 'there are three forms of unfilial conduct, of which the worst is to have no descendants' (2011, p. 264). Filial piety stresses continuation of the family name, with dogmatic obligations within Chinese families, and failure to reproduce is symbolized as an act of filial disobedience and a calamity. Additionally, within the family system, 'face' is seen as a vital component, hence individual needs/desires were not given priority over collective 'family face'. In regards to trans people, that their gender identities and expressions are different from their assigned sex are considered a violation of filial piety. This is a cultural principle of Chinese Confucianism, relating to respect for one's parents – to procreate in order to carry on the family title and to avoid harm to one's own body (Ma, 1999). Trans, gender nonconforming or gay children who are not compliant with family obligations and parental values are often seen as 'morally wrong' or bringing 'shame' to their parents and family members (Kwok, 2015, 2016, 2019a, 2019b; Kwok et al., 2013; Kwok and Wu, 2015).

Adding to the impacts of these Chinese family cultural values, Christianity has had a strong influence on Chinese sexual prejudice against sexual minorities (Chan, 2005; Kwok et al., 2013; Ng and Ma, 2006). Colonization by the British in the 19th century brought to Hong Kong a massive wave of religious missionaries (Ng and Ma, 2006). For some Christians in Hong Kong, monogamous heterosexual and life-long marriage appear to be a life prototype. Any nonconformity from this prototype, including same sex affections and sexual desires or identities, may be disallowed or could be seen as immoral, wrongful and sinful (Kwok and Wu, 2015; Kwok, 2019a). For example, there has been heated debate surrounding the establishment of a legal ordinance to protect the sexual and gender diverse population from discrimination in the past ten years. Hong Kong's Anti-Discrimination Ordinance based on sex, gender, and sexual orientation identities has not been enacted and is met with strong opposition. The arguments center on sexual- and gender-diverse individuals and whether they should be acknowledged as family units and have the usual citizens' rights of access to marriage, adoption, social services etc. Nowadays, trans identity has not been involved in sexuality education in Hong Kong, which is included under the 'moral and civic education' curriculum. If there is a gender education, the definition of gender is based on a binary conception (Kwok, 2019a; Winter and King, 2010).

Trans students in Hong Kong

On 8th July 2017, a young trans woman who dropped out of university a few years earlier jumped to her death from a railway bridge. It was reported that she felt distressed because she could not 'fit into society' and 'be herself authentically' (Lui and Poon, 2017). A study using the Minority Stress Model to examine the mental health of trans adults revealed that internalized phobia about individual's trans identity is significantly related to mental health (Ho, 2015). A study examining the experiences of 91 trans adults attending a gender clinic run by the Hong Kong Hospital Authority indicated that 46% of the informants suffered from a mental health condition such as depression (Chan, 2013). In a study on Chinese attitudes to trans people in Hong Kong, of 856 Chinese respondents 35% among believed that a man identifying as a woman is not 'normal' and 35% agreed that trans people's legal status should not be granted, even after sex reassignment surgery (King et al., 2009). An informant in another study expressed that trans people 'could not survive if there was no legislation against discrimination of them' (Equal Opportunities Commission, 2016, p. 110). Thus, social stigma faced by trans people in Hong Kong Chinese society appears to have impacts on their mental health.

Under this circumstance, trans individuals, including college students, continue to be marginalized. A survey conducted in Hong Kong trans communities with 106 participants (Suen et al., 2018, p. 1093) indicated that more than 50% of the informants had a university degree or higher education qualification. However, over 60% reported 'fair or poor quality of life' and 'had contemplated suicide'.

Discussion

Marine and Nicolazzo commented that multiple identities, experiences and needs of trans college students are likely to be 'silenced and ignored in favor of those who are cisgender' (2014, p. 266). We connect the concept of genderism and gender minority stress model to the current literature in understanding how genderism and trans non-inclusive campus environments have impacted the daily lives of trans university/college students. Trans students' academic and mental health difficulties could be perceived as consequences of gender minority stress they suffered in these higher institutions. These are additive to general stressors, and the suffering may be chronic, requiring extra adjustment for trans students to deal with these socially based stress

(Testa et al., 2017). For example, as reflected from the study by Suen et al. (2018), trans respondents in the study aged 15–24 were facing the highest rate of attempted (35.5%) and contemplated suicide (87.1%). Previous studies in the Asian region regarding the prevalence of attempted suicide among the trans population ranged from 16% in the Philippines (Winter, 2009), 32% in Japan (Terada et al., 2011) and 22% in Thailand (Winter, 2009). Suen et al. (2018) showed that the reported rates of suicidal ideation and attempted suicide for trans people in Hong Kong are comparable to those observed in other parts of the world. Unfortunately, the supports from college and higher education system are perceived by trans college students as cisgender-based and not relevant to them, and even worse, the campus environments were not safe and welcoming for them (Kwok, 2019b). While similar themes have been explored in both international and Hong Kong studies on manifestation of genderism and their possible impacts on the mental health of trans students, the situation appears to be difficult for Chinese trans college students in Hong Kong than their counterparts in countries (such as the US) where campus-based programs are present to support them in transgressing genderism and to cope with minority stress such as the college gay-straight alliances and Safe Space Allies (Goldstein and Davis, 2010) documented in the literature. The cultural context in Hong Kong may play a role in creating non-inclusive environment and additional socially-based stress for trans people in Hong Kong without policy and legal supports. The proposals from the Hong Kong Government for an anti-discrimination ordinance based on sexual orientation, gender identity and intersex status have been strongly opposed by both parents and religious groups (Kwok and Wu, 2015). At present, unlike racial minority college students or college students with disabilities who are protected from discrimination by legal protections, trans college students are subject to discrimination without legal and policy supports.

From the existing literature on gender minority stress and genderism, scholars discussed the perspective of counseling supports for minority college students need to address both individual based and institutional based supports. Campus support at the individual level from counselors (e.g. individual counseling sessions) can help to ameliorate the gender minority stress experienced by trans students due to the barriers they encountered. Besides individual intervention, trans students may need institutional support. We take the view of feminist scholars, who help us to extend our perspectives on the impacts of genderism, from individual to an institutional level, with social and political lenses. Szymanski et al. (2008) suggest that the personal difficulties sexual minority students experience in society can be seen as 'connected to the political, cultural, social and economic climate in which people live and that many of the problems experienced by persons with limited power in society can be conceptualized as reactions to oppression' (p. 513). Based on their perspective, the author perceives trans students' stress as a consequence of oppressive practices surrounded by prejudice toward trans people and a society without laws to safeguard their human rights. Therefore, university educators, counselors and administrators can go beyond emotional support, to promote structural and system change for trans students' wellbeing.

Up to the present day, mental health professionals in Hong Kong do not have any code of ethics that specially address educators' or counselors' possible transphobia within their practice. The Council on Professional Conduct in Education was established in the 1990s with the goal 'to draft operational criteria defining the conduct expected of an educator' (2015, p. 1). After all these years, respecting students' gender identity has not been included in the Code. Similarly, transphobia among social workers and its potential damage to their clients has not been addressed in the Hong Kong Social Workers Registration Board's (2015) code of practice. Likewise, in the Code of Ethics of the Hong Kong Professional Counselling Association (2011), where some campus counselors are registered, no guideline is to be found relating to the potential damage of counselor transphobia toward their service users. The absence of ethical guidelines relating to trans discrimination appears to cause additional difficulties for educators and mental health counselors in supporting trans students facing genderism.

This review of literature reveals themes similar to those identified in other countries regarding societal attitudes toward trans college students. For instance, even in the 21st century, genderism and transphobic attitudes have been found among the general public, and within the campus environment. Moreover, the manifestation of trans prejudice may also lie within institutions (Goldberg, 2018; Kwok, 2019b; Suen et al., 2018). There is evidence not only that genderism against trans students exist and are prevalent, but that, as consistent with the gender minority stress model, these prejudices can also impact upon their mental health (Testa et al., 2017). This has certainly been found to be the case for Chinese trans college students in Hong Kong, for whom facing multiple cultural barriers may internalize the transphobic message, which in turn will affect their mental health (Kwok and Wu, 2015). Here in Hong Kong, trans college students face a lot of cultural challenges, and the institutional context seems to have more barriers to accommodate Chinese trans students than other countries or jurisdictions with institutional and policy support in their colleges, such as university or high school-based associations/clubs (Heck et al., 2011). In Hong Kong, the heteronormative sociocultural climate makes it hard to create trans-inclusive projects on the college campus.

Recommendations

Gender diversity issues could be incorporated into the professional training curricula for educators, administrators and student service counselors, with anti-prejudice and advocacy perspectives. In addition, in developing their professional value systems and designing and delivering quality training programs, trainers in professional training programs should be fully aware of how Chinese cultural and religious factors affect the program participants and be ready to create a space for training participants to identify and discuss value dilemmas openly during their professional training (Kwok et al., 2013). There has been no anti-discriminative legislation targeting transphobic discrimination or genderism in Hong Kong. The existing codes of ethics for professional organizations do not spell out explicitly that transphobic prejudices and related stigmatized practices by educators, counselors and mental health practitioners should not be acceptable. Without legal protection and explicit code of ethics to prevent transphobic prejudice in higher institutions and practitioners, trans college students continue to encounter barriers to receiving mental health, learning and social supports.

Trans students may encounter difficulties, barriers or gender-based harassment due to genderism at both individual and institutional levels (e.g. campus facilities or policies). In regard to this, college educators and counselors should not only focus on mental health but actively challenge genderism and transphobia through advocating system change (Chavez-Korell and Johnson, 2010; Gonzalez and McNulty, 2010; Goodrich and Luke, 2009). Strategies at the individual level include affirming and acknowledging their trans experience and identities, raising trans college students' awareness on the harmful effects of genderism on their college lives. Moreover, coping skills and strategies to confront trans bullying are recommended. They may be connected to affirmative and useful medical and social services (Chavez-Korell and Johnson, 2010; Lennon and Mistler, 2010). At the same time, college counselors, educators and administrators may also undertake advocacy work to change oppressive policy in the university and society, as well as professional organizations that oppress trans people (Gonzalez and McNulty, 2010; Goodrich and Luke, 2009; Seelman, 2014a, 2014b; Szymanski et al., 2008). First, anti-harassment campaigns based on genderism can be initiated by collaborating with non-governmental organizations or the Equal Opportunities Commission. Second, society-based advocacy work can be carried out by drawing public attention to trans bullying cases and by promoting trans equality through conferences and media campaigns. Third, the existing practice guidelines should be reviewed to address transphobia and genderism among educators and counseling practitioners. Lastly, college administrators, educators and counselors may advocate for legal change through the enactment of anti-discrimination legislation.

Conclusion

Trans college students' experience is often overlooked in the literature compared with other minority group members, because of genderism, prejudice and comparatively small population size. Thus, existing LGBT literature on trans experiences may create incomplete accounts as some studies were not using trans informants. There were informants from lesbian, gay and bisexual groups, and sometimes non-campus informants are utilized to look at the campus experience retrospectively. Nonetheless, these studies are still valuable as they have generated groundwork for literature on trans youth, and prepared for future studies. The present chapter contributes to sexual and gender minority studies in higher education in East Asian cities, particularly in the Hong Kong Chinese cultural context, by adding to the existing body of work on the college and campus experiences. Genderism and prejudice toward trans people are structural and institutional barriers for trans students to achieve their educational aspirations. The literature review and discussion in this chapter provide higher education educators and counseling professionals with information about trans minority stress and campus experiences based on genderism in both the international and Hong Kong context. It also reveals a compelling need for administrators, educators and counselors in higher education to support trans students to navigate genderism, to reduce their feelings of exclusion and marginalization while going through social or medical transition during their higher education. The chapter also speaks to the need to expand the code of ethics for professionals, and the training and practice of professionals with trans students in advocating a safe and discrimination-free college campus environment in Hong Kong.

References

American Psychological Association (2011) *Answers to your questions about transgender people*, www.apa.org/topics/sexuality/orientation.aspx.

Beemyn, B. (2003) Serving the needs of transgender college students, *Journal of Gay & Lesbian Issues in Education* 1(1): 33–50.

Beemyn, B., A. Domingue, J. Pettit and T. Smith (2005) Suggested steps to make campuses more trans-inclusive, *Journal of Gay & Lesbian Issues in Education* 3(1): 89–94.

Beemyn, G. (2016). Transgender inclusion on college campuses, in A. Goldberg (ed.) *The Sage encyclopedia of LGBTQ studies* (pp. 1226–1229). Thousand Oaks: Sage.

Bilodeau, B. (2005) Beyond the gender binary: A case study of two transgender students at a Midwestern research university, *Journal of Gay & Lesbian Issues in Education* 3(1): 29–44.

Carabez, R., M. Pellegrini, A. Mankovitz, M. Eliason and M. Scott (2015) Does your organization use gender inclusive forms? Nurses' confusion about trans* terminology, *Journal of Clinical Nursing* 24(21–22): 3306–3317.

Carter, K. (2000) Transgenderism and college students: Issues of gender identity and its role on our campuses, in V. Wall (ed.) *Toward acceptance: Sexual orientation issues on campus* (pp. 261–282). Lanham: University Press of America.

Catalano, D. (2015) "Trans enough?": The pressures trans men negotiate in higher education, *Transgender Studies Quarterly* 2(3): 411–430.

Case, K., H. Kanenberg, S. Erich and J. Tittsworth (2012) Transgender inclusion in university nondiscrimination statements: challenging gender-conforming privilege through student activism, *Journal of Social Issues* 68(1): 145–161.

Chan, C.C. (2013) Prevalence of psychiatric morbidity in Chinese subjects with gender identity disorder in Hong Kong. Unpublished thesis, Hong Kong College of Psychiatrists.

Chan, C.W.P. (2005) The lack of sexual orientation anti-discrimination legislation in Hong Kong: Breach of international and domestic legal obligations, *International Journal of Human Rights* 9(1): 69–106.

Chavez-Korell, S. and L. Johnson (2010) Informing counselor training and competent counseling services through transgender narratives and the transgender community, *Journal of LGBT Issues in Counseling* 4(3-4): 202–213.

Council on Professional Conduct in Education (2015) *Code for the education profession of Hong Kong*. Hong Kong: Council on Professional Conduct in Education.

Donatone, B. and K. Rachlin (2013) An intake template for transgender, transsexual, genderqueer, gender nonconforming, and gender variant college students seeking mental health services, *Journal of College Student Psychotherapy* 27(3): 200–211.

Dugan, J., M. Kusel and D. Simounet (2012) Transgender college students: An exploratory study of perceptions, engagement, and educational outcomes, *Journal of College Student Development* 53(5): 719–736.

Effrig, J., K. Bieschke and B. Locke (2011) Examining victimization and psychological distress in transgender college students, *Journal of College Counseling* 14(2): 143–157.

Equal Opportunities Commission (2016) *Study on legislation against discrimination on the grounds of sexual orientation, gender identity and intersex status*. Hong Kong: Equal Opportunities Commission.

Goldberg, A. (2018) *Transgender students in higher education*. Los Angeles: Williams Institute, UCLA.

Goldberg, A., G. Beemyn and J. Smith (2018) What is needed, what is valued: Trans students' perspectives on trans-inclusive policies and practices in higher education, *Journal of Educational and Psychological Consultation* 29(1): 27–67.

Goldberg, A. and K. Kuvalanka (2018) Navigating identity development and community belonging when "there are only two boxes to check": An exploratory study of nonbinary trans college students, *Journal of LGBT Youth* 15(2): 106–131.

Gonzalez, M. and J. McNulty (2010) Achieving competency with transgender youth: School counselors as collaborative advocates, *Journal of LGBT Issues in Counseling* 4(3-4): 176–186.

Goodrich, K. and M. Luke (2009) LGBTQ responsive school counseling, *Journal of LGBT Issues in Counseling* 3(2): 113–127.

Goldstein, S. and D. Davis (2010) Heterosexual allies: A descriptive profile, *Equity & Excellence in Education* 43(4): 478–494.

Grant, J., L. Mottet, J. Tanis, J. Harrison, J. Herman and M. Keisling (2011) *Injustice at every turn: A report of the National Transgender Discrimination Survey*. Washington: National Center for Transgender Equality and National Gay and Lesbian Task Force.

Hendricks, M. and R. Testa (2012) A conceptual framework for clinical work with transgender and gender nonconforming clients: An adaptation of the Minority Stress Model, *Professional Psychology: Research and Practice* 43(5): 460–467.

Heck, N., A. Flentje and B. Cochran (2011) Offsetting risks: High school gay-straight alliances and lesbian, gay, bisexual, and transgender (LGBT) youth, *School Psychology Quarterly* 26(2): 161–174.

Hill, D. and B. Willoughby (2005) The development and validation of the genderism and transphobia scale, *Sex Roles* 53: 531–544.

Ho, W.Y. (2015) Collective self-esteem and stress coping in trans*, unpublished undergraduate dissertation, City University of Hong Kong.

Hong Kong Christian Institute (2006) 看得見的真相: 香港同志平權報告 [A report on discriminative cases on sexual minority groups]. Hong Kong: Hong Kong Christian Institute.

Hong Kong Professional Counselling Association (2011) *Code of ethics*. Hong Kong: Hong Kong Professional Counselling Association

Hong Kong Social Workers Registration Board (2015) *Guidelines on code of practice for registered social workers*. Hong Kong: Hong Kong Social Workers Registration Board.

King, M., S. Winter and B. Webster (2009) Contact reduces transprejudice: A study on attitudes towards transgenderism and transgender civil rights in Hong Kong, *International Journal of Sexual Health* 21(1): 17–34.

Klugman, S. (2014) An exploratory study of the experiences of transgender and gender nonconforming students at Rutgers University, Unpublished PhD thesis, Rutgers University.

Korell, S. and P. Lorah (2007) An overview of affirmative psychotherapy and counseling with transgender clients, in K. Bieschke, R. Perez and K. DeBord (eds.) *Handbook of counseling and psychotherapy with lesbian, gay, bisexual, and transgender clients* (pp. 271–288). Washington: American Psychological Association.

Kwok, D.K. (2015) *A research report on gender and sexual-orientation harassment experiences of LGBTQ students in Hong Kong secondary schools*. Hong Kong: Hong Kong Institute of Education.

Kwok, D.K. (2016) Conceptualizing transgender prejudice: Themes found from a qualitative study on sexual prejudice. *Abstract submitted to the biennial WPATH Symposium by the World Professional Association for Transgender Health*, University of Amsterdam, June 2016.

Kwok, D.K. (2019a). Sexuality and teacher education: LGBT students and teacher education, in M. Peters (ed.) *Encyclopedia of teacher education* [online]. Singapore: Springer.

Kwok, D.K. (2019b) Transgender college students seeking sexual health services: Barriers and opportunities, *10th Asia Pacific Conference on Reproductive and Sexual Health and Rights*, Siem Reap, Cambodia, 26th to 29th May.

Kwok, D.K. and J. Wu (2015) Chinese attitudes towards sexual minorities in Hong Kong: Implications for mental health, *International Review of Psychiatry* 27(5): 444–454.

Kwok, D.K., J. Wu and S. Shardlow (2013) Attitudes toward lesbians and gay men among Hong Kong Chinese social work students, *Journal of Social Work Education* 49(2): 337–352.

Lennon, E. and B. Mistler (2010) Breaking the binary: Providing effective counseling to transgender students in college and university settings, *Journal of LGBT Issues in Counseling* 4(3–4): 228–240.

Lui, Y.M. and O.K. Poon (2017) 飛墮大圍站:死者曾助市民追賊 平日愛穿女裝 嘆不入流感痛苦 [Falling from height at Tai Wai station: Helped catch a thief and liked to wear female clothes, sighed and felt distressed due to failure to fit into society], *HK01*, 9th July.

Ma, J.L.C. (1999) Social work practice with transsexuals in Hong Kong who apply for sex reassignment surgery, *Social Work in Health Care* 29(2): 85–103.

Marine, S. and Z. Nicolazzo (2014) Names that matter: Exploring the tensions of campus LGBTQ centers and trans* inclusion, *Journal of Diversity in Higher Education* 7(4): 265–281.

Marine, S., G. Helfrich and L. Randhawa (2017) Gender-inclusive practices in campus women's and gender centers: Benefits, challenges, and future prospects, *NASPA Journal About Women in Higher Education* 10(1): 45–63.

Messman, J. and L. Leslie (2019) Transgender college students: Academic resilience and striving to cope in the face of marginalized health, *Journal of American College Health* 67(2): 161–173.

Ng, M.L. and J.L.C. Ma (2006) Sexuality in Hong Kong special administrative region of the people's republic of China, in B. Francoeur and R. Noonan (eds.) *The Continuum complete international encyclopedia of sexuality* (pp. 489–502). New York: Continuum.

Nicolazzo, Z. (2016a) *Trans* in college: Transgender students' strategies for navigating campus life and the institutional politics of inclusion*. Sterling: Stylus.

Nicolazzo, Z. (2016b) 'It's a hard line to walk': Black non-binary trans* collegians' perspectives on passing, realness, and trans*-normativity, *International Journal of Qualitative Studies in Education* 29(9): 1173–1188.

Pryor, J. (2015) Out in the classroom: Transgender student experiences at a large public university, *Journal of College Student Development* 56(5): 440–455.

Seelman, K. (2014a) Recommendations of transgender students, staff, and faculty in the USA for improving college campuses, *Gender and Education* 26(6): 618–635.

Seelman, K. (2014b) Transgender individuals' access to college housing and bathrooms: Findings from the National Transgender Discrimination Survey, *Journal of Gay & Lesbian Social Services* 26(2): 186–206.

Seelman, K. (2016) Transgender adults' access to college bathrooms and housing and the relationship to suicidality, *Journal of Homosexuality* 63(10): 1378–1399.

Suen, Y.T. (2015) Methodological reflections on researching lesbian, gay, bisexual and transgender university students in Hong Kong: To what extent are they vulnerable interview subjects? *Higher Education Research & Development* 34(4): 722–734.

Suen, Y.T., R.C.H. Chan and E. Wong (2018) Mental health of transgender people in Hong Kong: A community-driven, large-scale quantitative study documenting demographics and correlates of quality of life and suicidality, *Journal of Homosexuality* 65(8): 1093–1113.

Szymanski, D., S. Kashubeck-West and J. Meyer (2008) Internalized heterosexism: A historical and theoretical overview, *Counseling Psychologist* 36(4): 510–524.

Terada, S., Y. Matsumoto, T. Sato, N. Okabe, Y. Kishimoto and Y. Uchitomi (2011) Suicidal ideation among patients with gender identity disorder, *Psychiatry Research* 190(1): 159–162.

Testa, R., M. Michaels, W. Bliss, M. Rogers, K. Balsam and T. Joiner (2017) Suicidal ideation in transgender people: Gender minority stress and interpersonal theory factors, *Journal of Abnormal Psychology* 126(1): 125–136.

Wernick, L., A. Kulick and M. Inglehart (2014) Influences of peers, teachers, and climate on students' willingness to intervene when witnessing anti-transgender harassment, *Journal of Adolescence* 37(6): 927–935.

Winter, S. (2009) Lost in transition: Transpeople, transprejudice and pathology in Asia, *The International Journal of Human Rights* 13(2–3): 365–390.

Winter, S. and M. King (2010) Hong Kong, in C. Stewart (ed.) *The Greenwood encyclopedia of LGBT issues worldwide* (pp. 375–390). Los Angeles: Greenwood Publishers.

Woodford, M., J. Joslin, E. Pitcher and K. Renn (2017) A mixed methods inquiry into trans* environmental microaggressions on college campuses: Experiences and outcomes, *Journal of Ethnic & Cultural Diversity in Social Work* 26(1-2): 95–111.

Yu, Y., S. Xiao and Y. Xiang (2011) Application and testing the reliability and validity of a modified version of Herek's attitudes toward lesbians and gay men scale in China, *Journal of Homosexuality* 58(2): 263–274.

Chapter 6

The marginalisation of religious students in higher education in the United Kingdom

Jacqueline Stevenson

Introduction

Unlike other chapters in this book, which seek to look at those communities under-represented in higher education, it might seem odd for the focus of this chapter to be on religious students. Globally, those who are 'religious' are the majority, with 84% of people considering themselves to have a religion (Pew Research Center, 2017). Although in the United Kingdom (UK) this number is lower, in the 2011 census over two thirds of people declared that they had a religion or belief[1] (Office for National Statistics, 2012). This data broadly accords with data on staff or students in UK higher education (HE), with just over two thirds of students stating that they have a religion or belief (Equality Challenge Unit, 2011; Guest et al., 2013).

What this chapter will argue, however, is that despite being on campus in high numbers, many religious students are marginalised by the policies and practice of UK higher education, and that these practices are framed by a set of prevailing assumptions: first, that UK higher education is (and should be) a secular space – despite the fact that some universities which have, and retain, religious foundations; second, that higher education secularises students, so that even if religious students start as a majority they will become a minority group; third, that being religious is an identity choice that students can (and should) divest; and finally, that religious students are the cause of (potential) threat and so need to be managed. As a result, religious students are frequently perceived as a minority group even if they are not, or subjected to 'unfreedoms' (Sen, 1999) and prevented from leading 'the kind of lives they have reason to value' (Sen, 1999, p. 10). In presenting this argument I will draw on both the existent literature and the 'Religion and Belief' policy documents of twenty UK higher education institutions (HEIs), and utilise the capabilities framework as a helpful heuristic through which to understand how religious freedom is, or is not, enabled on campus.

Before doing so, however, it is important to explain a little more about the terminology used in the chapter. First, it is difficult to agree a consensual definition of religion and religious. Identifying 'fixed' identity such as ethnicity is easier than determining a person's 'faith', 'religion', whether someone is 'religious', or their 'belief' (Perfect, 2011): these terms are not easy to define, are often used interchangeably and are asked in different ways by researchers. In addition, as Barker (1989) argues, some definitions of religion exclude beliefs and practices that others would consider clearly 'religious' – for example a definition which includes a belief in a God responsible for the creation of the universe and for its continuing operation would exclude non-theistic religions such as Buddhism. Moreover, there has been 'an explosion of popular interest in spirituality' (Hunt and West, 2007, p. 1) with many people increasingly describing themselves as 'spiritual' – a phrase that may acknowledge the existence of a God or may not (see Hunt, 2009).

There is also a difference, of course, in having a religion and being religious; moreover, when a person declares that they are 'religious' it is invariably a 'self-described identity', meaning different things to different individuals. It will also be determined by different phenomena (Purdam et al., 2007) such as membership of a church or other place of worship, affiliation to a community, and participation in sets of practices etc. which can be categorised in to beliefs, belonging and behaviour (Putnam and Campbell, 2010, among others). So, for example, whilst two-thirds of people named a religion when asked the question 'What is your religion?' in the 2011 Census, 52% of people answered 'no religion' when asked the question 'Do you regard yourself as belonging to any particular religion?' as part of the British Social Attitudes annual survey (Curtice et al., 2019). In short, religion is a multidimensional concept (Smart, 1989) and each dimension may have more significance to one person than another. This has been evidenced, for example, by the ways in which many Jews declare a strong Jewish cultural identity but have little or no contact with a synagogue (Coyle and Rafalin, 2000). In this chapter, however, I have used the following definitional framework: 'religious refers to both having a faith and undertaking some form of action related to that faith. The term 'religious students' is, therefore, used to refer to those students who self-identify as being religious' (Stevenson, 2012, p. 55).

The concept of marginalisation is also a complex one, and one that is rarely defined (Messiou, 2012). However, it, largely, relates to 'the state of being considered unimportant, undesirable, unworthy, insignificant and different resulting in inequity, unfairness, deprivation and enforced lack of access to mainstream power' (United Nations Development Programme, 1996; cited in Messiou, 2012, p. 1312). For Billson (1988), marginality can refer to cultural marginality (of which race, ethnicity, religion and other cultural differences are the defining variables), social role marginality (because of age, timing and/or situational constraints) and structural marginality, which 'refers to the political, social, and economic powerlessness of certain disenfranchised and/or disadvantaged segments within societies' (p. 2).

Moreover, marginalisation may be experienced by an individual (or group) which may or may not be recognised as such by the individual or by others.

Moreover, not all of those within any one group may be marginalised, whilst an individual may be marginalised in one or more aspects of their life but not necessarily in all (Messiou, 2012). Instead, as Mowat (2015, pp. 469–470) notes,

> it is how individuals interpret their life experiences (which in itself is framed through their past experience) and how they perceive their lives in relation to others and the 'ideals' which are a representation of cultural norms, expectations and values, shaped by and through political forces and the systems and structures (including legal systems) of society, which will determine whether or not they will experience their lives as marginalised.

For this reason, not all religious students may consider themselves to be marginalised. Perceptions, or experiences, of marginalisation can depend, for example, on the gender or ethnic background of an individual: the majority of all religious hate crimes[2] recorded by the Metropolitan Police Service is committed against those of Asian heritage (Walters and Krasodomski-Jones, 2018), whilst anti-Islam hate crime is more likely to be experienced by women (at 57%) than men (Faith Matters, 2019). It can also depend on whether an individual's religion is one that is more valorised or accepted within a UK HEI, such as Christianity, Hinduism or Buddhism, compared to, for example, Islam.

For this reason there will be many religious students who may not feel marginalised, for example, Christian students studying at one of the Cathedrals Group[3] of universities, whereas those students who do not have the freedom to achieve the quality of life they value may consider themselves to be so. This distinction is at the heart of the capability approach first articulated by the economist and philosopher Amartya Sen in the 1980s (Sen, 1989, 2003, 2004 amongst others).

The capabilities approach

The capabilities approach has, historically, provided a framework for the assessment of human development, most specifically in relation to economic wellbeing. For Sen, the quality of life that any individual is able to achieve should be analysed in relation to 'functionings' (made up of beings, for example, being educated, and doings, such as participating in social activities) and 'capabilities' (the opportunities to realise these functionings). For any individual therefore the notion of capability 'is essentially one of freedom – the range of options a person has in deciding what kind of life to lead' (Dreze and Sen, 1995, p. 11), with 'well-being freedom' (Sen, 1992, p. 40) both the means to, and the end goal of, development. The capabilities approach, therefore, allows for the evaluation of individual's capability to achieve the lives they have reason to value (Sen, 1999), with the evaluation of freedom also taking account of not just what people do but what they have the freedom to do and the possibilities they have for effecting change (Sen, 2006). Just as freedom should be central to the process of development, the role of development and the policies and interventions that frame developmental initiatives, should be to remove 'unfreedoms' (Sen, 1999). Factors such as poverty, poor sanitation, poor economic opportunities or poor public facilities are unfreedoms, as are intolerance, ethnic centricity, lack of security (Samuels, 2005) or repressive state apparatuses. Here, as Sen (1999, p. 4) notes,

> the violation of freedom results directly from a denial of political and civil liberties by authoritarian regimes and from imposed restrictions on the freedom to participate in the social, political and economic life of the community.

As noted by many, including both Sen and by Nussbaum, who has built on Sen's work, the capabilities approach is not methodologically individualistic, but it does support ethical individualism, with the notion of 'functionings' perceived as a conceptual category that is in itself morally neutral (Robeyns, 2016), and with each person counting as a moral equal (Nussbaum, 2000).

For this reason, Sen has not provided a definitive list of capabilities (although he does provide examples such as 'live long, escape avoidable morbidity, be well nourished, be able to read, write and communicate, take part in literary and scientific pursuits and so forth' (Sen, 1984, p. 497), as he argues that these depend on individual value judgements and that 'to have such a fixed list emanating entirely from pure theory, is to deny the possibility of fruitful public participation on what should be included and why' (Sen, 2004, p. 77).

This has led to a level of criticism of Sen's work since, as Clark (2005) notes, not all capabilities might be deemed valuable by all, and that some might be more valuable than others making it difficult to operationalise and evaluate the framework. In contrast, Martha Nussbaum has defined collections of capabilities, including, in addition to those noted by Sen above, 'protection for liberty of conscience', 'being able to participate effectively in political choices that govern one's life' and 'having the rights of political participation, free speech and freedom of association' (Nussbaum, 1999, p. 41–42).

In crafting her collection of capabilities Nussbaum has, however, taken what might be regarded as universally valued/valuable capabilities (e.g. to be well-nourished) and proposed capabilities which are contestable, by some and in certain contexts – for example, 'liberty of conscience'. This is particularly so for functionings since, as Robeyns (2016, n.p.) notes,

> Functionings can be univocally good (e.g. being in good health) or univocally bad (e.g. being raped). But the goodness or badness of various other functionings may not be so straightforward, but rather depend on the context and/or the normative theory which we endorse.

Instead Nussbaum, like Sen, calls for us to

> Respect the many different conceptions of the good citizens may have and to foster a political climate in which they will each be able to pursue the good (whether religious or ethical) according to their own lights. In other words we want universals that are facilitative rather than tyrannical, that create spaces for choice rather than dragooning people into a desired mode of functioning.
>
> (Nussbaum, 2000, p. 59)

The capability approach, therefore, evaluates policies and other changes according to their impact on people's capabilities as well as their actual functionings. Where functionings are contested, however, it can lead to conflict on multiple levels.

In her book, *The New Religious Intolerance* (2012), Nussbaum explores how religious freedom is being restrained in the face of post-9/11 fears of minorities and, in particular, Islamophobia. For Nussbaum, intense fear of minorities distorts anxiety and thus responses since fear is 'more narcissistic than other emotions'. As a result, fear of those whose functionings are different to our own, can, if left unchecked, become a 'dimming preoccupation' (p. 58), leading to intolerance and bigotry. And where fear becomes an overarching, or overwhelming societal concern, it can result in policy and practice being endorsed and enacted in ways which not only casts feared minorities into the shadows but keeps them there. As a result, fear allows for new forms of state-sanctioned religious intolerance such as the banning of burqas in France or minarets in Switzerland. One of the results of this politics of fear is rampant xenophobia or, in the case of Muslims, Islamophobia leading to cultural repression, or the ready attribution of acts of violence to those who are feared even when they are perpetrated by others, such as the Norwegian mass murders of 2011. For Nussbaum, therefore, 'however valuable and indeed essential it is in a genuinely dangerous world, [fear] is itself one of life's great dangers' (p. 58).

The higher education campus, whether in the UK or elsewhere, is a microcosm of the society within which it is located, and reflective of those communities who inhibit its spaces. It is perhaps not unreasonable, therefore, to wonder if and how the societal tensions in play off campus, are reflected – at least in some way – on campus. The second part of this chapter, therefore, draws on the Religion and Belief policies of twenty HEIs, qualitative data drawn from the author's own research (Stevenson, 2012, 2014, 2018), as well as the existent literature, to explore the ways in which in/tolerance of religion is being played out on the UK HE campus. The Religion and Belief policies were selected by virtue of the fact that they were the first twenty at the top of the results of a Google search using the term 'university religion and belief policy'. Brief characteristics on the HEIs are outlined in Table 6.1. Accurate data on the religion of students are not yet

Table 6.1 Institutional characteristics of the Religion and Belief policies analysed

University	Institutional characteristics
1.	A medium-sized Post-92[a] university located in the North of England; it has a significant number of local students, including those drawn from the city's Indian and Pakistani communities.
2.	A large Russell Group[b] university located in the South East of England; the university has a very high number of international students and, as a result, a high level of student diversity.
3.	A relatively large Post-92 university located in the Midlands, in a city with very high levels of ethnic diversity, primarily Muslims and Hindus of South Asian heritage.
4.	A medium-sized Pre-92 university located in the Midlands in a relatively rural area; although it has an ethnically diverse student population the majority are white.
5.	A large Post-92 university located in South West England in a metropolitan area. It has relatively low levels of ethnic diversity but this is reflective of its geographical location.
6.	A large Pre-92 university located in the Midlands with a relatively low number of students from ethnic minority backgrounds and few international students.
7.	A relatively large, Post-92 university located in South West England, in a predominantly white area and with few ethnic minority students.
8.	A large Russell Group university located in the North of England with relatively low levels of ethnic diversity amongst its home student population but a relatively high number of international students.
9.	A mid-sized Pre-92 university located in the South East of England. While predominantly white it has a mix of home ethnic minority and international students.
10.	A large Post-92 university located in South East England with almost half its students coming from an ethnic minority background.
11.	A mid-sized Post-92 university located in the South East of England with a very high number of white home students, whilst also having a sizeable proportion of international students.
12.	A small Post-92 university which is a member of the Cathedrals Group of universities. It is located in the East of England and has an almost-wholly white student body.
13.	A medium-sized Pre-92 university located in the North of England with a very high number of students from ethnic minority backgrounds drawn from its local communities.
14.	A medium-sized Pre-92 university located in Scotland/Wales/Northern Ireland[34]. It has a very small ethnic minority home study body, which is reflective of its geographical area, but a high number of mainly European international students.
15.	A medium-sized Post-92 university located in the South East of England and a member of the Cathedrals Group. Although it has an ethnically diverse student population the majority are white.

(*Continued*)

Table 6.1 (Continued)

University	Institutional characteristics
16.	A large urban university based in South East England. It is a member of the Russell Group. Its racial diversity for home students is below the national average but it has a large international student body.
17.	A mid-sized Post-92 university located in the North of England. It has very few ethnic minority or international students and mainly draws in local students from a predominantly white area.
18.	A large Post-92 university located in Scotland/Wales/Northern Ireland. It has relatively few home ethnic minority students but a large international student body.
19.	A Russell Group university located in the North of England. While predominantly white it has a mix of home ethnic minority and international students.
20.	A large Russell Group university located in Scotland/Wales/Northern Ireland. It has low levels of ethnic minority students and located in a predominantly white area.

[a] The post-92 universities were, primarily, previously called 'polytechnics'. They were given university status following the Further and Higher Education Act 1992 which allowed all polytechnics to award their own degrees. Pre-92 Universities are those which existed prior to the passing of the Act.
[b] The Russell Group comprises 24 research-intensive universities.

available, but information on ethnicity has been included to offer some level of insight into the diversity of the student body.

Religion and religious freedom on campus

The secularity of UK higher education has been much documented (see for example Aune and Stevenson, 2017; Bebbington, 2011; Gilliat-Ray, 2000). The first universities founded in the UK were the Universities of Oxford (c. 1170) and Cambridge (c. 1210). Both institutions were integral parts of the church with a key role being to educate parish priests, thus places to study were restricted to Anglicans from the Reformation onwards (Bebbington, 2011). Although secularist tendencies began to permeate higher education from the 16th century onwards, the European Age of Enlightenment, led to the rise of secularity over religion (Bebbington, 2011), whilst the commencement of the secular English Civic University movement of the 19th century furthered the decline (Jones, 1988). The founding of the explicitly secular 'new' universities of the 20th century finally positioned UK higher education, both intellectually and philosophically, as a 'secular space'.

The contemporary UK university sector now positions itself as global, international and plural, with institutions publicly committed to, variously, widening participation, social mobility and celebrating and valuing the diversity of their student body as noted within institutional Religion and Belief policy documents, designed to ensure that those with a religion or belief (or no religion or belief) do not face discrimination under the UK's equity legislation[5]:

> [Our University] celebrates and values the diversity brought by its individual members and aims to create an environment where religious beliefs are welcomed and respected. Members of any religion [...] will be treated with equal dignity, respect and fairness [University 18].

Despite its religious foundations, however, UK HE is positioned, both intellectually and philosophically, as a 'secular space' ('Students will need to be willing to portray a character or a role of any gender, race or faith; human and non-human [...] may involve touch and other forms of physical contact [...] these liberal, secular principles are fundamental to training for a successful career in the performing arts' [University 7]), where religion often exists solely in the guise of the multi-faith prayer room. Indeed, the HE sector has seen a rapid growth in student Atheist Societies (Guest et al., 2013) as well as the establishment of the National Federation of Atheist, Humanist and Secular Student Societies in 2009.

The perception that higher education is a secularising space remains an entrenched one – despite the fact that research by Guest et al. (2013) found that for 89% of the students they surveyed (both Christian and non-Christian) their perspective on religion had remained the same, or they had become more religious since starting university. Indeed, there is 'a major assumption about religion in universities: that it is a concern for only a minority of people'. (Aune and Stevenson, 2017, p. xx).

And yet, and of course, the contemporary campus is not wholly secular (Gilliat-Ray, 2000), not just because of the presence of religious staff and students on campus. Theology and religious studies, Islamic studies and to a lesser extent Jewish studies are taught across a number of universities, particularly at postgraduate level, whilst 'religion' is increasingly becoming a specific element of courses in other humanities and social sciences (British Academy, 2019). More overtly, a group of fifteen UK universities have formed the Cathedrals Group of universities which, collectively, teach around 100,000 students. Moreover, almost half a million non-UK students study in the UK, many of whom come from countries where the majority of people consider themselves to be religious (World Economic Forum, 2017); whilst for many of those educated in the UK, religion is one of the strongest aspects of their identity (Modood et al., 1997; O'Beirne, 2004; Tyrer and Ahmad, 2006).

This tension between religion and secularity is notable in the Religion and Belief policy documents (e.g., '[We are a] secular, non-political institution which celebrates and values the diversity of its community and aims to create an environment which respects the right of staff, students and visitors to hold cultural, religious, non-religious and philosophical beliefs' [University 2]).

At the same time, and perhaps because of this, religious discrimination also prevails on campus (Weller, 2006, 2011; National Union of Students, 2012) reflecting, at least to some degree, rising trends in global religious intolerance (Pew Research Center, 2018, 2019)[6]. A survey of Jewish students by the Institute for Jewish Policy Research, for example, found that one-fifth had been subjected to anti-Semitism in the year in which the survey took place, and a further third had witnessed an anti-Semitic incident on campus (Graham and Boyd, 2011). More recently, research by the National Union of Students (2018), found that one in three Muslim students had experienced some type of abuse or crime at their place of study, whilst over 40% either felt unable to express their views or had disengaged from political debate altogether. Such experiences rise sharply following major terrorist attacks in the UK or overseas (Stevenson, 2018):

> Every time there is something about "Muslims" on television I just think "oh no" because I know that they following day things will be much more difficult [Aisha, female, Pakistani heritage, 20, undergraduate].
> (reproduced from Stevenson, 2018, p. 7)

And yet religious students, in particular Muslim students, may be perceived more as the potential perpetrators of violence rather than the victims of it. Although the Home Office's 'Prevent' strategy (designed to challenge ideologies that support terrorism, and protect against the risks of radicalisation) was introduced in 2003 as part of the UK's overall post-9/11 counterterrorism approach (named 'CONTEST'), the London terrorist attacks of 2005 led to concerns that universities may actually be seedbeds for the growth of religious fundamentalism. Ever-increasing guidance has since been provided to universities on how to tackle violent extremism on campus (Home Office, 2011, 2019; Universities UK, 2005, 2011), with the Office for Students having delegated 'monitoring authority' (Hinds, 2018) under the Counter Terrorism and Security Act 2015. Although the evidence of radicalisation on campus is negligible, there is growing concern that the implementation of Prevent stifles freedom of speech and campus academic activism, and discriminates against Muslims in particular whilst failing to protect other more vulnerable groups (UCU Left, 2015). For some students this creates a real climate of fear, and, as a result, inhibits freedoms:

> You end up just not making yourself visible if you can get away with it. Better not to be noticed [Taj, male, Bangladeshi heritage, 21, undergraduate].
> (reproduced from Stevenson, 2018, p. 7)

Moreover, it is student-led Palestine Societies and Islamic Societies that have increasingly – according to Scott-Baumann (Neenan, 2018, n.p.) – become the focus of the Charity Commission which acts as 'an attack dog on behalf of Prevent', meaning that 'politically active student unions and their student societies are unable to show active interest in the world around them. This undermines a core task of universities, which is to protect free speech and encourage discussion of controversial issues (Neenan, 2018, n.p).

Article 9(1) of the European Convention on Human Rights states that 'Everyone has the right to freedom of thought, conscience and religion' and under Article 10(1) that:

> Everyone has the right to freedom of expression. This right shall include freedom to hold opinions and to receive and impart information and ideas without interference by public authority and regardless of frontiers.

In the UK, the Equality Act 2010[7] aims to protect people from discrimination because of their religious or philosophical beliefs, as well as those with no religion or belief. However, the right of any individual to *manifest* their religion and belief is qualified under Article 9(2) which notes that:

> Freedom to manifest one's religion or beliefs shall be subject only to such limitations as are prescribed by law and are necessary in a democratic society in the interests of public safety, for the protection of public order, health or morals, or for the protection of the rights and freedoms of others.

Freedom of expression, or freedom of speech is therefore not an absolute right and can be prevented under hate laws, for example ('Manifestation of freedom of thought, conscience and religion is not absolute and intervention may be justified where this is considered necessary to protect the rights of others' [University 20]). However, within the institutional policies, freedom of religious expression may be curtailed if it is contrary to the beliefs of others ('The right to manifest a belief may be qualified by the need to show respect for the differing worldviews, lifestyles and identities of others' [University 2]).

As a result, however, as a report by the freedom of expression campaigners Index on Censorship (2018, p. 4) has found,

> there has been a concerning rise in apparent attempts to shut down debates on certain subject areas in universities in the UK and elsewhere. Speakers whose views are deemed "offensive", "harmful" or even "dangerous" have been barred from speaking at events, conferences on particular topics cancelled and new laws introduced that some students and academics argue encourage an atmosphere of self-censorship that is inimical to the spirit of open debate essential for the testing and development of ideas.

Of more concern, however, is that some students recount that censorship is taking place just because the speaker happens to be Muslim:

> So we were planning an event and we wanted this particular speaker and suddenly there was all this requirement to prove that this person wasn't going to come on to campus and radicalise us all. So there was paperwork and paperwork to fill in but it was all just utter nonsense. I just kept telling them she was a feminist speaker who happened to be Muslim but I got nowhere […] it wouldn't have happened if she'd been a white feminist. I am sure of it. [Aisha, Pakistani heritage, female, 18, undergraduate].
>
> (reproduced from Stevenson, 2018, p. 9)

It is perhaps unsurprising then that the Religion and Belief policies reiterate an espoused but perhaps contradictory commitment to equality and equity. Across many of the policy documents, including those which make specific claims about secularity, commitment to only certain forms of religion remain valorised. Most notable is that tolerance towards Christianity remains a normative position for universities, with the framing of the academic year around a Christian calendar, largely taken for granted, whilst the provision of Halal or Kosher food is frequently only available as a 'special request'. In other words, the temporal and spatial functionings of religious students, which are likely to have the most effect on them, are generally those which are subject to most constraint, driving some students away from campus:

> I just socialise now with the friends I have where I live. I am from a large family and there is a close community and it just feels more accepting to be with them. [Zara, Sudanese, female, 20, undergraduate].
>
> (reproduced from Stevenson, 2018, p. 10)

Moreover, despite the opening framings of HEIs being welcoming and expansive spaces, the policy documents are clear that such possibilities are limited ('Examination period dates are fixed and publicised in advance […] it is not possible to change these dates in order to accommodate the full diversity of religious practices' [University 4]), whilst 'celebration' appears to be somewhat limited ('The university will not sanction students taking time out of the academic year to participate in religious celebrations or pilgrimages which are longer than two days' [University 6]). As a result, the universities hold ultimate power over the choices students are able to make ([requests for] time off to observe religious holidays that do not coincide with university holidays […] Where these are unable to be negotiated, students may need to formally interrupt their studies if they wish to continue with the leave of absence' [University 1]).

Indeed, throughout the documents it is clear that judgements will be made (though largely it is not clarified as to who will make them) as to what 'reasonable' behaviour is, or what forms of 'reasoned' debate might be allowed ('The University will make reasonable efforts ... The University will endeavour to bear in mind [...] consideration may be given' [University 1]). So, on the one hand, therefore, religious students are positioned as being welcome, and having rights, entitlement and equality in relation to functionings ('The University is concerned with permitting and facilitating the free practice of religion' [University 5]); however, where this might threaten the status quo universities will override this or threaten to take rights away – and not just where this might be against the law. Instead, what is suggested in the Religion and Belief Policy documents is: that secularity is rational and religion is not; that not all students are equal, or to be given equal treatment; that 'freedom' is only partially given – and that control is paramount; and that tolerance is countered by threat (veiled or otherwise).

In short, religious functionings are tolerated, but not if they create a problem for others, or threaten the good of the discipline, or the secularity of the university. In those cases, the university has complete power over the student and is able to curtail or deny religious functionings. In other words, students have the 'right' to exercise their religion and belief but not necessary the freedom to do so. Indeed, as Melanie Walker (2010a, p. 496) notes, within the contemporary university,

> Liberty, community, equity and security as policy values matter only in so far as they contribute to the main goals of human capital and efficiency.

Moving forward?

It is incontestable that religion divides, polarises and engenders strength of feeling. However, the marginalisation of religious students through the management and regulation of functionings not only contradicts the espoused equity positioning of universities as articulated in their Religion and Belief policies, but marginalises many religious students. In a context in which beliefs and practices are universally shared, functionings, and thus capabilities, are largely universally accepted; when these are contrary to the beliefs of others, it can, and does, lead to marginalisation, including the marginalisation of those who are present on campus in large numbers.

In her paper 'Critical Capability Pedagogies and University Education', Walker (2010b, p.899) draws on the capability approach,

> as a framework and criterion for equality and social justice because it arises from substantive concerns with improving the quality of people's lives, advancing human dignity and a fairer and more democratic world.

At the heart of capability theory is that people can, through greater understanding, and the application of universal principle of respect for conscience (Nussbaum, 2012), overcome intolerance. It also requires that we (as academics, educators, researchers and human beings) develop a greater understanding of those students we engage with. And yet religious literacy on campus remains minimal and the religious student experience is rarely listened to (Aune and Stevenson, 2017). Indeed, despite being one of the ten equity groups which require institutional policies to be developed, religious students are rarely consulted in the development of institutional policy or practice. Regardless of our own beliefs, religion can be a resource to be used to enable dialogue between different groups. Understanding religion and religious students has the potential to reduce intolerance, place higher education institutions in a better position to enable 'well-being freedoms' (Sen, 1992) for religious students, and ensure that they are not marginalised through fear or through ridicule.

Analysing these Religion and Belief policy documents has evidenced the tensions inherent in any application of the capability approach – that the functionings of one student has the inherent ability to restrict or remove the capabilities of others. This creates a challenge for universities who, rather than dealing with such tensions, retreat into a risk-avoidant or banal form of secularism. Reading across the policy documents also suggests, however, that (some) religious students form a type of 'symbolic threat' to universities. Despite institutional rhetoric ('we celebrate', 'we welcome', 'we value') most religious students are, in some way, positioned as posing a potential threat to universities, not so much in relation to radicalisation, but to Enlightenment rationalism. As a result, the institutional reaction is to constrain and to control. However, such positioning goes beyond thinking about functionings in relation to the individual. Rather it suggests that higher education institutions remain fearful about any, and all, religion which manifests in any other guise than Anglicanism.

Notes

1 When asked the question 'What is your religion?'
2 This is for hate crime recorded across London, not on campus.
3 The Cathedrals Group is an association of 15 universities and university colleges with Church foundations – see https://www.cathedralsgroup.ac.uk.
4 This term has been used in an attempt to maintain anonymity.
5 These have been deliberately left anonymous. Minor changes have been made to the quotes in an effort to retain this anonymity.
6 83 countries (42%) have high or very high levels of overall government restrictions or social hostilities on religion (Pew Research Center, 2018) with the largest increases in social hostilities being reported across Europe (Pew Research Center, 2019).
7 Under the recent Equality Act (2010), wherein religion and belief is a protected characteristic, higher education institutions have a legal duty to eliminate unlawful discrimination, harassment and victimisation and other conduct prohibited by the Act. They are also required to advance equality of opportunity between people who share a protected characteristic and those who do not, and to foster good relations between people who share a protected characteristic and those who do not. Responding to these new obligations all higher education institutions now have policies relating to religion and belief, one of the Act's protected characteristics.

References

Aune, K. and J. Stevenson (eds.) (2017) *Religion and higher education*, Abingdon/London: Routledge/Society for Research into Higher Education.

Barker, E. (1989) *New religious movements: A practical introduction*. London: HMSO.

Bebbington, D. (2011) Christian higher education in Europe: A historical analysis, *Christian Higher Education* 10(1): 10–24.

Billson, J. (1988) No owner of soil: The concept of marginality revisited on its sixtieth birthday, *International Review of Modern Sociology* 18(2): 183–204.

British Academy (2019) *Theology and religious studies provision in UK higher education*. London: British Academy.

Clark, D. (2005) *The capability approach: Its development, critiques and recent advances (GPRG working paper 32)*. Manchester/Oxford: Universities of Manchester and Oxford.

Coyle, A. and D. Rafalin (2000) Jewish gay men's accounts of negotiating cultural, religious, and sexual identity: a qualitative study, *Journal of Psychology & Human Sexuality* 12(4): 21–48.

Curtice, J., E. Clery, J. Perry, M. Phillips and N. Rahim (eds.) (2019) *British social attitudes: The 36th report*. London: National Centre for Social Research.

Dreze, J. and Sen, A. (1995) *India: Economic development and social opportunity*. Oxford: Oxford University Press.

Equality Challenge Unit (2011) *Religion and belief in higher education: The experiences of staff and students*. London: Equality Challenge Unit.

Faith Matters (2019) *Normalising hatred: Tell MAMA annual report 2018*. London: Faith Matters.

Gilliat-Ray, S. (2000) *Religion in higher education: The politics of the multi-faith campus*. Aldershot: Ashgate.

Graham, D. and J. Boyd (2011) *Home and away: Jewish journeys towards independence*. London: Institute for Jewish Policy Research.

Guest, M., K. Aune, S. Sharma and R. Warner (2013) *Christianity and the university experience: Understanding student faith*. London: Bloomsbury Academic.

Hinds, D. (2018) *Delegation of monitoring authority function to the Office for Students* [online], https://www.officeforstudents.org.uk/media/1301/prevent-ofs-delegation-letter.pdf.

Home Office (2011) *Prevent strategy (2011Cm 8092)*. London: Home Office.

Home Office (2019) *Revised Prevent duty guidance: For England and Wales* (updated 10th April) [online], https://www.gov.uk/government/publications/prevent-duty-guidance/revised-prevent-duty-guidance-for-england-and-wales.

Hunt, C. (2009) Seeking integration: Spirituality in the context of lifelong learning and professional reflective practice, in R. Lawrence (ed.) *Proceedings of the 50th Annual Adult Education Research Conference: Honoring our past, embracing our future* (pp. 155–160). Chicago: National-Louis University.

Hunt, C. and L. West (2007) Towards an understanding of what it might mean to research spiritually, in L. Servage and T. Fenwick (eds.) *Learning in community: proceedings of the joint international conference of the Adult Education Research Conference (48th national conference) and Canadian Association for the Study of Adult Education (26th national conference)* (pp. 301–306), Nova Scotia: Mount Saint Vincent University.

Index on Censorship (2018) *Uncomfortable, but educational: Freedom of expression in UK universities*. London: Index on Censorship.

Jones, D. (1988) *The origins of civic universities: Manchester, Leeds and Liverpool*: London: Routledge.

Messiou, K. (2012) Collaborating with children in exploring marginalisation: An approach to inclusive education, *International Journal of Inclusive Education* 16 (12): 1311–1322.

Mowat, J. (2015) Towards a new conceptualisation of marginalisation, *European Educational Research Journal* 14(5): 454–476.

National Union of Students (2012) *No place for hate – hate crimes and incidents in further and higher education: religion or belief*. London: National Union of Students.

National Union of Students (2018) *The experience of Muslim students in 2017–18*. London: National Union of Students.

Neenan, J. (2018) "Muslims are self-censoring" Prof Scott-Baumann on the battle for free speech on campus, SOAS Blog [online], https://www.soas.ac.uk/blogs/study/muslims-are-self-censoring.

Nussbaum, M. (1999) *Sex and social justice*. Oxford: Oxford University Press.

Nussbaum, M. (2000) *Women and human development: The capabilities approach*. Cambridge: Cambridge University Press.

Nussbaum, M. (2012) *The new religious intolerance: Overcoming the politics of fear in an anxious age*. Cambridge: Harvard University Press.

O'Beirne, M. (2004) *Findings from the home office citizenship survey*. London: Home Office.

Office for National Statistics (2012) *Religion in England and Wales 2011* [online], https://www.ons.gov.uk/peoplepopulationandcommunity/culturalidentity/religion/articles/religioninenglandandwales2011/2012-12-11.

Perfect, D. (2011) *Religion or belief (Equality and Human Rights Commission Briefing Paper 1)*. Manchester: Equality and Human Rights Commission.

Pew Research Center (2017) *The changing global religious landscape*. Washington: Pew Research Center.

Pew Research Center (2018) *Global uptick in government restrictions on religion in 2016*. Washington: Pew Research Center.

Pew Research Center (2019) *A closer look at how religious restrictions have risen around the world*. Washington: Pew Research Center.

Purdam, K., R. Afkhami, A. Crockett and W. Olsen (2007) Religion in the UK: An overview of equality statistics and evidence gaps, *Journal of Contemporary Religion* 22(2): 147–168.

Putnam, R. and D. Campbell (2010) *American grace: How religion divides and unites us*. New York: Simon and Schuster.

Robeyns, I. (2016) The capability approach, in E. Zalta (ed.) *The Stanford encyclopedia of philosophy* (Winter 2016 Edition) [online], https://plato.stanford.edu/archives/win2016/entries/capability-approach.

Samuels, J. (2005) *Removing unfreedoms: Citizens as agents of change: Sharing new policy frameworks for urban development*. London: Intermediate Technology Development Group.

Sen, A. (1984) *Resources, values and development*. Oxford: Basil Blackwell.

Sen, A. (1989) Development as capability expansion, *Journal of Development Planning* 19(41): 41–58.

Sen, A. (1992) *Inequality reexamined*. Oxford: Clarendon Press.
Sen, A. (1999) *Development as freedom*. Oxford: Oxford University Press.
Sen A. (2003) Development as capability expansion, in S. Fukuda-Parr and A. Shiva Kumar (eds.) *Readings in human development: Concepts, measures, and policies for a development paradigm* (pp. 3–16). New Delhi/New York: Oxford University Press.
Sen, A. (2004) Capabilities, lists, and public reason: Continuing the conversation, *Feminist Economics* 10(3): 77–80.
Sen, A. (2006) Capability and well-being, in M. Nussbaum and A. Sen (eds.) *The quality of life* (pp. 30–53). Oxford: Clarendon Press.
Smart, N. (1989) *The world's religions*. Cambridge: Cambridge University Press.
Stevenson, J. (2012) Religion and higher education: Making sense of the experience of religious students at secular universities through a Bourdieuian lens, unpublished EdD thesis, University of Leeds.
Stevenson, J. (2014) Internationalisation and religious inclusion in UK higher education, *Higher Education Quarterly* 68(1): 46–64.
Stevenson, J. (2018) *Muslim students in UK higher education: Issues of inequality and inequity*. London: Bridge Institute.
Tyrer, D. and F. Ahmad (2006) *Muslim women and higher education: Identities, experiences and prospects*. Liverpool: Liverpool John Moores University.
UCU Left (2015) *Challenging the prevent agenda* [online], https://uculeft.org/2015/09/challenging-the-prevent-agenda.
United Nations Development Programme (1996) *Georgia human development report 1996: Glossary*. New York: United Nations.
Universities UK (2005) *Promoting good campus relations: Dealing with hate crimes and intolerance*. London: Universities UK.
Universities UK (2011) *Freedom of speech on campus: Rights and responsibilities in UK universities*. London: Universities UK.
Walker, M. (2010a) A human development and capabilities 'prospective analysis' of global higher education policy, *Journal of Education Policy* 25(4): 485–501.
Walker, M. (2010b) Critical capability pedagogies and university education, *Educational Philosophy and Theory* 42(8): 898–917.
Walters, M. and A. Krasodomski-Jones (2018) *Patterns of hate crime: Who, what, when and where?* Brighton/London: University of Sussex and Demos.
Weller, P. (2006) Addressing religious discrimination and Islamophobia: Muslims and liberal democracies. The case of the United Kingdom, *Journal of Islamic Studies* 17(3): 295–325.
Weller, P. (2011) *Religious discrimination in Britain: A review of research evidence, 2000–10*. Manchester: Equality and Human Rights Commission.
World Economic Forum (2017) *Losing their religion? These are the world's most atheistic countries* [online], https://www.weforum.org/agenda/2017/07/losing-their-religion-these-are-the-world-s-most-atheistic-countries.

Section II

Mobility

Chapter 7

Expectations, experiences and anticipated outcomes of supporting refugee students in Germany

Systems theoretical analysis of organizational semantics

Jana Berg

Introduction

Soon after they registered an influx of applicants from a refugee background in 2015 and 2016, German higher education organizations (HEOs) started to support prospective refugee students, mostly with measures of study preparation. After first initiatives of counseling and social integration were often offered voluntarily, quickly-established public and private funding schemes provided the resources to formalize offers and create support structures for refugees, including counseling positions and preparatory courses (Berg et al., in press).

Before 2016, refugee students were formally treated as international students and not individually addressed by HEOs. With the initiation and formalization of support structures for refugees, a new differentiation was introduced. In order to be included into and able to access specific support, residence status became relevant. Refugee students were now – at least in the context of support structures – formally differentiated from international students. Simultaneously, support structures were formalized. Central to this support were newly established positions of *first contacts* for refugees: those positions were created in order to communicate with prospective refugee students, as well as internal and external personnel relevant to support and the processing of their requests (Berg et al., in press).

This chapter looks into semantic associations and potential discourses on refugee students within German HEOs. The perspectives of first contacts as well as heads of international offices are analyzed in order to understand organizational rationales for supporting refugees and the understanding of refugee students. Further, the chapter asks whether and how refugees are seen within the context of the internationalization of German HEO.

I will first give an overview of higher education for refugees in Germany and international research on refugees in higher education. After describing the theoretical framework and empirical basis of this chapter, I show what reasons my interview partners give for supporting refugee students. Further, I discuss whether and how refugees are seen in the context of HEOs' internationalization and then broach the issue of changes and developments in semantics of refugee students. Finally, I discuss my results in reference to the initial research questions.

Higher education for refugees in Germany: an overview

While other countries mostly take in resettlement refugees from other countries, the vast majority of refugees in Germany apply for asylum on arrival. Usually, asylum seekers register after entering the country. They are then distributed to one of the sixteen German states ('*Bundesländer*'), where they can apply for asylum and go through a lengthy process, including personal interviews and case examination. The process can result in one of three forms of protection: refugee protection, entitlement to asylum and subsidiary protection. Alternatively it can result in a national ban on deportation ('*Duldung*' or 'toleration'), which usually allows them to remain in the country for a certain time, or finally in the application being declined (Bundesamt für Migration und Flüchtlinge [BAMF], 2018).

The specific situation of refugees differs widely, depending on their status, available resources, infrastructure and networks, individual decisions of case workers and other factors. As all newly-arriving migrants, refugees are obliged to participate in 700 hours of Integration Courses, which include training in basic language skills (BAMF, 2018). After a certain time and depending on their status, refugees are eligible for public financial student support[1].

When refugees apply for German higher education, they are registered as non-EU international students (Grüttner et al., 2018a) and must meet the general application criteria. German HEOs do not collect information on the residence status of their applicants. This information only becomes available if they apply for support that is dependent on residence status and is not further saved or used apart from support measures. Thus, in the following, the term 'refugee' is used according to how HEO practitioners use it and does not refer to a specific legal outcome of an asylum procedure.

Applicants generally must hold an entrance qualification and proof of language proficiency. Most programs require proof of fluent German on a C1 level referring to the Common European Framework of Reference (Council of Europe, 2020) for language and mostly also an intermediate level of English. Additionally, subject-specific criteria, such as additional language skills, can become relevant. If their documents are not validated as an entrance qualification, international students can enroll in preparatory colleges ('*Studienkollegs*') and take an assessment test ('*Feststellungsprüfung*'), which will count as an entrance qualification. As soon as they fulfill the formal criteria, refugees can regularly apply for higher education. They then have to compete with all other international applicants for limited study places. Bureaucratic requirements, individual cases and the complex system of HEO-dependent rules create various and partly complicated pathways to German higher education (Schröder et al., 2019).

A study of newly arriving refugees that was conducted in 2016 shows that about one-third (32%) held school degrees that were likely to allow access to higher education and many more had high educational aspirations (Brücker et al., 2016). This interest in higher education was warmly welcomed by German politicians: (higher) education is understood to be crucial for the social and economic integration of migrants and refugees. First reactions to the influx of asylum seekers framed them as a source of new hope for the German labor market (Streitwieser and Brück, 2018). Further, higher education is seen as a basis of hope and for building a new life – either in a new country, or for taking part in re-building their country of origin by refugee students themselves as well as practitioners (Grüttner et al., 2018b). Regardless of the positive framing, few academic studies had looked into higher education for refugees, and there was little practical experience with the topic at German HEOs before 2016.

During the last years, many Germany HEOs developed support structures for refugees. This engagement was initially based on voluntary work right after the refugee influx and was further developed with the support of federal, state-level, private and partly also HEO-internal funding schemes (Berg et al., in press). On the federal level, the Federal Ministry of Education and Research (BMBF) started the programs 'Integra' and 'WELCOME' in order to support offers for refugees at HEOs and preparatory colleges. These are managed by the German Academic Exchange Service (Deutscher Akademischer Austauschdienst [DAAD]). The first round of Integra was funded with 100,000,000€ from 2016 to 2019 and supports academic preparation as well as language courses. WELCOME supports offers for refugees that are organized by students, e.g. by financing paid student positions (DAAD, 2018).

Research on higher education for refugees

Academic studies mainly focus on challenges posed to refugees seeking to enter or obtain higher education and on the description or evaluation of support programs for (prospective) refugee students (for literature reviews, see Berg et al., 2018; Ramsay and Baker, 2019). While studies previously mainly focused on Canada, the USA, the UK and Australia (Berg et al., 2018), the war in Syria and a growing public and academic interest in the topic led to additional publications from a variety of countries, with an increasing focus on Germany (Grüttner et al., 2018b; Schneider, 2018; Unangst, 2019), Jordan (AbduRazak et al., 2019; Steinhilber, 2019) as well as Turkey (Akbasli and Mavi, 2021; Erdoğan and Erdoğan, 2018).

Among the main challenges for refugee students are language proficiency, meeting formal entrance criteria, inflexible and repressive aspects of the asylum regime, and access to correct information. Based on those interdependent challenges (Bajwa et al., 2018; Berg, 2018), studies have argued that refugees need specific support in order to meet their often high academic goals. This should be granted due to a 'moral obligation [and] socioeconomic' rationales, as Lenette (2016, p. 1312) points out for the Australian context.

In order to support refugees, many HEOs and other organizations have started specific programs. The conditions vary, depending on whether those programs are set within refugee camps (Abdo and Craven, 2018; Bellino and Hure, 2018) or at HEOs, if and how they are funded, who is involved and other factors. Due to large funding schemes and broad offers for refugees, German higher education has recently been noted to effectively support refugee students (United Nations Educational, Scientific and Cultural Organization, 2018). Offers for refugee students at German HEOs mostly include language classes, academic preparatory courses and access to university facilities and wi-fi as well as offers to support the social integration of refugees (Beigang et al., 2018).

Only a few studies analyze perspectives on refugee students. Some take the perspective of practitioners and members of HEOs into account, mostly asking about challenges and experiences with specific support structures (Crea and Sparnon, 2017; Grüttner et al., 2018b; Nayton et al., 2019). Streitwieser and Brück (2018) discuss HEOs' engagement with refugees in the context of public debates around solidarity as well as a right-wing backlash in Germany.

Anderson's (2020) analysis of media representations of international and refugee students in Canada shows that media reports on international students in general differ from reports on refugee students. Those reports on refugee students seem to emphasize welfare and support, while those on international students show a greater variety in topics and both very positive as well as very critical positions:

> It seems [...] that the positive framing of international students [...] – and their possible transitions to Canadian society as "ideal" immigrants – was closely linked to their real or perceived financial and labor contributions as members of the global "best and the brightest", unlike refugee students who are allowed into the country as expressions of Canada's benevolence.
>
> (Anderson, 2020, p. 18)

Similar differentiations can be found in Ergin's (2016) study of the perspective of Turkish students regarding their fellow Syrian students. Showing a generally positive attitude toward internationalization, they feared that the admission of Syrian refugees might lower their own chances of admission and on the labor market. Nonetheless, Ergin describes that the students welcomed the support for refugees in order to ensure their right to education. Furthermore, 'the participants believed that if their Syrian classmates would return to Syria in the future, they would play a crucial role in rebuilding the post-war Syria and maintaining good diplomatic relations with Turkey' (Ergin, 2016, p. 412).

Based on the assumption that perspectives on refugees play a crucial role in the implementation and design of support structures, this study focuses on the emerging discourse on refugees at German HEOs. While some papers discuss refugees in the context of the internationalization of the higher education system (Berg, 2018; Ergin et al., 2019; Streitwieser, 2019), this study specifically asks about HEOs' motives and rationales for supporting refugees and the understanding of refugees within HEOs.

Theoretical framework

This chapter is based on a systems theoretical approach to the sociology of knowledge. The focus of this approach is the interconnectedness of social differentiation and evolutionary developments of semantics (Keller, 2011, p. 64). In other words, it asks how structural changes are interconnected with and depend on semantics and discourses (Luhmann, 1980, p. 7). With this focus, it allows an analysis of individual as well as organizational motivations and operations within their organizational setting and underlying semantics. Luhmann's systems theory is based on *communication*. In his understanding, communication includes information, utterance and understanding (Luhmann, 2018 [2011], p. 68). The intended meaning of utterance and the perceived meaning of understanding are independent from each other and can vary. Communications are observable, they process differentiations and therefore notations (Keller, 2011, p. 65).

All communications regarding a specific topic or function build *systems*: Each interaction between people builds *interactive systems*. *Organizational systems* follow structured communications and are generally decision-driven. The main task of such systems is to reduce complexity: they set limits to what is possible and thereby create communicative expectations. Communicative acts have to match those expectations in order to be compatible and thus processable by a system. Systems constantly observe themselves and draw distinctions between themselves and everything outside their boundaries, meaning all non-compatible communication. They create generalized *self-descriptions* as an orientation for possible communications (Luhmann, 2018 [2011], pp. 347–348). Within organizations, those self-descriptions can be formalized, such as mission statements or strategy papers.

All communications that are not compatible to a system build its *environment*, including all other systems. Thus, within society, environment is not one entity, but differs for each system within that society. The communications of different systems follow different communicative expectations and are thus not compatible with each other. Society is understood to be a social system, including all other systems and all environments. The systems of one society each follow their own expectations and logics, unable to fully understand each other. Since systems limit complexity by limiting communicative possibilities, they are always less complex than their environment.

Systems constantly observe themselves and their environment. If an environmental communication does not meet the systems expectation, it will either be ignored as irrelevant or can create an *irritation*. Such irritations can create *conflicts* and result in the need to adjust a system's structures. That means that systems and their communicative expectations are not static, but *flexible*.

In order to deal with environmental complexity, systems build programs that break down complex topics in order to match their communicative expectations and to enable them to make decisions. There are two categories of decision programs: *Conditional programs* are 'primarily input-oriented [and] distinguish between conditions and consequences' (Luhmann, 2018 [2011], p. 213). In the context of HEOs, an example would be regular admission procedures. If all criteria are met, an applicant can be accepted. *Goal programs* are 'primarily output-oriented programs [and distinguish] between means and ends' (Luhmann, 2018 [2011], p. 213). They are implemented in order to meet certain ends. To stick with our example, this could be measures to support the inclusion of specific applicants. Further, systems can get more complex themselves by *internal differentiation* (Luhmann, 1970, p. 123.). Additional system-internal structures can become sub-systems themselves. At the boundaries of systems, *boundary positions* can fulfill the task of translating environmental communications and thus ensure working communication between systems. Finally, some *media of communication*, such as money, can be used to set conditions or communicate between systems (Luhmann, 1970, p. 127 and 1982, p. 95). Nonetheless, the communication will be received and processed within the boundaries of each system's possibilities of understanding. Information remains within the boundaries of a system (Luhmann, 2018 [2011], p. 37).

The process of building new systems or new structures within systems is referred to as functional differentiation. It is understood to be a flexible process, following functional needs. It is evolutionary in the sense that it is socially caused but not controlled, and it is allowed by mechanisms of variation, selection and stabilization (Luhmann, 1980, p. 41). The formalization of support for refugee students can be seen as a flexible reaction to an emerging functional need in combination with the new availability of resources. In this context, I ask about motivations and anticipated consequences of those new structures within higher education organization. This shifts the focus to semantics.

As Stichweh sums up several explanations for the term, semantics can be understood as generalized meaning ('*Sinn*'), offering a range of topics, forms and differentiations that build the basis for all communication and thus all possible operations. Social systems depend on semantics to offer them meaning and to reproduce the logics of functional differentiation and complexity reduction (Luhmann, 1980, p. 18; Stichweh, 2000, p. 238). Semantics provide the differentiations and expectations that communication is based on and are therefore crucial for structure formation and operations of any social system (Stichweh, 2000, p. 242). They can metaphorically be understood as a generalized catalog, or a rulebook of producing, choosing and operating with meaning (Luhmann, 1980, p. 19). In order to be operational, semantics have to be understood and processed in connection with social systems, or, in other words, in relation to a specific function (Luhmann, 1980, p. 45).

Knowledge is the product and at the same time the premise of communication; it consists of all expectations that can be irritated and challenged (Keller, 2011, p. 65). Changes in ideas and common sense are accompanied and caused by the variation, selection and stabilization of semantics. Due to this evolutionary development, change and learning are possible (Luhmann, 1980, p. 24 and p. 41). Changes in the framework of possible ideas, operations and structural changes are interconnected and can cause each other (Luhmann, 1980, p. 44).

In this context, discourses are understood to be systems of semantics-production that became independent social systems of their own through a process of differentiation (Stichweh, 2000, p. 239). They can be structurally coupled ('*strukturelle Kopplung*') with other systems, which means they can irritate them and thus cause them to change their semantics (Stichweh, 2000, p. 240).

By providing meaning and expectations, semantics often are the basis for building structures. Thus, in order to understand the development of functional structures and social systems, it is important to analyze their underlying semantics, self-description and expectations as well as potential discursive influences.

Methods

According to Keller (2007, 2011), discourse analysis looks into statements and expressions as representations, realizations and updates of discourses. It aims to analyze how discourses are created and strategically used by social actors as well as how they are related to and interdependent with social practices. His approach is closely oriented toward social constructivist perspectives from the sociology of knowledge (Keller, 2011).

The systems theoretical background differs from Keller's theoretical argumentation. Nonetheless, Keller's approach allows the structural analysis of semantics and associations within discourses. Hermeneutic semantic analysis often focuses on levels of meanings of individual words (Scarvaglieri and Zech, 2013; Wojtkiewicz and Heiland, 2012). In order to analyze a broader context and look into several semantic and discursive aspects, I modeled my methodical approach on Keller's discourse analysis.

This chapter is based on expert interviews with eighteen members of eight German HEOs, including four universities and four universities of applied sciences. Between late summer 2017 and summer 2018, first contacts for refugees and heads of international offices were interviewed at each HEO. One university has two first contacts and at one university of applied sciences the first contact changed during the field period, which is why there are three interviews included for both HEOs. The interview partners were chosen based on the assumption that their position allows them specific insights into and a certain influence on the development and characteristics of support structures for refugee students (Liebold and Trinczek, 2009, p. 35). Their HEOs were selected based on their regional distribution, covering cities of different sizes in various areas in Germany. The sample includes HEOs from seven German states. While most are widely distributed across the country, one university and one university of applied sciences were chosen from within the same city. Other sampling criteria were diverse mission statements, focusing on diversity, internationalization and excellence (Berg et al., in press).

All interviews were fully transcribed. They are given codes based on institution (U=University, FH=University of applied sciences) with chronological reference to the participants (E1, E2 and E3). In order to organize the data for analysis, the interviews had been topically coded with MAXQDA. Thus, open coding was mainly focused on pre-selected sequences dealing with the perception/description of refugees, the understanding of internationalization, diversification and social responsibility, as well as reasons for and challenges during the initiation and formalization of support structures for refugees. Based on the MAXQDA-coding, an Excel table was created to give an overview of dimensions and content, as well as additional categories: semantic associations, irritations and the development of an independent discourse. Further, individual cases were compared depending on the time of the interview and with a specific focus on indicators of the development of arguments and knowledge.

The aim was to analyze the emergence and potential development of the participants' knowledge about refugees within HEOs and comprehend potential consequences on an organizational level. The research questions were as follows:

- What are organizational rationales for and the expected benefits of supporting refugee students?
- Are refugees seen as international students?
- Do experiences with refugees change the discourse on the challenges, needs and potential of international students?

Results

In this section, I first give an overview of organizational rationales for supporting refugees. Then, I analyze how refugees are understood in comparison to international students with no experience of forced migration. Finally, I show the prospects of further developments and describe organizational benefits of the programs for refugees that were mentioned throughout the interviews.

Why support refugee students?

> Yes, the question is indeed asked, just why we do it. Meaning, exactly this question: "Just what do we gain from it?" [...] This aspect of social responsibility, I believe most see that. That we just have a certain responsibility. But they have asked very specifically, "What does it do for [the university]?" [...] And indeed many question it and say, "Well, actually we gain nothing from it. It creates tons of work, we have to deal with specific topics. Really, we do not actually gain anything from it." [...] As mentioned, this is not how I see it. [...] We gain a lot from it. We also just have to do it and have a responsibility, but there are tendencies that also say: "Yeah, if we do not do it, nothing is lost" (U1E2, head of international office)[2].

The rising number of refugees who were presumed to need support or contacted HEOs with requests, as well as the motivation of members of HEOs to provide assistance caused an increase of mostly voluntary engagement for prospective refugee students. After funding became available, this led to the formalization of goal programs and support structures (Berg et al., in press). Next to practical necessities resulting from the irritation of existing conditional programs as well as expectations and motivations in environmental communications, such as the expectation to educate more professionals for the German labor market, HEOs followed system-internal rationales when they created support structures for refugees.

Some interview partners do describe challenges for their HEO in realizing support for refugees, such as scarcity of resources. This included the availability of rooms, teaching personnel and funding, but also insecurities about legal frameworks and their individual ability to maneuver within partly unclear formal regulations. In some cases, this led to discussions about the legitimation of support for this rather small group. On the other hand, the interviewees framed support for refugees within the self-description of their HEO and argued for potential benefits for their organization and other systems.

Organizational rationales for supporting refugees are closely connected to system-internal semantics and discourses that are part of formal documents of self-description, mainly meaning an increased internationalization, but also diversification. Furthermore, prospective benefits for HEOs were discussed. For example, refugees were often credited with helping to create a more international and diverse campus, which was also understood to be beneficial for domestic students, allowing intercultural experiences and potentially motivating them to go abroad. Refugees were expected to become highly motivated, and therefore hopefully successful, students. In addition, humanitarian reasons were given, referring to HEOs' third mission of acting socially responsibly:

> So, first the [HEO] of course profits because they are qualified people who come to this [HEO]. Who, yes, bring great motivation and then, I think, one also profits, because the students become, yes, more international. That just the entire environment becomes more diverse. I think, that will probably also benefit the mechanical engineers—who are all from this region—if there are some other people participating.
>
> (FH1E3, head of international office)

The argument of social responsibility was often connected to environmental semantics that are mostly structurally interconnected with semantic goals of HEOs, such as the hope that refugees would become professionals in the German labor market:

> And ehm, if you look at it from an economic perspective, [...] everybody is complaining about a lack of professionals and a lack of younger professionals. And this of course is a huge chance. Ehm that they are of course potentially prospective professionals. Who can be trained here. And who also, yes, really can be integrated and because of this, this is a huge chance.
>
> (FH1E1, first contact)

It seems fair to argue that the formalization of goal programs in order to offer support for refugee students can be seen as an indicator for the emergence of a discourse on refugees within HEOs. Based on initial semantic associations and expectations, support structures were created, parallel to forming a specialized discourse. This includes expectations about the characteristics and needs of refugee students, about adequate support, about potential benefits for the HEO and partly also about reasons to support refugees. It is closely linked to HEOs' self-descriptions and sub-systems' discourses, e.g., on internationalization or diversification, but also to system-environmental semantics and discourses that present external expectations, e.g., on the lack of professionals or public opinions of refugees.

International refugee students?

The internationalization of higher education is understood as a process rather than a condition or outcome (Knight, 1994), including the mobility of students and academic staff, but also the internationalization of academics, including research cooperation, publications and events[3]. Other aspects are common international methods of quality assurance and the transfer and compatibility of research and educational models or international study programs (Larsen, 2016; Robson, 2011; Seeber and Lepori, 2014). It is of great importance for HEOs within a globalized academia. Academically, it is connected to a broad and interdisciplinary body of research, for example, in the fields of transnationalism, of European identity building (van Mol, 2013) and of migration. On the other hand, the term offers space for interpretation and very different realizations (Knight, 2011).

One of the central questions of my research is whether refugee students are understood as international students. While there mostly seemed to be no question that refugee students increase the diversity of the student body and that supporting them is an important part of their HEO's third mission, the interviewees' opinions differed more strongly on the question of whether refugees were part of the internationalization of their HEO. Some of the multiple facets of internationalization are reflected in topics that came up throughout the interviews.

First, refugees are often referred to within the context of 'internationalisation at home' (U1E2, head of international office) in the sense of creating a more international student body, including additional international perspectives in comparison to more common countries of origin (Larsen 2016). Increasingly, HEOs do not only focus on the mobility of students and staff, but also on creating a more international study experience, focusing on intercultural exchange, but also including intercultural topics in their range of studies:

> Besides [student mobility], I think it is also important [...] to create offers here for students that do not go abroad. Meaning that they can participate in intercultural workshops or in various presentations about different countries or regions. That they are in touch with exchange students or with international full-time students [...] That they blend, get to know each other and also work together'.
> (FH1E3, head of international office)

Second, even though *internationalization strategies* are named as a reason to support refugees and an argument why supporting refugee students is indeed based on organizational self-description and embedded in HEOs' goals, refugees are generally not understood to become an explicit aspect of internationalization strategies. The main reason for this seems to be that existing internationalization strategies are understood to cover the general support for refugees and there simply is no need to formalize this specific support within the description of sub-systems such as international offices. More specific approaches, such as projects to support refugees, are rather seen as temporary goal programs and described in terms of existing self-descriptions. Those are broad enough to allow flexible reactions, which can be seen in the way refugee students are connected to existing goals such as internationalization at home. Semantics and thereafter structures can be created in order to meet specific needs, but that does not necessarily change the entire organization. This flexibility ascribes the responsibility and competence for organizing support to individual actors rather than making it 'a recorded strategy' (U2E1, first contact); support programs for refugees are 'not such a focus topic of internationalisation [strategies]' (U2E1, first contact). Thus, their realization rather follows 'implicit [...] strategies of actors' (U1E3, first contact).

Third, the *formal classification of refugee students as international students* has organizational consequences. It allows them to access structures that are specifically provided for international students[4]. For refugees, some additional rules apply. For example, they can request that the international students' fees be waived. By creating specific offers for refugees, funding providers and HEOs introduced an *additional differentiation for refugee students*. Thus, especially during study preparation, residence status can become relevant in order to access specific support:

> [...] as a part of our strategy we do not want to isolate refugees. But of course one has to check which residence status or, for example, if they want to do a language class with us. That is a language class for refugees. Meaning we just have to know whether one has asylum or not. But once they are in and during the application procedure, all are the same.
> (FH3E1, first contact)

Fourth, the interview partners describe a different set of *challenges and needs* of refugee students compared with international visa students as a reason to offer the mentioned specific support. They understand refugees as a group of international students that is defined by its own characteristics (Berg, 2018), such as less preparation to study in Germany before they arrived in the country, but also benefits such as access to public student loans that are not granted to other international students. Additional challenges arise from the circumstances of their migration to Germany. To name a few, some refugees are missing the documents, they mostly did not prepare to study in Germany, the flight itself and time spent in Germany before study preparations or studies cause gaps in their educational biography, and traumatizing experiences as well as concern for friends and relatives in their home countries can cause psychological distress. The combination, accumulation and interdependence of those challenges can be seen as specific for refugees and is understood to create the need for additional support structures (Berg, 2018):

> It is really mainly all those questions regarding the asylum procedure, which then impact questions like finances and participation in language classes and place of living.
> (U2E2, head international office)

> I mean, the other possible points are the psycho-social challenges, which I assume occurs more often among refugees.
> (U1E3, first contact)

> Partly they also have advantages compared to other foreign students. Because they can receive BAföG [public student funding], for example,
> (FH1E1, first contact)

Finally, the interviewed HEO-members assume that refugees would not want to be labelled as such due to potential *stigmatization*. Repeatedly, it was stated as an objective to *treat refugee students as international students* as quickly as possible in order to support their quick social integration.

> Even though I do not know whether one should see it that separately. Because, in the end they all are international students and I am having a bit of a hard time to always see that so separately [...] I believe that they themselves probably do not want that in the long term. And, because I think that they, well, have special counselling needs. But I believe maybe more so during study preparation. But I believe during the next years it will rather be the case that they belong to the full time students. Hopefully. And then it is a part of the internationalisation.
>
> (FH1E3, head international office)

Irritations and adjustments, insecurities and prospects

A previous explorative study showed great uncertainty on which structures are actually meeting the needs of refugee students (Berg, 2018). Based on experiences, hearsay, guidelines and anticipations, support structures were initiated in accordance to system-internal and environmental semantics about the needs of refugee students. Further planning and realization of support structures showed the importance of personnel in organizational decision making and structural changes (Berg et al., in press).

One of the goal programs implemented and formalized by HEOs in order to support refugee students is the position of first contacts. They are usually in charge of counseling as well as managing support offers as well as creating and maintaining communication structures within and outside their organization (Berg et al., in press). Experiences with refugee students sometimes do not fit and thus irritate the expectations support structures were based on (Keller, 2011, p. 65). This can influence organizational semantics regarding refugee students and cause the adjustment of support structures, often with first contacts as boundary positions in charge of communicating irritations, initiating adaptions and therefore minimizing uncertainty and irritations (Luhmann, 1976, 2018 [2011], p. 178), which points to the importance of personnel and on-topic communication channels for the experience-based adjustment of programs:

> Then there is this mathematics preparation course, which also goes on for six months. But we will shorten that. So, we do collect experiences and are learning from what we are doing here. It was just too long. During Ramadan many dropped the course. And we will shorten this to two periods of six weeks.
>
> (U2E1, first contact)

Throughout the interviews conducted in late spring and summer 2018, most interviewees seemed to have overcome initial uncertainties and to be fairly certain that the progression of semantic and structural changes had dealt with most irritations. Sometimes, they also had very specific ideas of prospective structural changes. Most of them were, however, rather uncertain about whether and how to sustain support structures for refugees.

Throughout the interviews, there were three main prospects for the development of support structures for refugee students:

- First, some HEOs planned to maintain their support for refugees, but were depending on external funding in order to do so. Funding has been crucial for the formalization of initially often voluntary support (Berg et al., in press). In 2017, the interviewees did not know whether public support would be extended after 2019. In 2018, some HEOs were planning to apply for further public funding, ideally in order to keep offering study preparation support, but also to 'accompany this new phase' (FH2E1, first contact) of enrolled refugee students. However, nobody knew whether or to what extent they could continue.

- Second, some HEOs were planning on merging offers for refugee students and other groups. This often meant either including refugees in existing structures for international students or learning from the experiences with refugees in order to provide improved support structures for a diverse student body. This was understood to be a chance for organizational change:

    So, they might maybe [...] become a group in diversity strategies for a while. Because, ehm, they are here and there will always be more refugees [...] And because of this it just is one of those many groups on their way to university. And this is good, it is to some extent normality. This is why I said, the experiences we made here bring innovation to the university [...] And thoughts about designing university life against the background of diverse groups.
    (U4E2, head of international office)

- And third, at some HEOs, not enough refugees participated in courses in order to maintain them. Therefore, no further specific support will be offered. This can also result in a merging of structures, which seems to rather depend on structural than semantic changes:

    I think the numbers rather decrease. So, ehm, for this reason we could not apply for [external funding] anymore. And even if there is a handful of people in [specific offer for refugees], then one has to consider whether to just include them into the regular offers for international students, where they are welcome anyway. So, if there are offers, they will never be excluded.
    (FH2E2, head of international office)

Generally, the interview partners described positive effects of their HEO's engagement for refugees. Most interview partners refer to a *more diverse and international student body*, which is even understood to motivate domestic students to go abroad and help them to reach internationalization objectives. Another aspect is *stronger voluntary student engagement*. Some HEOs tried to maintain this engagement by creating intercultural classes that allow students to earn credit points for their studies, or by creating paid jobs for students, e.g., within the federally funded WELCOME program that is focused on student support.

Further, refugees are discussed as an *opportunity to learn more about the situation and potential needs* of other international *students*. The experience with supporting refugees can provide the opportunity to improve general programs and other groups, especially international students, are expected to benefit from this as well. In addition to increased awareness for the social needs of international students and study preparation as an episode of education with specific needs (Berg et al., 2019), support structures for refugees are expected to point out and *create awareness for challenging and unnecessarily complicated organizational structures*, mostly referring to conditional programs:

> Maybe […] that we, ehm, also notice, ehm, that our procedures are very, ehm, complicated and bureaucratic, and that we could probably consider, that what is clear to us, ehm, is not as clear to others, ehm, or foreign groups. And one should consider how we could communicate better. And how we then could, ehm, make our own procedures simpler. For example in order to be even more attractive for, ehm, other groups too.
> (U4E1, first contact)

Discussion

The initiation of differentiation and a discourse on refugee students within German HEOs can be seen as an example of structural differentiation and the development and adjustments of semantics, discourses and structures. A systems theoretical perspective was used in analyzing the interconnectedness of emerging semantics and the differentiation of a discourse on refugees and the formalization and changes of support structures.

Reconsidering the research questions, organizational rationales for, and expected benefits of, supporting international students are mentioned within the context of supporting refugee students. Assuming independent discourses on international as well as refugee students, their semantic associations and topics differ, but are closely linked.

What are organizational rationales for and expected benefits of supporting refugee students?

Initial voluntary support was presumably often based on HEO-external semantics, such as the wish to support people in need. Further formalizations of programs for refugees are often described while referring to internationalization, diversification and a third mission of social responsibility. This links supporting refugees to general HEO strategies, since all three topics are part of HEOs' formal self-description such as mission statements and strategy papers. It can also be seen as an example of the flexibility of those self-descriptions and mission statements, as a new group was targeted based on general mission statements.

The expected benefits of supporting refugee students include rationales of fulfilling a third mission of social responsibility, increasing the student body's diversity and the HEO's internationalization by winning highly skilled and motivated students. They are expected to increase the 'internationalisation at home' (U1E2, head of international office, also see Harrison, 2015), adding more diverse international perspectives compared to traditional countries of origin (for the most important countries of origin see Wissenschaft Weltoffen, 2019) and possibility motivating domestic students to go abroad. Ideally, refugees are expected to stay for their academic career and as professionals in the labor market.

Are refugees seen as international students?

While refugees are formally treated as international students when applying for higher education, a differentiation was made in order to create and manage access to specific support: in the context of support, their residence status becomes relevant. Associations between refugee students and HEOs' internationalization can be seen on several levels. The interviewees perceive refugee students as an addition to the international student body and argue for supporting them partly based on the organization's objective of internationalization. However, it is also stated that refugee students face a distinctive set of challenges which differ from the experience of other international students who specifically planned and prepared to study in Germany (Berg, 2018; Streitwieser, 2019).

Even though the perception of refugee students is explicitly closely linked to the discourse on international students and one reason to support them is the argument of supporting potential experts for the labor market, semantic associations throughout the interviews rather referred to the context of diversification. This includes that refugees are perceived as needing help. Academically productive outcomes are hardly mentioned in this context, which could be expected in the general semantics of internationalization as a means to win highly-productive students. This is similar to Anderson's (2020) description of differences between representations of refugee students and international students in Canadian media discourses.

Ultimately, the objective seems to be to include refugee students into the general student body and help them to overcome the focus on their residence status, which is assumed to hold the potential of stigmatization. Nonetheless, those HEOs who want to continue their offers often discuss how they could also support refugees throughout their studies. If there is an independent discourse on refugees, it seems fair to assume that it will continue to produce occasions of support, for a discourse cannot end itself (Stichweh, 2000).

Therefore, it seems fair to state that refugees are indeed seen as a part of HEOs' internationalization but are still perceived as distinctive from other international students. A distinction is often drawn depending on the stage of their transition into higher education: prospective refugee students become refugee applicants and then international students. This refers to the extent to which they are treated as a specific group on an organizational level. The participants usually assume that on an individual level, most refugees will likely continue to struggle with specific challenges such as psychological distress, difficulties concerning their housing, language barriers etc. But most of those issues will either be addressed in general student services, such as psychological counselors, or are perceived not to be part of HEOs' responsibility.

The classification as international students influences the situation of refugees in higher education: in comparison to, for example, the United Kingdom, where refugee students are registered as domestic students (Stevenson and Willott, 2007), it allows access to service offers for international students. Furthermore, certain exceptions are made for refugees: They do not have to pay tuition fees for international students[5] and can become eligible for public financial student support. This creates a specific situation for refugees: they are classified as international students, but can also access refugee-specific offers and are partly treated as similar to domestic students (see Schneider, 2018; Webb et al., 2019, p. 113).

Do experiences with refugees change the discourse on the challenges, needs and potential of international students?

Indeed, one potential benefit that is ascribed to supporting refugee students is the possibility to learn from the experiences in order to learn about the service needs of international students, combine strategies of diversification and internationalization, and also to identify unnecessarily complicated formal procedures. This is understood to benefit all other students:

> Based on our experiences with refugees, we learn a lot about us, and what is clear and obvious to us is possibly not as clear and obvious and likely one has to consider what one should change, simplify and explain better.
>
> (U4E1, first contact)

Whether the experiences will have a lasting impact, whether the potential of merging and changing support structures is realized and whether semantics of internationalization and diversification become more closely connected remain questions for the further investigation of future developments.

Conclusion

This chapter has provided an insight to organizational semantics and discourses surrounding refugee students at eight German HEOs in 2017 and 2018. It shows the importance of general mission statements on internationalization, diversification and third missions when it comes to including new target groups, since arguments for supporting refugees are generally on those topics. Formal strategies thus allowed support for an additional target group they were not initially meant to address. This shows how general self-descriptions allow organizations to flexibly adapt to new situations and functional needs. Nonetheless, some interview partners referred to internal discussions on the organizational benefits of supporting refugees. This shows that support structures are not formalized altruistically but based on strategic goals and self-description.

Some interview partners state that experiences with refugee students hold the potential of changing and improving semantics and practices of internationalization and diversification and create more diverse, aware and service-oriented HEOs. New federal and state-level funding schemes are designed to include offers for refugee students and international students. Whether experiences with refugees will have a lasting and sustainable impact will have to be observed throughout coming years. On a short term basis, emerging networks, closer contact to students, refugees as highly motivated potential new students and an increase in student engagement were emphasized as positive outcomes of recent developments.

Acknowledgments

First, I thank Michael Grüttner and Stefanie Schröder. Our discussions and their feedback are always inspiring and helpful to me. Also, I developed the guidelines for early interviews in orientation on the guidelines we developed for the exploratory study of the WeGe-projekt on pathways of refugees into German higher education (https://www.wege.dzhw.eu/). Next, I thank Dr. Anja Gottburgsen and PD Dr. Bernd Kleimann. Together, we developed an interview guideline I used when conducting some of the interviews on which this chapter is based. They also took part in the first round of topical coding that prepared the pre-selection of sequences. Also, I thank Olivia Laska and Renny Osuna for supporting the development of this chapter by researching relevant literature.

Funding

The article is based on research funded by the German Federal Ministry of Education and Research [01PX16015] and was partly carried out at the German Center for Higher Education Research and Science Studies in Hannover, Germany, and partly at George Washington University in Washington, D.C., US.

Notes

1 The federal law for the support of education ('*Bundesausbildungsförderungsgesetz*' or, in short form, *BAföG*) provides public support for students from low income families. Half of it is granted as an interest-free loan, the other half is publicly funded. The maximum allowance is 853€ per month.
2 All interviews were conducted in German and all quotes translated by the author.
3 It should be mentioned that at some of the sampled HEOs, new research projects were initiated and some HEOs directly address refugee academics with additional support structures, such as networking offers etc. Due to the focus of my research, I have specifically looked into perceptions of incoming degree-seeking refugee students. Nonetheless, research topics or staff mobility and further aspects of the internationalisation of higher education, such as new migration related study programs, could be interesting to look into.
4 Refugee students' access to BAföG can be understood as an environmental factor, since it is not based on formal classifications within the educational system but depends on the political system.
5 German higher education is mostly tuition free. Students pay semester fees of up to 450€/semester that cover administrative costs. In international comparison, those fees are rather cheap and often include regional tickets for public transportation as well as HEO-specific additional offers. Additionally, international students often have to pay tuition fees, depending on their HEO's state ('*Bundesland*').

References

Abdo, D., and K. Craven (2018) Every campus a refuge, *Migration and Society* 1(1): 135–146.
AbduRazak, L., R. Al Mawdieh, A. Karam, A. Yousef Aljaafreh and M. Elias Al-Azzaw (2019) Determining the challenges faced by Syrian refugees students at Jordanian camps according to their perspective: A case of universities role to supporting [online], *Modern Applied Science* 13(8): 176.
Akbasli, S. and D. Mavi (2021) Conditions of Syrian asylum seeker students in a Turkish university, *International Journal of Inclusive Education* 25(7): 763–778.
Anderson, T. (2020) News media representations of international and refugee postsecondary students, *The Journal of Higher Education* 91(1): 58–83.
Bajwa, J., M. Abai, S. Kidd, S. Couto, A. Akbari-Dibavar and K. McKenzie (2018) Examining the intersection of race, gender, class, and age on post-secondary education and career trajectories of refugees, *Refuge* 34(2): 113–123.
Beigang, S., J. von Blumenthal and L. Lambert (2018) *Studium für Geflüchtete: Aufgaben für Hochschulen und Politik* [Higher education for refugees: Tasks for higher education institutions and politics]. Osnabrück: Institut für Migrationsfroschung und Interkulturelle Studien.
Bellino, M. and M. Hure (2018) Pursuing higher education in exile: A pilot partnership in Kakuma refugee camp, *Childhood Education* 94(5): 46–51.
Berg, J. (2018) A new aspect of internationalisation? Specific challenges and support structures for refugees on their way to German higher education, in A. Curaj, L. Deca and R. Pricopie (eds.) *European Higher Education Area: The impact of past and future policies* (pp. 219–235). Cham: Springer International Publishing.
Berg, J., A. Gottburgsen and B. Kleimann (in press) Formalising organisational responsibility for refugees in German higher education: The case of 'first contacts'. Awaiting publication in *Studies in Higher Education*.

Berg, J., M. Grüttner and S. Schröder (2018) Zwischen Befähigung und Stigmatisierung? Die Situation von Geflüchteten beim Hochschulzugang und im Studium. Ein internationaler Forschungsüberblick [Between ability and stigmatisation? The situation of refugees on their way to and in higher education: An international research overview], *Zeitschrift Für Flüchtlingsforschung*, 2(1): 57–90.

Berg, J., S. Schröder and M. Grüttner (2019) Studienvorbereitung für Geflüchtete in Deutschland – Herausforderungen eines besonderen Bildungsabschnitts [Study preparations for refugees in Germany – Challenges of a specific educational stage], *Schulheft* 176: 132–137.

Brücker, H., N. Rother and J. Schupp (eds.) (2016) *IAB-BAMF-SOEP-Befragung von Geflüchteten: Überblick und erste Ergebnisse* [IAB-BAMF-SOEP-survey of refugees: Overview and first results]. Berlin: Deutsches Institut für Wirtschaftsforschung.

Bundesamt für Migration und Flüchtlinge (2018) *Ausländer mit Aufenthaltstitel ab 2005* [Foreigners with residence permits since 2015] [online], http://www.bamf.de/DE/Willkommen/DeutschLernen/Integrationskurse/TeilnahmeKosten/Aufenthaltstitel_nach/aufenthaltstitel_nach-node.html.

Council of Europe (2020) *The CEFR levels* [online], https://www.coe.int/en/web/common-european-framework-reference-languages/level-descriptions

Crea, T. and N. Sparnon (2017). Democratizing education at the margins: Faculty and practitioner perspectives on delivering online tertiary education for refugees, *International Journal of Educational Technology in Higher Education* [online] 14: 43.

Deutscher Akademischer Austauschdienst (2018) *Zukunftswege: Erfolge und Herausforderungen bei der Integration von Geflüchteten ins Studium* [Future-paths: Successes and challenges of integrating refugees into higher education]. Bonn: Deutscher Akademischer Austauschdienst.

Erdoğan, A. and M. Erdoğan (2018) Access, qualifications and social dimension of Syrian refugee students in Turkish higher education. In A. Curaj, L. Deca and R. Pricopie (eds.) *European Higher Education Area: The impact of past and future policies* (pp. 259–276). Cham: Springer International Publishing. s

Ergin, H. (2016) Turkish university students' perceptions towards their Syrian classmates. *TED Eğitim ve Bilim* 41(184): 399–415.

Ergin, H., H. de Witt, H. and B. Leask (2019) Forced internationalisation of higher education: An emerging phenomenon, *International Higher Education* 97: 9–10.

Grüttner, M., S. Schröder, J. Berg and C. Otto (2018a) *Die Situation von Geflüchteten auf dem Weg ins Studium: Erste Einsichten aus dem Projekt WeGe* [The situation of refugees on their way to higher education: First insights of the WeGe-projects]. Hannover: Deutsches Zentrum für Hochschul- und Wissenschaftsforschung GmbH.

Grüttner, M., S. Schröder, J. Berg and C. Otto (2018b) Refugees on their way to German higher education: A capabilities and engagements perspective on aspirations, challenges and support, *Global Education Review* 5(4): 115–135.

Harrison, N. (2015) Practice, problems and power in 'internationalisation at home': Critical reflections on recent research evidence, *Teaching in Higher Education* 20(4): 412–430.

Keller, R. (2007) Diskurse und Dispositive analysieren: Die Wissenssoziologische Diskursanalyse als Beitrag zu einer wissensanalytischen Profilierung der Diskursforschung [Analysing discourses and dispositives: Knowledge-sociological discourse analysis as a contribution to a knowledge-analytical profilation of discourse analysis], *Forum Qualitative Sozialforschung* [online] 8(2): 19.

Keller, R. (2011) *Wissenssoziologische Diskursanalyse: Interdisziplinäre Diskursforschung* [Knowledge-sociological discourse analysis: Interdisciplinary discourse analysis]. Wiesbaden: Springer Fachmedien.

Knight, J. (1994) *Internationalization: Elements and checkpoints*. Ottawa: Canadian Bureau for International Education.

Knight, J. (2011) Five myths about internationalization, *International Higher Education* 62: 14–15.

Larsen, M. (2016) *Internationalization of higher education: An analysis through spatial, network, and mobilities theories*. New York: Palgrave Macmillan.

Lenette, C. (2016). University students from refugee backgrounds: Why should we care? *Higher Education Research & Development* 35(6): 1311–1315.

Liebold, R. and R. Trinczek. (2009) Experteninterview [Expert interviews], in S. Kühl, P. Strodtholz and A. Taffertshofer (eds.) *Handbuch Methoden der Organisationsforschung* [Handbook of methods of organisational research] (pp. 32–56). Wiesbaden: VS Verlag für Sozialwissenschaften.

Luhmann, N. (1970) Soziologie als Theorie sozialer Systeme [Sociology as theory of social systems], in N. Luhmann (ed.) *Soziologische Aufklärung* [Sociological enlightenment] (pp. 113–136). Opladen: Westdeutscher Verlag.

Luhmann, N. (1976) *Funktionen und Folgen formaler Organisation* [Functions and results of formal organisations]. Berlin: Duncker und Humblot.

Luhmann, N. (1980) *Gesellschaftsstruktur und Semantik: Studien zur Wissenssoziologie der modernen Gesellschaft* [Social structure and semantic: Studies about the sociologiy of knowledge of modern society]. Frankfurt: Suhrkamp.

Luhmann, N. (1982) *Politische theorie im wohlfahrtsstaat* [Political theory in the welfare state]. München: Olzog.

Luhmann, N. (2018 [2011]) *Organization and decision*. Cambridge: Cambridge University Press.

Nayton, C., G. Meek and R. Foletta (2019) Language education for people seeking asylum aspiring to higher education in Australia: Practitioner perspectives from the Asylum Seeker Resource Centre (ASRC), *Widening Participation and Lifelong Learning* 21(2): 209–221.

Ramsay, G. and S. Baker (2019) Higher education and students from refugee backgrounds: A meta-scoping study, *Refugee Survey Quarterly* 38(1): 55–82.

Robson, S. (2011) Internationalization: A transformative agenda for higher education? *Teachers and Teaching* 17(6): 619–630.

Scarvaglieri, C. and C. Zech (2013) "ganz normale Jugendliche, allerdings meist mit Migrationshintergrund". Eine funktional-semantische Analyse von "Migrationshintergrund" ["Regular youths, but mostly with a migration background" A functional-semantic analysis of "migration background"]. *Zeitschrift Für Angewandte Linguistik* 58(1): 201–227.

Schneider, L. (2018) Access and aspirations: Syrian refugees' experiences of entering higher education in Germany, *Research in Comparative and International Education* 13(3): 457–478.

Schröder, S., M. Grüttner and J. Berg (2019) Study preparation for refugees in German 'Studienkollegs': Interpretative patterns of access, life-wide (language) learning and performance, *Widening Participation and Lifelong Learning* 21(2): 67–85.

Seeber, M. and B. Lepori (2014) The internationalization of European higher education institutions, in A. Bonaccorsi (ed.) *Knowledge, diversity and perfomance in European higher education: A changing landscape* (pp. 138–163). Cheltenham: Edward Elgar Publishing.

Steinhilber, A. (2019) Higher education and forced migration: An evaluation of psychosocial support provided for Syrian refugees and the Jordanian host community, *Intervention* 17(1): 96–102.

Stevenson, J. and J. Willott (2007) The aspiration and access to higher education of teenage refugees in the UK, *Compare: A Journal of Comparative and International Education* 37(5): 671–687.

Stichweh, R. (2000) Semantik und Sozialstruktur [Semantic and social structure], *Soziale Systeme* 6: 237–250.

Streitwieser, B. (2019) International education for enlightenment, for opportunity and for survival: Where students, migrants and refugees diverge, *Journal of Comparative and International Higher Education* 11: 4–9.

Streitwieser, B. and L. Brück (2018) Competing motivations in Germany's higher education response to the "refugee crisis", *Refuge* 34(2): 38–51.

Unangst, L. (2019) Refugees in the German higher education system: Implications and recommendations for policy change, *Policy Reviews in Higher Education* 3(2): 144–166.

United Nations Educational, Scientific and Cultural Organization (2018) *Migration, displacement and education: Building bridges, not walls (Global Education Monitoring Report 2019)*. Paris: UNESCO Publishing.

Van Mol, C. (2013) Intra-European student mobility and European identity: A successful marriage? *Population, Space and Place* 19(2): 209–222.

Webb, S., K. Dunwoodie and J. Wilkinson (2019) Unsettling equity frames in Australian universities to embrace people seeking asylum, *International Journal of Lifelong Education* 38(1): 103–120.

Wissenschaft Weltoffen (2019) *Wissenschaft Weltoffen 2019 Abbildungen* [online], http://www.wissenschaftweltoffen.de/wwo2019.

Wojtkiewicz, W. and S. Heiland (2012) Landschaftsverständnisse in der Landschaftsplanung: Eine semantische Analyse der Verwendung des Wortes "Landschaft" in kommunalen Landschaftsplänen [The notions of landscape in landscape planning: A semantic analysis of the usage of the word "landscape" in municipal landscape plans], *Raumforschung Und Raumordnung* 70(2): 133–145.

Chapter 8

Irish Travellers and higher education

Andrew Loxley and Fergal Finnegan

'Pavee Point holds that any strategy must be underpinned by an intercultural approach and by principles of equality, diversity and anti-racism. Strategies and implementation programmes must be inclusive, culturally appropriate, and appropriate to the needs of groups in society, including Travellers and Roma'.

(Pavee Point, 2014, p. 4)

'Recognition of the distinct heritage, culture and identity of Travellers and their special place in Irish society will be hugely and symbolically important to their pride and self-esteem and overcoming the legacy of economic marginalisation, discrimination and low self-esteem with which the Traveller community has struggled'.

(Government of Ireland [GoI], 2017)

Introduction

The purpose of this chapter is to offer a profile of the Irish Traveller community (TC) in Irish higher education (HE). We will locate this within the context of Irish HE widening participation and access policy (WPA). Despite the availability of data relevant to understanding the position of the TC in Irish society and education, it is uneven and not applied in a way to make much sense of WPA. We say uneven because little systematic empirical research has been undertaken with the TC vis-a-vis their engagement with compulsory education let alone HE; though there are a few insightful studies which do capture the educational (and otherwise) lives of Travellers (see Binchy and Healy, 2005; Boyle, 2006; Devine and McGillicuddy, 2019; Forkan, 2006; Hourigan and Campbell, 2010; Kenny, 1997; O'Mahony, 2017). For this chapter we have gathered together what is known and germane to WPA and provide a trigger for further research. Specifically, we offer a narrative constructed through the 'prism' of policy and associated documents. Much of our discussion is set out as a chronological account to communicate the extent to which current WPA concerns are nested within continuities and changes in policy making with regard to the TC. The chapter is broken into five sections: (1) we set out the broad social and policy context vis-à-vis the TC[1], (2) provide a brief overview of Irish HE, (3) provide a brief overview of WPA policy, (4) examine WPA in relation to the TC and (5) explore the current limits and future possibilities for research on Travellers and WPA. This long and wide focus is the only way to properly make sense of HE policy vis-a-vis Travellers' low participation rates. Historically, much of the Irish state's, as well as the TC's emphasis (due to low participation, progression and completion rates), has justifiably been on the compulsory education system. This remains a salient issue and we discuss this sector's role in not only providing routes into HE, but mediating and reproducing social and educational inequalities. This cuts across the macro, meso and micro levels; schools have often been key sites of conflict between the state and the TC over cultural norms, social expectations and useful knowledge (Ryan, 1998).

Setting the scene: demographics, persistent inequalities and changing policy imperatives

Being visible to the state: some basic demographics

Historically the generation of numerical data on the TC has been a 'patchy' process, with their inclusion as a distinct group in the Irish census (which began in 1812), only occurring from 2002 onwards[2]. Before that data was generated intermittently from the 1940s onwards by the Garda Síochána (the Irish police service) in 1944, 1952 and 1956 (Dempsey and Geary, 1979; Rottman, Tussing and Wiley., 1986) and only comprised of basic 'head count' enumerations. The national 1960 'Commission on Itinerancy' (sic) (GoI, 1963) saw the first attempt by the state to construct a profile of the TC in regard to accommodation conditions, employment and occupational status, education and health via two censuses taken 1960 and 1961. Following this, in 1971, annual surveys were undertaken by the Department of Local Government[3]. The next major survey and as a follow-up to the 1963 Commission occurred in 1981 (GoI, 1983; Rottman, Tussing and Wiley, 1986) as part of the remit of the Traveller People Review Body. The next survey was undertaken as part of another national review entitled the 'Report of the Task Force of the Travelling Community' (GoI, 1995). However, it was with the use of national census data in 2002, 2006, 2011 and 2016 (albeit methodological and politically problematic), began to offer a relatively consistent, if not always comparable, profile of the TC. Two further reports worth noting are: (1) The 'All Ireland Traveller Health Study' (University College Dublin, 2010) and (2) 'A Social Portrait of Travellers in Ireland' (Watson et al., 2017). Whereas the former was a bespoke census of the TC vis-à-vis health conditions in both the Republic and Northern Ireland, the latter was a re-analysis of the 2011 census data with a remit to compare TC and settled communities. These widely cited reports presented a very detailed 'picture' of the TC which re-highlighted the extent of disadvantage not only in comparison with the settled community, but importantly within the TC. A key finding and a common refrain across the reports from 1963 onwards, are like any other community, differentiated and stratified along a range of dimensions such as educational outcomes, gender roles and health status.

The first major state sponsored enquiry into the TC, the 1963 'Commission on Itinerancy' reported that the TC comprised of 6,591 individuals or 1,198 families (GoI, 1963). In 1971 this had grown to 7,778 and by 1981 doubled to 14,821 and 2,432 families. In 2002, the Irish census enumerated 23,681 individuals, in 2011 29,495 and in 2016, 39,987 were recorded as 'White Traveller' or 0.6% of the Irish population of 4,689,921 (Central Statistics Office [CSO], 2017). In terms of age profile, the proportion aged over 65 is 2.9%; significantly below 12.6% for the non-TC. In contrast 'nearly 6 in 10 (58.1%) Travellers were under 25 (0–24) compared to 3 in 10 (33.4%) in the general population' (CSO, 2017). This is a pattern which has not changed much since the 1981 census: 50% were under the age of fifteen and 5.5% were 50 or over rising to 11% in 2016, but below the rest of the population at 31%. The life expectancy of a Traveller male is 61 compared to 76 for non-TC males; for females this is 70 and for non-TC females this is 81. Of the 10,653 Travellers in the work force, 80.2% were unemployed (CSO, 2017); a statistic which has remained a constant since the 1963 Commission. The rate for the non-TC is currently 4.2%.

Becoming visible: becoming seen and wanting to be seen

How large-scale research of this sort is conducted and its attendant purpose is an important part of the story (see Foucault, 2004, 2007; Scott, 1998). Travellers only became fully visible – legible and potentially manageable – to the state from the 1960s onwards during a period of economic and cultural 'late modernisation' (see Cleary, 2006; Garvin, 2004, Sweeney, 1998). State policy was largely underpinned by the idea that Travellers, or at least sections of the TC, constituted a 'problem'. The reports referred to above not only described the conditions of the TC, but contained within them 'solutions' (to education, employment, health care etc.) which have morphed through various ideological and political frames which in turn echo the dominant sociocultural and political discourses of the time periods in which they were written. Broadly, we can characterise them as three policy 'moments': (1) 'assimilationist' (1960s to mid-1980s), (2) 'integrationist' (1980s to late-1990s) and (3) 'inclusionist' (mid-1990s onwards). To this latter period, we can add as further layers 'multiculturalism' and 'rights-based' approaches (see Boyle, 2006; Boyle et al., 2018; Hourigan and Campbell, 2010; Pavee Point, 2014). We would argue that this latter change in policy orientation emerged through Traveller organisations mobilising and articulating concerns and interests of the community and not through the munificence of the state. Additionally, there have been several waves of activism which materialised as part of movements for civil rights in the 1960s and 1970s and widespread radical community development groups in the 1970s and 1980s in Ireland (see Powell and Geoghegan, 2004; Zappone, 1998). This has created space for the emergence of national and local Traveller organisations rooted in egalitarian values and politics such as the Irish Traveller Movement and Pavee Point. The emergence of an inclusionist zeitgeist within Irish society more generally also lies behind the glacial move in policy towards treating the TC as a distinct cultural and ethnic group whose traditions, as well as identity and needs (material and non-material) are promoted and respected; this was recognised in law in 2017. Moreover, this position along other policy provisions (including education and anti-discrimination related legislation: see Table 8.1) from the mid-1990s, has generated a space in which

Table 8.1 Main reports, policy documents, legislation and committees

Date	Title
1960	Establishment of the Commission on Itinerancy
1963	Report of the Commission on Itinerancy
1974	Post of National Co-ordinator for the Education of Travellers established
1985	Travelling People Review Body
1992	Post of National Education Officer for Travellers created
1993	Establishment of the Task Force on the Travelling Community
1995	Task Force on the Travelling Community (report)
1996	National Strategy for Traveller Accommodation
1998	First Report of the National Traveller Monitoring and Advisory Committee
1998	National Traveller Health Advisory Committee
1999	National Traveller Monitoring and Advisory Intercultural Education Strategy
1999	National Traveller Accommodation Consultative Committee
2000	Second Report of the National Traveller Monitoring and Advisory Committee
2000	Equal Status Act
2002	National Traveller Health Strategy
2002	National Primary and Post-Primary School Guidelines
2003	High Level Officials Group on Travellers
2004	Equality Act
2006	Report on Towards a Traveller Education Strategy Reconstituted
2008	National Intercultural Health Strategy
2010	All-Ireland Traveller Health Study (UCD, 2010)
2012	National Roma and Traveller Integration Strategy
2017	National Traveller and Roma Inclusion Strategy 2017–2021
2017	A Social Portrait of Travellers in Ireland (Watson et al., 2017)
2019	Action Plan for Travellers Participation in Higher Education 2019–2021

Source: Pavee Point (2013) and updated and augmented by the authors for this chapter.

Traveller organisations have the status as legitimate partners in the policy process. As noted by the 1995 Task Force report:

> [we] acknowledge the important role played by Traveller organisations. They have made a significant contribution to creating conditions needed for new initiatives to be developed in response to the situation of Travellers and for these new initiatives to succeed.
>
> (GoI, 1995, p. 4)

While this shift in policymaking is significant it should be noted that the social partnership model (seen to be partially responsible for the 'Celtic Tiger' years) fell apart during the crisis and austerity years (i.e. 2008 onwards) which had a particularly dramatic impact on community-based organisations (Harvey, 2012) including many Traveller groups and education and training initiatives for the TC.

The Irish higher education system: a quick tour

Although higher education has been part of the Irish cultural and political landscape since the late 16th century starting with the foundation of the University of Dublin (also known as Trinity College Dublin) in 1592, up until the 1990s in terms of participation rates, it had remained relatively small-scale, comprising of seven universities and fourteen institutes of technology (IoTs) and a number of teacher education colleges. However, as noted by Walsh and Loxley (2015) one of the defining features of Irish HE has been the considerable expansion in terms of full-time student numbers. In 1965 there was an undergraduate population of 21,000 full-time students distributed across five universities, in 1991 this was 51,000 (including postgraduates) and had risen by 2009 to 153,329 full-time undergraduates and 22,419 full-time postgraduates located in 40 state supported institutions; for 2017–18 (latest data) this was 159,823 and 29,823, respectively. A similar pattern is evident in regard to research which expanded over the past twenty years from a very low starting point. Using the number of doctorate holders as a proxy indicator, this category of graduate has grown from 443 in 1997 to 810 in 2005 and 1,445 in 2017. And at 1.3% the proportion of 25–64-year-olds holding doctorates is above the Organisation for Economic Cooperation and Development (OECD) average of 1.1% (OECD, 2019). Not unsurprisingly 76% of doctoral graduates from 2005 onwards have come from the sciences, engineering, ICT and health care disciplines, in which the state invested heavily in full-time scholarships and cognate research programmes worth €1.3 billion over a twenty-year period; the remaining 24% are from the social sciences, business and education. In relation to overall funding (as of 2019) the state spent €1.7 billion (or 17% of the total education budget) on HE which accounts for 0.7% of GDP (well below the OECD average of 1.4% and the third lowest; Norway comes 'top' on 2.5%). The annual per capita spend per undergraduate student of €11,844 is also below the OECD average of €13,919. However, to put this into context, Irish HE was badly affected by the financial crash of 2008 and subjected to nearly a 25% reduction in funding after twenty years of continual growth.[4] This was accompanied by enlarged state regulation of the sector and new restrictions regarding institutional expenditure on hitherto relatively autonomous institutions. There was no reduction in student numbers, only in academic and support staff, and a marked deterioration in pay and conditions of employment (see for instance Clancy, 2015; HEA, 2011, 2012; Walsh, 2019; Walsh and Loxley, 2015).

In terms of organisational structure, Irish HE is categorised as a binary system (OECD, 2004; Walsh, 2019). This is split between seven universities and eleven IoTs and more recently a new category, the 'technological university' though this is still regarded as part of the IoT sector[5]. Space precludes a detailed overview of the recent structural changes (partly precipitated by the financial crash), but a key recommendation as part of a system level review in 2011 (HEA, 2011; see Walsh and Loxley, 2015 for a critical commentary) was for mergers and rationalisations of the IoTs into 'technological universities'. The report also reaffirmed two further 'big ticket' items which had long been part of the Irish HE narrative. Firstly, a continuing identification with HE as being a progenitor and conduit to constructing a knowledge-based economy via research and human capital formation. Secondly, a renewed commitment to the WPA agenda. In short Irish policy makers (in concert with EU and OECD policy and other advanced capitalist countries), have viewed HE as a vehicle through which to combine a desire for economic transformation and the pursuit of some mode of social justice through HE participation; both of which have remained an ideological constant within an ostensibly very fluid system.

Access and participation: the Irish story – a very short précis

Along with the usual 'growing pains' associated with shifting from an 'elite to an elite plus mass system' (Trow, 1973, 2010), expansionism had largely benefited those individuals from socioeconomic groups (SEGs) and communities who had already been disproportionately represented in HE. Some methodological quirks around categorisation notwithstanding, Table 8.2 shows the relative stability or intransigence of participation rates over time.

Despite nearly twenty years of WPA policy initiatives, Irish HE witnessed a deepening, rather than a widening of participation. The abolition of undergraduate tuition fees from 1996 onwards (a very significant policy move) did little as far as we can tell to draw into HE those groups that traditionally had not formed part of the undergraduate student 'body' (Fleming et al., 2017). However, this should not be seen as a simplistic supply-side explanation for the increase in participation, as the expansion also needs to be located within

Table 8.2 %SEG Irish population and new entrants to HE: As per 2011 Census (CSO, 2017) and HEA Equal Access Surveys (2015)[a]

	1996 all pop^	% of pop 1996^	2011 all pop^	% of pop 2011^	% HE new entrants 1998***	% HE new entrants 2002***	% HE new entrants 2011*	% HE new entrants 2015*
A. Employers and managers	412,516	11.38	705,132	15.37	21.6	23.1	18.7	16.9
B. Higher professional	160,801	4.43	295,586	6.44	10.1	11.1	10.7	10.5
C. Lower professional	290,373	8.01	556,587	12.13	11.1	11.5	9.3	8.6
D. Non-manual	613,285	16.91	931,068	20.29	9.4	8.9	9.3	10.0
E. Manual skilled	513,682	14.17	386,742	8.43	13.6	13.5	12	10.0
F. Semi-skilled	346,415	9.55	359,725	7.84	11.2	11.1	5.4	5.3
G. Unskilled	277,061	7.64	151,949	3.31	-	-	2.4	4.7
H. Own account workers	203,172	5.60	196,774	4.29	7.2	8.2	8.4	7.4
I. Farmers	309,102	8.52	166,231	3.62	16.2	21.7	7.7	6.8
J. Agricultural workers	76,296	2.10	23,504	0.51	-	-	0.8	0.4
Z. All others gainfully occupied and unknown	423,384	11.68	814,954	17.76	-	-	15	19.4

*** From O'Connell et al. (2006) based on their new entrant surveys 1998 and 2004.
* From HEA (2016).
^ CSO (2017). Note the '% of new entrants' is calculated by using a numerator derived from the difference between the access survey respondents minus the non-respondents to the SEG question and not the actual number of new entrants.
[a] Table taken from Fleming et al. (2017).

the context of significant and long-term transformations taking place within the Irish economy more generally vis-à-vis occupational and sectorial restructuring (see Loxley, 2014). This reformation was predicated on the 'necessity' to shift away from a traditionally low-trust low-skill economy towards one re-constructed around a high-trust high-skill economy. This is of course an ideological construct and there is considerable debate about the shape of the labour market and the key drivers of change (see, for example, Breathnach, 2007; Wickham and Bobek, 2016). Needless to say, within this storyline, the Irish state in common with other advanced (and not so advanced) capitalist countries gave HE one of the 'starring roles' (Fleming et al., 2017; Walsh, 2019; Walsh and Loxley, 2015). However, in relation to the TC this shift is important as it highlights the dynamic and integral relationship between employability and education which is referred to in all of the reports discussed above. Added to this, is the effect of the imperative for HEI accreditation (beyond compulsory schooling) by labour markets, which in turn generates an even more marginal status for Travellers through their lack of participation.

Towards the end of the 1990s, the HEA – the statutory body with responsibility for the oversight of state-supported HEIs – commissioned a number of reports to explore the extent of and suggest possible solutions to manage and ameliorate under-representation (Fleming et al., 2017). In summary, the key measures introduced in the early 2000s were: (1) establishment of the National Office for Equity and Access in 2003 (though now closed down) to develop and co-ordinate policy, (2) the publication of access plans and interim evaluations (three plans so far: HEA, 2004, 2008, 2015) and (3) the construction of a number of equity groups, i.e. the 'under-represented'[6]. The setting up of this policy regime (replete with targets, monitoring procedures and some financial incentives), very much left HEIs to develop locally contextualised forms of intervention which encompassed a mixed economy of 'outreach' programmes in schools and further education colleges, as well as access programmes provided within HEIs (see Fleming et al., 2017 for details). Though it is useful to note that in concert with the current micro-interventionist model of state-HE governance, recent measures have seen the tying of financial penalties to HEIs in the form of negotiated 'compacts' vis-à-vis targets across a range of activities which includes WPA (HEA, 2012).

Access and participation and Irish Travellers: key trajectories and trends across the education system

Although Travellers have constituted one of the state's so-called 'equity groups' vis-à-vis under-representation within HE, in terms of participation rates they remain very low and fairly static. In 2019, 61 people who self-identified as a Traveller[7] were enrolled in HE and only 1.4% (n = 167) members of the TC aged fifteen and over in the 2016 census reported they held a Bachelor's or postgraduate qualification. In comparison, for the settled community the proportion of graduates is 31% and 21% for sub-degree qualifications; for Travellers the latter is 1.4%. It was estimated that in 2004 there were 28 Travellers in HE; by 2015 this was 35, rising to 61 in 2019 (Department of Education and Science [DES], 2005; HEA, 2019a) with the HEA slightly missing the target of 80 which was set in 2015. However, due to the way in which this data is generated (i.e. based on enrolments only), it is difficult to ascertain how many Travellers remain in HE to completion.

In order to understand this situation, it is important to expand on the broader (as well historical) context of the TC's engagement with education. Hence it comes as no great revelation that low levels of participation in HE are connected with low school completion rates and early school leaving. Although this was seen as problematic with some of the other equity groups (e.g. low SEGs), for the TC the scale and magnitude of this issue has been and still is disproportionate vis-à-vis the settled communities (HEA, 2018). In relation to progression and retention in compulsory education, the 2005 Traveller Education Strategy (DES, 2005) reported that 84% of Traveller children enrolled in primary schools transferred to post-primary institutions. However, they estimated that only 46% (n = 1,845) out of 4,000 Traveller students of post-primary age (ages twelve to nineteen) remained in school, of which 45% (n = 830) stay in school after the age of fifteen and/or sixteen and over half are female. The latest publicly available data (DES, 2017) reported that there were 8,202 children in primary school; most of the relevant age group. 2,689 Traveller students were enrolled in post-primary schools or approximately 60% of that age cohort. However, only 12% (337) stay on in school after the age of sixteen in comparison with a post-sixteen retention rate of 94.5% for settled students (DES, 2017).[8] Unfortunately, there are no data showing how many of these post-sixteen-year-old Travellers stay on and complete the Leaving Certificate examination (the usual gateway into HE for approximately 90% of new entrants), but it would not be too difficult to surmise that this is a small pool of young adults who can or wish to make the transition to HE and would not be out of line with the tiny number of undergraduates in the system. Lastly in relation to attainment this is seen to be well below that of non-Traveller students. Data from the 2005 review of provision (DES, 2005) showed that two-thirds of primary-age students were in the bottom 20% for mathematics, the same was also found for English (DES, 2005). This pattern was repeated in subsequent 2011 report in which the authors overserved that 'in 2007 and 2010, the average test scores of pupils from the Traveller community were significantly below those of non-Travellers at every grade level in both reading and mathematics, and the magnitude of the difference between the scores of the two groups is large in every case' (Weir and Archer, 2011, p. 45). This would appear to be the latest publicly available data in respect of attainment. A further point to note is that Traveller students (in relation to settled students) are disproportionally enrolled in schools which are located in designated disadvantaged geographical areas (Smyth et al., 2015). Historically, the proxy indicator of location has long

Table 8.3 Traveller community highest education level attained: 2002–2016

	2002 Male	2002 Female	2006 Male	2006 Female	2011 Male	2011 Female	2016 Male	2016 Female
Primary (incl. no formal education)	3,786	3,705	3,411	3,521	1,030	1,002	3,697	3,741
Lower secondary (12–16)	632	812	765	858	1,139	1,355	1,461	1,514
Upper secondary (16–18)	138	200	159	211	258	417	525	711
Third level non-degree	33	48	11	31	412	170	67	101
Third level degree or higher	62	54	14	19	8	16	62	105
Totals who reported	4,651	4,819	4,360	4,640	2,847	2,960	5,812	6,172
Totals all Travellers 15 plus	6,620	7,060	6,276	6,858	8,401	9,008	9,055	9,687

Source: Central Statistics Office.

been associated with low participation rates vis-à-vis the SEG equity groups (HEA, 2019b) so it comes as no surprise that this can be seen as a compounding 'variable' in respect of the TC. An obvious effect of poor progression and retention is also related to attainment more generally; Table 8.3 shows the distribution of levels of attainment from 2002 to 2016 broken down by gender. As can be seen there are significant numbers of people reporting having no formal or primary as their highest level of education. In 2016 this was 65% (a decrease from 79% in 2002), but a massive gap when compared with the settled community of 13.3% as shown on Table 8.4.

The relationship between employment status and education was also well rehearsed across the reports. Watson et al. (2017) analysis of the 2011 national census data suggested that Travellers 'have 19 times the odds of being non-employed compared to the general population' (p. 39). However, they argue that when adjusted for 'education' this drops to '8.5' and quite significantly if they possess a HE qualification (2.2) or a post-primary qualification (3.8). Put another way, they calculated that 80% of non-Travellers holding a HE qualification were in employment compared with 57% of Travellers; for those with primary education it was just 9% as opposed to 41% for non-Travellers (Watson et al., 2017, p. 40). This suggests that education is a factor in increasing the likelihood of being employed, though there is still a substantial difference between the two communities.

Part of the explanation for the above lies in the history of differential provision which has shaped TC responses to education. The 1963 Commission adopted a segregationist approach arguing for separate education (schooling

Table 8.4 Highest education level attained (%): Traveller and settled communities 2016

	Settled Community			Traveller Community		
	Male and Female	Male	Female	Male and Female	Male	Female
Primary (incl. no formal education)	12.3	13.3	14.4	62.1	63.6	60.6
Lower secondary (12–16)	15.5	17.1	13.9	24.8	25.1	24.5
Upper secondary (16–18)	19.8	19.0	20.5	10.3	9.0	11.5
Third level non-degree	29.0	21.8	20.1	1.4	1.2	1.6
Third level degree or higher	22.2	27.5	33.1	1.4	1.1	1.7
All reporting completing education 15plus (n)	2,898,384	1,414,362	1,484,022	11,984	5,812	6,172
All Population 15 plus (n)	3,755,313	1,839,849	1,915,464	18,742	9,055	9,687

Source: Central Statistics Office.

and training) facilities. What began to develop post-1963 over a period of 30 years was ironically a system of largely, though not exclusively, provision constructed around separate schools for Travellers (pre-primary and post-primary) as an attempt at social, cultural and economic assimilation. The 1983 Travelling People Review Body (GoI, 1983) edged towards an integrationist orientation at post-primary and proposed a range of recommendations such as an adapted curriculum, greater use of (on a temporary basis) separate facilities and recommended enrolling more Traveller students in mainstream settings though remained advocates of the use of 'special classes' (GoI, 1983, p. 69–70). Enrolment in mainstream primary schools was not seen as being problematic 'but the need for additional special schools must be considered' (GoI, 1983, p. 69). The 'Teacher Guidelines' issued to schools by the DES a decade later took a more explicit integrationist position arguing that 'Traveller children have full access to education' (DES, 1994). However, it was the 1995 Task Force report (GoI, 1995) which provided the most thorough going, highly critical and at times scathing evaluation of provision and practice. Of their 333 main recommendations, 167 focused on education ranging from initial teacher education, curriculum, assessment and pedagogy, enrolment, discrimination, accommodation, transport, over-reliance on special educational needs provision, lack of funding, lack of professional development and so on. The volume of recommendations indicated the scale of the problems endemic within the system for the TC; the next largest set recommendations was 49 and these related to 'accommodation'. The Task Force document was followed by two progress reports in 2000 and 2005 which we refer to below in the context of HE.

The state giveth and the state taketh away

Despite an array of initiatives and interventions which had been developed since the 1970s this, and to echo Boyle (2018), proved to be a fragile and asymmetrical 'compact'. In following the financial downturn circa 2008, the state was quick to cease or reduce funding for what were considered successful programmes. Prior to 2008, state funding for Traveller education initiatives totalled €55 million (DES, 2005), in 2013 the Traveller organisation Pavee Point (2013) in a justifiably forthright and well-argued critique of these reductions calculated that the allocation had decreased from an apogee of €76 million in 2008 to €10 million in 2013. The three biggest changes were the loss of pre-school provision funding which had been merged with mainstream provision, a significant reduction on teaching resources from €48 million to €8.5 million. This included closing, with the loss of 40 posts, the Visiting Teacher Service for Travellers (VTST); a home-liaison project started in the 1970s which 'assisted both children and parents in engaging with the schools and education system' (Pavee Point, 2014, p. 14) and was well regarded by the Task Force (GoI, 1995) and singled out for praise in the Monitoring Committee's 2000 Progress Report (GoI, 2000). It is worth noting with irony that the authors of the 1995 Task Force report expressed concern that 'appropriate measures be put in place to ensure teachers [...] do not suffer from "burn out"' (GoI, 1995, p. 42). A review in 2015 of a cognate project (The School Completion Programme – see Smyth et al., 2015) concluded that a falloff in retention of TC students was a direct effect of the loss of the VTST. Secondly, there was the closure of the Resource Teachers for Travellers initiative (set up in 1996 as per the Task Force Report) and accounted for 710 posts and €34,000,000. The third most significant change was the closure of the Senior Traveller Training Centres; in 2009 they received €26,800,000. None of these initiatives have been reinstated. Coincidently, or ironically, some of them were closed due to the DES referring to simply enacting a well-established policy of mainstreaming.

And onto into higher education

In historically placing Travellers and their involvement in HE within the Irish policy narrative, the first mention came in the Task Force on Travelling Community (GoI, 1995). Prior to that the emphasis was firmly on developing different modes of intervention to support participation, progression and retention in the pre-school and compulsory schooling system. Given the high rates of early school leaving and non-completion this would seem a logical step to take. As part of the authors' summary they noted that:

> The main reason [for lack of participation] has to do with poor performance [...] in primary and second-level schools at the present time [re. early 1990s] third level education is not a possibility for the vast majority of Travellers [...] given that access to third-level education is determined to a large extent by high levels of achievement in second-level it is not surprising that few Travellers go on to third-level.
> (GoI, 1995, p. 205)

There was a recognition that there needed also to better data to support any subsequent initiatives but commented anecdotally that a small number of Travellers had participated in HE programmes. Given what the Task Force saw as its significant mission to restructure and develop the compulsory system, it is not unexpected in this context to see that only four out of the 167 education-focused recommendations allude to HE. More specifically these centred on 'access' and 'funding' (GoI, 1995, p. 53):

1) In the short term it is possible for more Travellers to benefit from third level education. Universities and other third level and post second level institutions should be encouraged to take positive action in this regard;
2) The Department of Education should encourage Traveller participation in third level education by targeting Travellers through the Higher Education Grants Scheme and by ensuring that grants are adequate to cover the costs involved;
3) A national trust should be established, with Government support and private sector sponsorship, to facilitate and encourage Travellers to avail of third level education; and
4) The Traveller Education service should identify where Travellers have gained access to and successfully completed third level courses in order to derive lessons for the future.

They also noted that the 'financial costs [...] are prohibitive for most Traveller families and those who have availed of third level education have only been able to do so because of voluntary support and grants' (GoI, 1995, p. 206). In the follow-up progress reports published in 2000 and 2005, HE is only mentioned in the former. The report is critical of the lack of progress with Travellers vis-à-vis other disadvantaged groups and bemoans poor to non-existent data on participation. Incidentally this was improved upon at school level but it would take at least another 15 years before anything like systematic data was generated for HE. Nothing was achieved in regards in the setting up of a national trust.

Following the publication in 2002 of the Teacher Guidelines (DES, 2002a, 2002b), the next significant education-focused document came in the form of the 2005 Traveller Education Strategy (DES, 2005) which also appeared at the same time as the first HEA WPA action plan (HEA, 2004). Similar to the other reports, the main emphasis was placed on pre-school and compulsory schooling with HE initiatives being less prominent. The authors estimated that in 2002 there were twenty Travellers in HE, 28 in 2004 mostly mature participants; in 2017 these account for only four of the 48 new entrants (HEA, 2020). They also noted that a number of HEI access initiatives had prioritised working with primary and post-primary schools when most Travellers had left the system which they saw as being not the best use of resources. However, attention was drawn to two school-focused initiatives specifically with Travellers operated by Trinity College Dublin and Dublin City University, in partnership with the VTST. The work of other HEIs was noted: National University of Ireland Maynooth and the relatively high participation rates (n = 16) in their Department of Applied Social Studies, the development of support materials for working with schools and community groups produced by Mary Immaculate College in Limerick and an outreach centre operated National University of Ireland Galway[9]. Beyond documenting these initiatives the authors offered seven main recommendations which they wished to see implemented and attained over a five year period. Each of these contained a number of areas broken down into what they saw as being the key issues: (1) attempt to foster change in attitudes towards education and especially HE in the TC, (2) review of extant access programmes and their applicability to TC needs, (3) generate cultural sensitivity and awareness with respect to the TC, (4) focus on mentoring with a view to supporting workplace transition, (5) role modelling for the TC and (6) and the old problem of data to assist planning.

With the establishment in 2003 of the National Access Office, the development, implementation and monitoring of policy passed from the DES to the HEA. The three plans produced between 2004 and 2015 (HEA, 2004, 2008, 2015) all made reference to the need to increase the levels of participation. The three plans also echoed each other in the rationale for the inclusion of Travellers which have been largely couched in the discourse of human capital development and social justice. However, in terms of 'meeting the targets' set this has proved difficult to attain and in the words of the latest evaluation report 'a significant challenge remains in achieving the target in respect of the Traveller[s], but the target of 80 should be retained' (HEA, 2018, p. 34). In light of this 'challenge' and unlike the other equity groups, the TC have been granted their own (imaginatively entitled 'Action Plan for Traveller Participation in Higher Education 2019–21' – HEA, 2019a) plan which was launched by the Minister for Higher Education in late 2019. Although largely an echo of the other policies and reports on Traveller education, it is a mark of the seriousness which the DES, HEA and in conjunction with Traveller groups has taken the extreme under-representation of Travellers in HE to create a separate document. In an attempt to offer what the authors refer to as a 'whole education approach' (i.e. the inclusion of all sectors and a range of stakeholders – parents/carers, teachers, academics etc.), the plan is made up of nine main goals, replete with cognate (and labyrinthine subsets of) 'objectives', 'priority actions' and 'implementation partners'. Three of the goals focus on enhancing or creating partnerships (with Traveller groups, home-school liaison teachers, career guidance teachers and access officers in HEIs). A further three are concerned with structural matters under the heading of 'coherent pathways' – largely aimed at supporting retention and transition from post-primary settings, facilitating access for mature Travellers and interestingly, transitions into the workplace post-graduation. The next two concern the seemingly intractable problem of data generation within both schools and HEIs and in particular the problem of non-identification. The last goal is the obtusely entitled 'mainstream the delivery of access'. This can roughly be translated into exploring ways of transposing and embedding access practices into the normal routines of HEIs, an ideal which has been around since the late 1990s (see, for example, Skilbeck and Connell, 2000 for their model for Irish higher education).

In more specific terms, and as an attempt to partially reverse the deleterious effects the state imposed on HE post-financial crash, a new access initiative which included specific reference to the TC, was launched in 2017 by the then Minister for Education Richard Bruton. Going under the title of 'Programme for Access to Higher Education' (PATH) and comprising of three strands, with an allocation of €16.6 million over three years. Although operating under the auspice of the 2015–16 'National Plan for Equity of Access to Higher Education' (HEA, 2015) each of the strands provided distinct initiatives aimed at (though not exclusively) the TC. In summary, PATH 1 was created to begin to address the issue of under-represented of the equity groups in the Irish teaching labour force (see Keane and Heinz, 2015; Kearns and Loxley, 2019). HEIs which provided initial teacher education programmes competed for funding to set up new initiatives to encourage (including the other equity groups) Travellers to enter the teaching profession. It is useful to note that this was a policy echo of previous aspirations which advocated the need for teachers from the TC to act as role models and hence encourage TC students to stay on in school as well as to foster intercultural understanding. The second and third PATH initiatives provided targeted funding in the form of the '1916 bursaries' (PATH 2)[10] and resources to create regional clusters of HEIs (PATH 3)[11] to develop partnerships with schools, FE colleges and community groups, again with the intention of facilitating new or extending existing routes into HE. Given the glacial-like progress in increasing Traveller participation, both the 2018 interim evaluation report (HEA, 2018) and the 2019 'Action Plan for Traveller Participation in Higher Education' (HEA, 2019a) were highly optimistic that the PATH projects might ameliorate this position.

In place of a conclusion: an incomplete story, missing voices and potential lines of future research

Despite the fact there are a lot of data on the TC and clear evidence of a problem with barriers to participation we know far too little about Travellers in HE. This is somewhat ironic given the Irish state's effort over the past 20 years to attract more Travellers into HE, very little of that momentum has found its way into a meaningful programme of research. Qualitative research on Travellers' experiences as undergraduate or postgraduate students is scarce so we are left making (and probably part-spurious) inferences. What is discernible however, is that low-levels of participation is the 'product' of a number of intermeshed factors around cultural attitudes towards the value, role and purpose of education, early school leaving, financial barriers, the structure of the Traveller economy and gender roles. Given the ambivalent role of formal education in the life of the TC and the high level of diversity, differentiation and stratification within the TC there is almost no way of advancing WPA without a great deal more fine-grained research.

As we have argued elsewhere this is not just a 'gap' in the research but part of wider disconnect between the formation and elaboration of access policies and students and graduates' voices (Finnegan et al., 2014; Fleming et al., 2017). Despite decades of access policy there is a weak level of consultation with 'target groups' and very little sense of where education fits in terms of wider life experience of non-traditional students. When we consider the position of Irish Travellers in society as a whole, and the demands and arguments made by Traveller organisations for a meaningful say in Irish institutions there are clear scientific, ethical and political reasons to approach such research in a collaborative and genuinely participatory way. By definition this agenda needs to be negotiated over time and will take considerable planning and would work most effectively if universities take their lead from Traveller groups. In this regard even though there are very few pieces of in-depth research which can be directly drawn upon to develop WPA for the TC there are a number of ongoing research projects on Traveller history and culture being conducted by Travellers (Pavee Point, 2019) and Traveller academics such as the sociologist Sindy Joyce (Raleigh, 2019) that offer useful models on how this might be approached.

In this regard, it is worth noting that last year a brief report on educational needs was drawn up collaboratively between academics (Maynooth University, 2017). Alongside this there are plans, at a relatively advanced stage (linked to HEA funding) for two IoTs and two universities to do an extensive 'community needs analysis' with Travellers in late 2020 on how WPA can build pathways through education that lead to individual and community empowerment.

Notes

1 It is beyond this chapter to offer a broader history of the TC in Ireland not least because this is complex and contested territory (Shuinéar, 2004) which is actively being worked on by Traveller researchers.
2 This was based on a recommendation made by the Task Force. However, it was not entirely welcomed by the TC as they were the only ethnic group to be included. A review of the use of ethnic categories for the 2021 census has also reinforced this position.
3 Traveller organisations played an active role as enumerators (Rottman, Tussing and Wiley, 1986).
4 See the National Recovery Plan (GoI, 2011) for details of the significant funding cuts across most areas of state expenditure as well.
5 There were previously fourteen IoTs established in the 1970s offering technical and vocational degree and sub-degree programmes. A merger in 2019 of three IoTs created the Technological University of Dublin; negotiations are underway to create two more.
6 This is an umbrella label given by the state to those groups deemed to be under-represented in HE. The categories and types of social groups have changed over the past twenty years; currently they are as follows: Mature age adults, people with a disability, people from lower socio-economic groups, people on part-time and flexible programmes usually based in further education colleges. With Travellers being recognised as a distinct ethnic group this makes them unique within the WPA policy arena as other groups can be seen as administrate categories created partly out of methodological necessity (i.e. simple to count) and largely political imperatives (Fleming et al., 2017).
7 Since 2007, the HEA have conducted what they refer to as 'equal access survey': a self-report instrument administered to all new undergraduate higher education entrants in order to profile the ethnic and socio-economic groups present within the system.
8 This data needs to be treated with caution as the enumeration was based on students attending additional needs support classes as a Traveller rather than self-identifying as a member of the school community irrespective of 'need'. Hence there might well be an underreporting which is acknowledged by the DES.
9 Both Galway and Limerick are locations outside of Dublin with high numbers of Travellers.
10 This amounted to 200 bursaries of €5,000 per year offered to full or part-time undergraduates for the duration of their programme: a total of €6 million.
11 €7.5 million was allocated to this project and distributed via a competitive process.

References

Binchy, J. and C. Healy (2005) *Achieving equity of access to higher education in Ireland: The case of Travellers*. Limerick: Mary Immaculate College, University of Limerick.

Boyle, A. (2006) Traveller education in Ireland: Parental involvement in preschool education, *Aesthethika: International Journal on Culture Subjectivity and Aesthetics* 2(2): 33–43.

Boyle, A., M. Flynn and J. Hannifin (2018) From absorption to inclusion: The evolution of Irish state policy on Traveller education, in É. Ní Shé, L. Burton and P. Danaher (eds.) *Social capital and enterprise in the modern state* (pp. 75–115). Basingstoke: Palgrave MacMillan.

Breathnach, P. (2007) Occupational change and social polarisation in Ireland: Further evidence, *Irish Journal of Sociology* 16(1): 22–42.
Central Statistics Office (2017) *Census of population 2016 – profile 8: Irish Travellers, ethnicity and religion.* Cork: Central Statistics Office.
Clancy, P. (2015) *Irish higher education: A comparative perspective.* Dublin: Institute of Public Administration.
Cleary, J. (2006). *Outrageous fortune: Capital and culture in modern Ireland.* Dublin: Field Day Publications.
Dempsey, M. and R. Geary (1979) *The Irish itinerants: Some demographic, economic and educational aspects.* Dublin: Economic and Social Research Institute.
Department of Education and Science (1994) *The education of Traveller children in national schools: Guidelines.* Dublin: Stationery Office.
Department of Education and Science (2002a) *Guidelines on Traveller education in primary schools.* Dublin: Department of Education and Science.
Department of Education and Science (2002b) *Guidelines on Traveller education in second-level schools.* Dublin: Department of Education and Science.
Department of Education and Science (2005) *Report and recommendations for a Traveller education strategy.* Dublin: Government Publications.
Department of Education and Science (2017) *Number of pupils who are members of the Traveller community.* Dublin: Department of Education and Science.
Devine, D. and D. McGillicuddy (2019) Explorations of care and care injustice in the everyday lives of Irish Traveller children, *Gender and Education* 31(5): 618–630.
Finnegan, F., B. Merrill and C. Thunborg (eds.) (2014) *Student voices on inequalities in European higher education: Challenges for theory, policy and practice in a time of change.* London: Routledge.
Fleming, T., A. Loxley and F. Finnegan (2017) *Access and participation in Irish higher education.* London: Palgrave Macmillan.
Forkan, C. (2006) Traveller children and education: progress and problems, *Journal of Youth Studies Ireland* 1(1): 77–92.
Foucault, M. (2004) *Society must be defended: lectures at the Collège de France, 1975–76.* London: Penguin.
Foucault, M. (2007) *Security, territory, population: lectures at the Collège de France, 1977–78.* Basingstoke/New York: Palgrave Macmillan.
Garvin, T. (2004) *Preventing the future: Why was Ireland so poor for so long?* Dublin: Gill & Macmillan.
Government of Ireland (1963) *Report of the Commission on Itinerancy.* Dublin: Stationery Office.
Government of Ireland (1983) *Report of the travelling people review body.* Dublin: Stationery Office.
Government of Ireland (1995) *Report of the task force on the travelling community.* Dublin: Stationery Office.
Government of Ireland (2000) *Second progress report of the committee to monitor and co-ordinate the implementation of the recommendations of the task force on the Travelling community.* Dublin: Stationary Office.
Government of Ireland (2011) *National recovery plan: 2011–2014.* Dublin: Stationary Office.
Government of Ireland (2017) *National Traveller and Roma Inclusion Strategy 2017–2021.* Dublin: Stationery Office.

Harvey, B. (2012) *Downsizing the community sector: changes in employment and services in the voluntary and community sector in Ireland, 2008–2012*. Dublin: Irish Congress of Trade Unions.

Higher Education Authority (2004) *Achieving equity of access to higher education in Ireland, action plan 2005–2007*. Dublin: National Office for Equity of Access to Higher Education and the Higher Education Authority.

Higher Education Authority (2008) *National plan for equity of access to higher education 2008–2013*. Dublin: Higher Education Authority.

Higher Education Authority (2011) *National strategy for higher education to 2030: Implementation plan*. Dublin: Higher Education Authority.

Higher Education Authority (2012) *Towards a higher education landscape*. Dublin: Higher Education Authority.

Higher Education Authority (2015) *National plan for equity of access to higher education 2015–19*. Dublin: Higher Education Authority.

Higher Education Authority (2016) *Equal Access Survey data* – 'raw' dataset shared via private communication with authors.

Higher Education Authority (2018) *Progress review of the National Access Plan and Priorities to 2021*. Dublin: Higher Education Authority.

Higher Education Authority (2019a). *Action plan for Traveller participation in higher education 2019–21*. Dublin: Higher Education Authority.

Higher Education Authority (2019b) *A spatial and socio-economic profile of higher education institutions in Ireland*. Dublin: Higher Education Authority.

Higher Education Authority (2020) Private communication with authors, January 2020.

Hourigan, N. and M. Campbell (2010) *The TEACH report: Traveller education and adults: Crisis, challenge and change*. Dublin: National Association of Travellers' Centres.

Keane, E. and M. Heinz (2015) Diversity in initial teacher education in Ireland: The socio-demographic backgrounds of postgraduate post-primary entrants in 2013 and 2014, *Irish Educational Studies* 34(3): 281–301.

Kearns, M. and A. Loxley (2019) *Exploring mature students' intentions (motivations) towards ITE, Diversity in Teaching (DiT) Research Symposium*, 14th November, National University of Ireland, Galway.

Kenny, M. (1997) *The routes of resistance: Travellers and second-level schooling*. Aldershot: Ashgate.

Loxley, A. (2014) From seaweed & peat to pills & very small things: Knowledge production and higher education in the Irish context, in A. Loxley, A. Seery and J. Walsh (eds.) *Higher education in Ireland: practices, policies and possibilities* (pp. 55–85). Basingstoke: Palgrave MacMillan.

Maynooth University (2017) *Travellers in higher education: Seminar report*. Maynooth: Maynooth University.

O'Connell, P., D. Clancy and S. McCoy (2006) *Who went to college in 2004: A national survey of new entrants to higher education*. Dublin: Higher Education Authority.

O'Mahony, J. (2017) *Traveller Community national survey*. Dublin: The Community Foundation for Ireland.

Organisation for Economic Cooperation and Development (2004) *Review of national policies for education: review of higher education in Ireland. Examiners' report*. Paris: Organisation for Economic Cooperation and Development.

Organisation for Economic Cooperation and Development (2019) *Education at a glance: OECD Indicators*. Paris: Organisation for Economic Cooperation and Development.

Pavee Point (2013) *Travelling with austerity: Impact of cuts on Travellers, Traveller services and projects*. Dublin: Pavee Point Publications.

Pavee Point (2014) *Submission to dept of education re: Strategy statement*. Dublin: Pavee Point Publications.

Pavee Point (2019) *Traveller family histories give visibility to Traveller culture at National Library* [online], https://www.paveepoint.ie/traveller-researched-family-histories-added-to-national-library-archive.

Powell, F. and M. Geoghegan (2004) *The politics of community development: Reclaiming civil society or reinventing governance?* Dublin: A. & A. Farmar.

Raleigh, D. (2019) Sindy Joyce is first Traveller to graduate with a PhD in Ireland [online], *Irish Times*, 15th March, https://www.irishtimes.com/news/ireland/irish-news/sindy-joyce-is-first-traveller-to-graduate-with-a-phd-in-ireland-1.3759198.

Rottman, D., A. Tussing and M. Wiley (1986) *The population structure and living circumstances of Irish Travellers: Results from the 1981 Census of Travelling families*. Dublin: Economic and Social Research Institute.

Ryan A. (1998) Teachers, Travellers and education: A sociological perspective, *Irish Journal of Educational Studies* 17(1): 161–174.

Scott, J. (1998) *Seeing like a state: How certain schemes to improve the human condition have failed*. New Haven/London: Yale University Press.

Skilbeck, M. and H. Connell (2000) *Access and equity in higher education: An international perspective on issues and strategies*. Dublin: Higher Education Authority.

Shuinéar, S. (2004) Apocrypha to canon: Inventing Irish Traveller history, *History Ireland* 12(4): 15–19.

Smyth, E., J. Banks, A. Whelan, M. Darmody and S. McCoy (2015) *Review of the school completion programme*. Dublin: Economic and Social Research Institute.

Sweeney, P. (1998) *The Celtic tiger: Ireland's economic miracle explained*. Dublin: Oak Tree Press.

Trow, M. (1973) *Problems in the transition from elite to mass higher education*. Berkeley: Carnegie Commission on Higher Education.

Trow, M. (2010) *Twentieth-century higher education: Elite to mass to universal*. Baltimore: Johns Hopkins University Press.

University College Dublin (2010) *All Ireland Traveller health study: Our geels*. Dublin: University College Dublin.

Walsh, J. and A. Loxley (2015) The Hunt Report: an Irish solution to an Irish problem, *Studies in Higher Education* 40(6): 1128–1145.

Walsh, J. (2019) *Higher education in Ireland: 1922–2016*. Palgrave: Basingstoke.

Watson, D., O. Kenny and F. McGinnity (2017) *A social portrait of Travellers in Ireland*. Dublin: Economic and Social Research Institute.

Weir, S. and P. Archer (2011) *A report on the first phase of the evaluation of DEIS*. Dublin: Educational Research Centre.

Wickham, J. and A. Bobek (2016) *Enforced flexibility? Working in Ireland today*. Dublin: Think-tank for Action on Social Change.

Zappone, K. (1998) Top-down or bottom-up: The involvement of the community sector in partnerships, in P. Jacobson, P. Kirby and D. O'Broin (eds.) *In the shadow of the tiger: New approaches to combatting social exclusion* (pp. 50–59). Dublin: Dublin City University.

Chapter 9

Sámi peoples' educational challenges in higher education and migration in Finland

Pigga Keskitalo

Introduction

This chapter examines the relationship between higher education and human migration, in which people move from one place to another with the intention of settling, permanently or temporarily, in a new location to study. For the Sámi people, migration has meant moving to larger towns and cities in Finland, Sweden and Norway (e.g. Lindgren, 2000; see also United Nations, 2008). The Sámi people are indigenous people of the European Union (Lehtola, 2005). According to Sanders' (1999) definition, indigenous people – also known as first people, aboriginal people or native people – are ethnic groups who originally inhabited a given region. Historically, Sámi people lived all over Finland, including in the southern areas (see Aikio, 2012). Currently, evidence suggests that a large number of Sámi people have moved to the capitals of Finland, Sweden and Norway. Lindgren (2000) has highlighted that this migration has meant for many Sámi changes in terms of lifestyle, livelihood and language (see also Keskitalo, 2019a, 2019b).

The Sámi peoples live in central and northern Sweden and Norway, northern Finland and on Russia's Kola Peninsula, and have long held connections to other populations. The area the Sámi inhabit is called *Sápmi* in the North Sámi language. Depending on how this group is defined, there are approximately 100,000 Sámi living in these countries, although the data collection processes that arrived at that number have proven to be inadequate; hence, there is a lack of reliable demographic information about the Sámi people. What can be asserted quite categorically is that the Sámi – as with many other indigenous peoples – comprise a minority in the countries they live. They are recognised and protected under international conventions and declarations concerning the rights of indigenous peoples as well as through national laws and acts (Sarivaara and Keskitalo, 2019).

Sámi livelihoods have historically been connected to the land and water. Originating from hunter-gathering tribes, the Sámi have traditionally been involved with fishing, hunting, reindeer herding and, later in history, small scale farming. According to the most recent research, the Sámi languages emerged during the second millennium BC at the latest, which also gave birth to Sámi culture (Aikio, 2006, 2012). The Sámi languages are Finno-Ugric languages; they are, therefore, related, for example, to the Finnish language.

The primordial Finnish and Sámi are assumed to have separated at the end of Stone Age. The history of the Sámi is identified by various changes; notable ones include a move from collecting culture to reindeer herding one (from 1400–1600) and the disruption of their traditional ways caused by the arrival of settlers, together with the introduction of epidemic diseases and Christianity (Sarivaara and Keskitalo, 2019). Of interest is that Sámi peoples are connected not only linguistically but also genealogically. Genetic studies on Sámi have pointed out that the frequency of blood groups and protein polymorphisms in different Sámi groups differ significantly from the general Northern European population (Beckman et al., 2001).

Studying migration

Mobility and borders are mutually constitutive but appear as uneven, complex and precarious in the 21st century. It is important to question how mobility and stability, borders and border crossings as multi-level practices are shaped and reshaped by various structures and drivers in addition to the global flows of people. People who migrate, often with family members, hope to reach individual or collective goals or to achieve a dignified self-realisation and/or a preferred way of life (Chaichian, 2014; Wahlbeck, 2016).

There are still large gaps in the understanding of Arctic demography – for example, variations in in- and out-migration, male and female migration, designs of settlement (urban vs. rural) and nomadic patterns (indigenous vs. non-indigenous) in the cross-territorial framework. Moreover, the lack of vital statistical data at the regional and municipal levels similarly remains inadequate (Rautio et al., 2014). There are no official statistics on Sámi migration, but data should be gathered from Sámi language speakers and those who live in or migrate from the Sámi home areas in Finland. The Sámi home areas consist of the municipalities of Utsjoki, Inari, Enontekiö and the northern area of Sodankylä.

Sámi migration

Migration occurs as a multifaceted fashion within the Sámi context. Traditionally, in Sámi culture, migration has always been closely connected with the traditional seasonal movement within a specific pastoral area or the longer journeys between summer and winter pastures (Heikkinen, 2003; International Centre for Reindeer Husbandry, 2018; Kortesalmi, 2008). Wars, changing state borders and a novel method for organising reindeer herding created a new order in Finland in the 1800s and 1900s (Kortesalmi, 2008; also Anttonen, 1999; Hirvonen, 2010). Furthermore, modern life pressures – for example, relocating from areas newly dedicated to hydropower (Lähteenmäki, 2014; Linkola, 1967) – have caused many changes for the Sámi people since the 1950s (Brattrein and Niemi, 1994; Seurujärvi-Kari, 2011).

Changes came to the Sámi lands after World War II, when reconstruction started. Some of the Sámis had already moved to southern Finland to work and study (Ahokas, 2013; Lindgren, 2000), despite the official Sámi area being understood as northern Finland. Greater movement to the south took place gradually in 1950s and culminated in the 1960s, since it became clear that not everyone could cope with a traditional lifestyle. Migration to towns in southern Finland continued from the 1970s through the 2000s so that nowadays over 75% of Sámi children live outside traditional Sámi areas. The same kind of movement also happened in Norway and Sweden (Blindh, 1979; Eidheim, 1997; Hovland, 1996). The forms of migration undertaken by Sámi people are both diverse and individual. However, despite this large-scale migration and threats to cultural traditions, Lindgren (2000) highlights that even in a suburban context, pluralism can arise and language revitalisation can occur.

In 2003, there were fewer than 8,000 Sámi, of whom 54% lived outside traditional Sámi areas. In 1992, the proportion was 38%; in 1995, it was 41% and in 1999, 45%. At the same time, 90% of Sámi people over the age of 75 lived in traditional Sámi areas, but more than 70% of those under the age of 10 lived outside these areas. According to the Sámi Parliament, the erosion of traditional livelihoods causes migration, especially if there are no decent lifestyles available for those who wish to work within traditional areas or work in northern areas more generally. When increasing numbers of people are divorced from their traditional way of life, the future of the Sámi language becomes endangered (Sámi Parliament, 2006).

According to Latomaa (2010), how migrants can retain their languages depends on a country's minority and language policies and what kind of mainstream attitudes there are towards their languages. She points out that if a state's policies, as well as its citizens' attitudes, are strongly assimilative, minority or migrant languages can be seen as worthless and dispensable. In contrast, when social policy supports cultural and linguistic pluralism, minority representatives or migrants can more freely choose which languages they use in their homes. Latomaa further highlights that those who live in new places need to consider their past and future prospects. They must choose what connections they maintain with their home areas, what they need in order to be able to succeed in their new environment and whether they continue to speak their own language or speak the mainstream language at home. Finally, Latomaa argues that similar changes concern not only migrants but also older Finnish minorities (Latomaa 2010). Such issues are particularly relevant for the Sámi, since the number of Sámi language speakers decreased throughout the 1900s.

Sámi language modification was caused by changes in the education system. The former school rotation organisation was changed, and the teacher visits to villages were abolished. People born in 1940s and 1950s were forced to move to other, larger villages to attend Finnish-language elementary schools, where they lived in dormitories. Conditions were such that the Finnish language became the main language for many of the children, and many families changed their language of communication at home from Sámi to Finnish. The language situation improved in the 1970s, when Sámi language instruction began after a long period of nationalism (Keskitalo et al., 2014a; Latomaa, 2010). The language revival resulted from its development in schools; schools started to provide Sámi-language classes, and the Sámi language also became a subject of study (Aikio-Puoskari, 2007; Rahko-Ravantti, 2016). Furthermore, Sámi early childhood education was conducted in Sámi, and language revitalisation was also fostered by *language nests* (Äärelä, 2016). The Sámi language has also increasingly been used in the media, in different associations, and in cultural life, and Sámi literature is now published more extensively than it was before the 1980s (Hirvonen, 2010; Lehtola, 2005).

The Finnish curriculum has not accommodated the migration from Sámi traditional areas to the towns and cities. The right to attend Sámi-speaking classes only exists in the Sámi areas. Outside of these, only two hours of Sámi language instruction is provided per week (Rahko-Ravantti, 2016), which causes a hierarchy in language importance, despite the pluralist reality. The minority and migrant languages in Finland have only been used outside the formal curriculum since 2004 beyond the Sámi core areas (Latomaa, 2010).

According to Hirvonen, societal changes have affected Sámi societies. Many Sámi people have been absent from their traditional lands for decades because of study, work or other personal reasons. Living in a new area may be challenging because it often does not provide good opportunities to study, use or maintain the Sámi language and culture. Those Sámi who live outside their traditional lands can be referred to as members of a diaspora, as they have a strong relationship to their home area. After relocation, the connection to Sámi lands and to Sámi people might change, and the identity of those who moved might be questioned. This can cause a measure of negotiation and redefinition Sámi identity within the Sámi community. The Sámi connection to the mainstream culture involves feelings of both empowerment and subordination, which affects how they see themselves in relation to other people and how they cope in the new environment (Hirvonen, 2010). According to Gröndahl (2010), the Sámi migrants' situation is intersectional, as it simultaneously consists of connection and disconnection to their background.

Intersectionality attempts to identify how interlocking systems of power impact those who are most marginalised in society. Various forms of social stratification do not exist separately but are rather interwoven, such as class, race, sexual orientation, age, religion, disability and gender. Intersectionality originally explored the oppression of women of colour, but today the analysis can be potentially applied to all social categories and identities (Cooper, 2016).

Schweitzer et al. (2014, p. 144) in the Nordic Council of Ministers' *Arctic Human Development Report* summarise the present situation of the Sámi in the Arctic region:

> On the one hand, there is a trend toward the revitalization of indigenous languages and cultures and the strengthening of northern identities. On the other hand, there is a growing threat to circumpolar cultures and identities through modernization, globalization and (urban) migration.

Scandinavian higher education policies towards the Sámi people

There are long roots tight to universities and Sámi people in higher education at least when it comes to the tradition of studying the Sámi people. Already in 1600s, Sámi men were educated to work as teachers among the Sámi people (Keskitalo et al., 2014b). At a very early stage, the Sámi people were subject to 'civilisation' processes and migration. For example, the first Sámi writer, Pedar Jalvi, moved to southern Finland to study at Jyväskylä Teachers' College, from which he graduated in 1915 (Aikio, 1966). Some of these first students stayed permanently in southern Finland, resulting in third-generation Sámi residence in that region. In the 20th century, the church proceeded to recruit young Sámi as teachers to teach Sámi children. Jouni Guttorm worked in Kylmäkoski because he was not able to find a job in the Sámi areas. The Guttorm family changed its surname to Keva so that the children would not be teased on account of their Sámi family name (Ahokas, 2013).

The Sámi languages have long been taught at the different universities in Finland; for example, the Faculty of Humanities at the University of Helsinki. Teaching and research on the Sámi languages have been conducted at the University of Helsinki for as almost as long as the study of the Finnish language – from the mid-19th century onwards. Many of the internationally renowned scholars of Finno-Ugric studies started their careers specifically studying the Sámi languages at the University of Helsinki. Since 1986, Helsinki University has had a lecturer in Sámi languages, and from 1993, the school has had a Sámi studies programme (Seurujärvi-Kari, 2014a).

At the University of Oulu, the tradition of teaching the Sámi language and culture extended to the end of the 1960s, when the Sámi language, called at that time the Lappish language, began to be taught by the Finnish language department. It developed into a major university subject in the early 1980s when teaching focused mainly on educating native speakers of the Sámi language. Most graduates focused on Sámi language teaching. The teaching of Sámi culture began to strengthen in the 1990s – particularly with the Giellagas Institute being established in 2001 – when Sámi culture studies became another major subject alongside the Sámi language. In 1970, the

University of Oulu hired a lecturer in the Lappish language, which was the first in Finland (Lehtola 2014).

Lapland College was founded in 1979, and, included in the curriculum, teacher training was a natural continuation of the women's seminar in Tornio (1921–1970) and the Kemijärvi Seminar (1950–1970). The Sámi language teaching was part of the teaching offering of the Lapland College (now the University of Lapland) from the beginning (Rantala 2014).

Today, some of the studies are also conducted in traditional Sámi areas (such as Inari). There has been debate about creating more higher education programmes in this region. Today, still, universities demand that their students move to towns to study. However, some programmes have been offered, through online study and some classes have been organised in traditional Sámi area, such as Sámi kindergarten teacher education courses (Peltola et al., 2019).

In Norway, in traditional Sámi areas, Sámi higher education has been offered at the Sámi University of Applied Sciences since its establishment in 1989 (Guttorm et al., 2016). At Umeå University, in Sweden, it is also possible to study the Sámi language.

Methods

This research is concerned with Sámi people's experiences of migration, and it uses qualitative, narrative interviews to collect people's ideas and thoughts about migration. This study examines what kind of stories people tell about their migration and how the phenomenon is constructed as a story (Hyvärinen, 2006). The study also uses Sámi research (Seurujärvi-Kari, 2014b) as a means to open up, engage with and resolve the legacy of assimilation and, in particular, language shift. Sámi education that is based on a mediating role plays a vital part in struggles to revive indigenous languages and cultures (Keskitalo and Sarivaara, 2016).

For this research, 23 people were interviewed through a narrative method. The interviewees represented adults of all ages: students and young people, middle-aged people of working age and retired people. They were chosen through snowball sampling to acquire narratives from a wide-range of Sámi people, not to make generalizable conclusions about the Sámi people of Finland.

Sámi migrants can be analysed through the concept of intersectionality, which expresses social categories' collective and distinctive features (Gröndahl, 2010; Hancock, 2016). Intersectional analysis considers how categories of cultural, societal and discursive affect and influence one another (de los Reyes et al., 2005).

The data were examined by identifying meaningful criteria and relevant stories that arose from the interviews: the reasons for moving, how life is perceived in the post-migration circumstances, what role Sámihood has in the new area and what kind of ideas migrant people have about their futures.

The data were given no numbers or dates in order to avoid combining elements and identifying interviewees. Because there are so few interviewees and the come from close-knit communities, the need for anonymity is high (see Nystad, 2003).

The reliability of the study depends on the fact that the researcher is a Sámi and has a unique insight into the meaning of Sámi people's experience of migration. Furthermore, the research was conducted according to ethical principles of research, including its concepts, approaches, methods and conclusions. Sámi and indigenous research aim to privilege the personal experiences of the researcher and interviewees, and the quality of research is established through this kind of interaction.

Migration

Reasons for relocating

The Sámi interviewees mentioned many reasons for moving to a new area; the reasons often related to their age. Other factors included work, studies, love, wanting to experience adventure and new challenges, career choices, family changes and the poor situation in traditional Sámi areas. In the 1950s, especially, the living conditions in these areas deteriorated and people sought work opportunities elsewhere (Lindgren, 2000). People wanted to escape either from unemployment or their poor earning levels (Korkiasaari and Tarkiainen, 2000).

There were many kinds of relocations according to interviewees: within villages, between villages, moving short distances, moving to larger settlements and moving further south in Finland; some even moved between Nordic countries and even abroad.

Even if people decided to move, their family sometimes called the migrant back home to the Sámi area. Families worked hard, and it was not easy to let the young people move away because families needed their labour. One student interviewee said, 'My grandfather wrote to his son: "Please, you need to stop your education and come back from school. There are so many wolves in the reindeer herd"'. Now, due to mechanisation, there is probably less need for workers. Traditional means of earning a living no longer provide a livelihood.

One elderly person said that he moved away when he was in his twenties and Sámi society had already begun to transform. Finnish identity and the Finnish language started to predominate. Those who were educated or working in traditional Sámi areas, had traditional livelihoods, or spoke Sámi and preferred to live in that area stayed. The modernisation process and its consequences for society caused people to move (Lindgren, 2000). Assimilation, language change and societal changes affected feelings of belonging to Sámi society. The rise of Sámi political action was mentioned by interviewees. These stories concern those earlier times in 1950s and 1960s. One participant said the following:

> I felt that I did not belong to that [Sámi] society and those groups, as I could not speak Sámi. There was also a lot of confrontation, which was concealed. Political action started to rise as did differences between groups. Those who were academically educated started to get ahead. I think the change of society and its decomposition affected those days a lot, in hidden forms. Hidden inner conflicts, disputes and competition were the reasons I left, among others. As I was young, the world was calling me.

Today, as in earlier times, most of the students who relocated felt that they had to move because there were not enough opportunities in the north. Many migrants needed to move because there is only limited vocational education in the north of Finland. Regardless of the time, youth seem to want to see the world, earn money and find suitable opportunities for their life. Travelling between home and the study location has made interviewees realise that maybe northern areas need to develop their education options so that people do not need to travel extensively to study.

The types of people who relocate

The kind of expectations families have, the kind of livelihood the families pursue and the kind of opportunities, educational or otherwise, traditional Sámi lands offer affect decisions to migrate. As one participant stated:

> Those who choose to work in their communities and care about Sámihood and the Sámi language, those stay, so that I can understand it, but it is not that black and white.

Since the great migration, especially in the 2000s, the need for education development and Sámi-language services outside the Sámi core areas has been a subject of great debate. The situation had deteriorated, but many new developments have occurred. Helsinki has started Sámi classes; Kittilä, Helsinki, Sodankylä, Rovaniemi and Oulu have started Sámi kindergartens and Rovaniemi has started Sámi language education after a long break. Sámi language distance education also has great potential. People try to connect with those who have moved away, as they worry about their Sámihood and Sámi language ability. One student said the following:

> I often worry and wonder. Those who move, do they care enough, do they come home regularly, do they keep their connections? I assume that usually those who stay have a strong Sámi identity, but sometimes also those who move or live outside the Sámi core areas have a strong identity. It depends on the family background and person.

Many motivations for relocation were explained by better opportunities and wider experiences in the new location:

> Those who leave would like to study. There are very few opportunities in the north. If you want to experience new things, you might want to leave. If you stay, you choose something that you can study in the north, and then you get a job. Those who do not need an adventurous lifestyle stay.

Some mentioned also that parity grew after relocation to the south:

> When I left, a lot of those who drank too much were living in the north. Those concentrating on career development lived in the south. At the same time, I can say that I am putting things too simply, but this is one thing I realised.

The interviewees are clear about the motivation to stay or leave. Those who stay are more interested in things that the home area provides and those who leave tend to seek something else.

Issues that worried interviewees

Interviewees mentioned many negative consequences of relocation. Settling in towns and suburban areas seemed to be achieved sometimes with difficulties and sometimes without them. As one student stated: 'I really am worried about migration's effects on Sámihood. I am afraid of assimilation.'

This is not an unfounded fear, as only 1,900 people have claimed Sámi as their mother tongue, out of roughly 10,000 Sámi people living in Finland. This means that only approximately 20% of Sámi people speak Sámi as their first language. Of course, it should not be assumed that everybody has announced Sámi as mother tongue because of how the concept of mother tongue is understood.

In addition, travelling long distances can cause complications, according to interviewees. Travelling is expensive, difficult and time-consuming, and travellers need to plan ahead. Travelling between the study location and home in the north can cause a sense of anxiety.

Adapting to new demands and having concerns about maintaining Sámi culture made people feel stressed, yet the new environment also brought a lot of pleasure and new opportunities. Despite these benefits, the existing challenges still bring conflicting feelings to people and cause a great deal of stress and feelings of 'otherness':

> In a way, I feel that I do not belong anymore to the society I left and that I am not part of the society I came to. I feel like an outcast and disturbed. I miss the north and travel there often, and it helps, but I cannot return.

People feel also that they are alone in south, that no one cares and that they do not get any help if it is needed, a sentiment the following student articulated: 'I feel like in the north, everybody is so helpful. Here they do not stop if you ask for help'.

Many of the stories mention the diasporic connection to the Sámi areas. Migrants miss their home, the nature and the people, but, conversely, they are still happy to live outside these areas. Despite some difficult feelings, people still choose to stay away from home and tolerate the loneliness and the longing for the natural environment. Some of the interviewees said that it is not possible to return. Still, many of those who were living in the south felt that their move was not permanent. Many dreamed about moving to the north but had no such opportunity; many had built their lives in the south, so it was not possible to move.

Plans to return

When talking about their dreams of returning home, many interviewees felt positive about this, but they used such phrases as 'later', 'when the kids are bigger', 'when retiring' and 'not yet'. Even if they saw the north in positive terms, they were kept in the south by such things as careers, home, people, climate and way of life. As one participant stated, 'My family [husband and kids] will not return. I will return, I will return alone – but later'.

Of their experiences in the north and south, interviewees explained that they feel both places as their home and wander between them. One student said, 'Once I decided to move suddenly from south to north, to my childhood home, as I missed the snowmobile riding'.

Many of the students plan to move back home after graduation, as was the case for this student:

> It is very certain that I will not stay at my study location but I will return to my home area. I want to go back to my people. I cannot imagine that I'll stay. Study time itself is nice, and the distance to home is something that I can manage.

There are no statistics about the actual number of students who return north after graduating. South study places are one way that students eventually stay in their study towns.

Life after relocation

In this next section, the study highlights what kind of consequences and expectations Sámi people perceive that migration has brought them. Interviewees mentioned many good aspects of living in big cities, as did this student:

> [There are] so many chances to study and work in different kinds of workplaces. In the north you need to get along with everybody. Here I can choose who I socialise with. It's easy to travel, and I can get to know things I did not know before.

Many of the things that people report are positive. They feel that relocation, after all, is quite harmless and that, after a while, it brought positive benefits to their lives. But still they missed home. Despite the problems experienced by earlier migrants in settling, they still felt that relocation brought positive benefits to their life, including stability and a feeling of progress.

Problems settling down

One student explained how difficult it is to settle down in at a new school:

> If you knew any people beforehand, it helps you to adapt to the community. I could ask for help, and there were many people from my home area. I got to know them very well at my place of study, even though I was not even talking to them before getting to know them well at the place of study. Having the same origin and village brought us closer.

Others discussed the difficulties and challenges of relocating without knowing anyone: 'The first days were tough. It was dark and it was raining. I felt so lonely and I was crying when walking in the empty town'. One student suggested a kind of Sámi godfather/godmother system so that there are people to take care of Sámi youth arriving to the towns and cities.

Connection to Sámi culture and Sámi community

The next section deals with the connection to Sámi culture and community. Interviewees represented two kinds of people: those who could speak Sámi actively and those who could not. One interviewee mentioned that, 'Sámihood is not the same here as in the north. It is imagined, constructed, and pretentious'. Maintaining connections to relatives and to the Sámi speaking society is important. Little things can bring joy to the life of a student who is living in the city, as one student expressed: 'I love talking to my dog in Sámi. When relatives send me reindeer meat, I feel very supported and loved'.

Interviewees felt that they could stay connected to Sámi culture and retain and language despite the distance:

> Despite the fact that I live far away and I have not had so many Sámi things in my life recently, I do not think I will lose anything. I know who I am, and my background stays with me. Distance does not damage my connection to my background. I am not worried at all. Sáminess stays with me wherever I go.

Connection to family and relatives

Many of interviewees come from traditional Sámi backgrounds, the north, and participate in that life every time they go back home. As one participant exclaimed, 'My soul sings when I go home. Still, I have not been there for two years'. The interviewees reported strong feelings and connections in relation to their home areas in the north. For one participant, it felt like their real home: 'I feel like this study town is my home, but my village home up north is my home, a real true home'.

Children's bond to Sámihood

Many of the interviewees were concerned about their children and their children's language capability:

> If we do not go regularly, I feel that, because they were not born in the north, they get only a minimal amount of Sámihood, and that makes me sad. We can travel only for one week per year to the north. I cannot move because it's complicated.

Others decided they would move to the north when they had children, as they see their children as the future of Sámi culture:

> With my future kids, I'd rather live in the Sámi lands. I've seen when working with kids in Sámi areas that their eyes are shining.

The interviewees also mentioned that it is not easy dealing with children and the Sámi language in suburban areas. One participant said the following:

> I am the only person who is speaking to my kids in Sámi. They surely lose out because they cannot attend Sámi language kindergarten. I want to make sure that they will later get Sámi language distance teaching. But I try to travel with them regularly to Sápmi.

Nowadays, it may be easier to preserve the Sámi language and Sámi culture. In many places, Sámi kindergartens and Sámi language classes are available. As one interviewee stated, 'For us as a family, it was absolutely expected that the kid would learn Sámi. It generated a better quality of life, when we could continue with Sámi language education after we moved'. The existence of a Sámi language kindergarten made decision about moving very easy for the interviewee.

Further measures

Many of the interviewees said that issues related to migration and cultural maintenance could have been better planned, given the reality of large-scale migration. They raised concerns that the local Sámi education system needs to be developed and supported in order to prevent migration. Still, there has been little action regarding this. They even said their self-determination is not being realised, as they cannot effectively decide about education possibilities:

> It's hard to become educated. Education institutions do not take enough account of the wishes of those who live in remote areas. It's very complicated to move to towns or to travel to other study locations. I'd rather study as much as possible via distance learning. I need to study further in order to get a permanent job.

They also felt that distance learning has not been effectively implemented:

> I would like to live in the north, but my education institution refuses to send lecturers to the north. They urge me to stay in town and study. That's bad. I would love to live in the north and undertake internet-based study.

When students are educated away from their home, there are few links between the school and the home and between the school and the culture of the home community. Hence, the loss of culture and indigenous language seems to continue in the Arctic areas (Hirshberg and Petrov, 2014).

Conclusion

Education is a meaningful category explaining Sámi people's migration. Education is an essential part of fate control. Resilient fate control may reinforce communities, at least for a while, permitting them to resist the pressure from outside. It may, however, be less reactive to the marked differences in both gender and generational foci in relation to the development process. Indeed, this may to result in unexpected and unwanted out-migration patterns and, thus, the loss of the new human capital gained, for example, through the expansion of educational prospects. Additional probable significance of formal education is the loss of cultural identity and loss of contact with nature (Battiste, 2000; Hirshberg and Petrov, 2014).

Hirshberg and Petrov (2014) further state that with a higher level of education, the capacity and wish of local residents to find employment or new educational chances in another place grows as well. A growing number of people, specifically women, move away from the Arctic to obtain their education or to work elsewhere. Simultaneously, many Arctic regions are attracting human capital from the south, as professionals take advantage of high salaries in certain Arctic sectors (e.g. mining and oil). Regrettably, most of them stay in the Arctic simply for a limited time (Hirshberg and Petrov, 2014; Voswinkel, 2012). According to Petrov and Vlasova (2010), departing educated native northerners and a lack of returning migrants create a problem of brain drain from the Arctic.

Acknowledgments

Some of the data used in this chapter were previously published in my chapter in *Human Migration in the Arctic* (2019) edited by S. Uusiautti and N. Yeasmin and published by Palgrave.

References

Äärelä, R. (2016) "Dat ii leat dušše dat giella"/"Se ei ole vain se kieli": Tapaustutkimus saamenkielisestä kielipesästä saamelaisessa varhaiskasvatuksessa [It's not just a language: A case study of a Sámi language nest in Sámi early childhood education], *Acta Universitatis Lapponiensis 335*. Rovaniemi: Lapin Yliopistokustannus.

Ahokas, L. (2013) Nilla Keva oli paljon muutakin kuin opettaja [Nilla Keva was much more than just a teacher], *Akaan Seutu* [online], https://akaanseutu.fi/2013/04/06/nilla-keva-oli-paljon-muutakin-kuin-opettaja.

Aikio, A. (2006). On Germanic-Saami contacts and Saami prehistory, *Suomalais-Ugrilaisen Seuran Aikakauskirja* 91: 9–55.

Aikio, A. (2012). An essay on Saami ethnolinguistic prehistory, in R. Grünthal and P. Kallio (eds.) *A linguistic map of prehistoric Northern Europe* (pp. 63–117). Helsinki: Suomalais-Ugrilaisen Seuran Toimituksia.

Aikio, S. (1966) Piirteitä Pedar Jalvin kirjallisesta tuotannosta [Features from the literary production of Pedar Jalvi]. *Lapin Kansa*, 29th November, p. 9.

Aikio-Puoskari, U. (2007) Saamelaisopetus osana suomalaista peruskoulua – kielenvaihdon vai revitalisaation edistäjä? [Sámi education as part of a Finnish primary school – a promoter of language exchange or revitalization], in *Sámit, sánit, sátnehámit: Riepmočála Pekka Sammallahtii miessemánu 21. beaivve 2007* [Sámi, words, wordings. Commemorative book for Pekka Sammallahti on 21st May 2007]. (pp. 73–84). Helsinki: Suomalais-Ugrilaisen Seuran Toimituksia.

Anttonen, M. (1999) *Etnopolitiikkaa Ruijassa. Suomalaislähtöisen väestön identiteettien politisoituminen 1990-luvulla* [Ethnic policy in Finnmark. The politicization of the identity of a Finnish-based population in the 1990s]. Helsinki: Suomalaisen Kirjallisuuden Seura.

Battiste, M. (2000) Maintaining aboriginal identity, language, and culture in modern society, in M. Battiste (ed.) *Reclaiming indigenous voice and vision* (pp. 192–208). Vancouver: University of British Columbia Press.

Beckman L., K. Sjoberg, S. Eriksson and L. Beckman (2001) Haemochromatosis gene mutations in Finns, Swedes and Swedish Saamis, *Human Heredity* 52(2): 110–112.

Blindh, I. (1979) *Samer i Stockholm: En undersökning om utflyttade samers kulturella behov* [The Sámi in Stockholm: research about migrated Sámi peoples' cultural needs]. Guovdageaidnu: Sámi Instituhtta.

Brattrein, H. and E. Niemi (1994) Inn i riket [In a country], in E. Drivenes, M. Hauan and H. Wold (eds.) *Politisk og økonomisk integrasjoen gjennom tusen år* [Political and economic integration across a thousand years] (pp. 146–209). Oslo: Gyldendal Norsk Forlag.

Chaichian, M. (2014) *Empires and walls: Globalisation, migration, and colonial control*. Leiden: Brill.

Cooper, B. (2016) Intersectionality, in L. Disch and M. Hawkesworth (eds.) *The Oxford handbook of feminist theory* (pp. 385–406). Oxford: Oxford University Press.

de los Reyes, P., I. Molina and D. Mulinari (2005) *Intersektionalitet: Kritiska reflektioner över (o)jämlikhetens landskap* [Intersectionality: Critical reflections about the landscape of (in)equality]. Malmö: Liber.

Eidheim, H. (1997) Ethno-political development among the Sami after World War II: the invention of selfhood, in H. Gaski (ed.) *Sámi culture in a new era: the Norwegian Sami experience* (pp. 29–61). Karasjok: Davvi Girji.

Gröndahl, S. (2010). *Erilaisuuden kokemuksesta moniarvoisuuteen: Romanien ja matkaajien kirjallisuus Pohjoismaissa* [From diversity to experience of pluralism: Literature of roamers and travellers in Scandinavia], in E. Rantonen (ed.) *Vähemmistöt ja monikulttuurisuus kirjallisuudessa* [Minorities and multiculturalism in literature] (pp. 106–131). Tampere: Tampere University Press.

Guttorm, H., P. Keskitalo and A. Bergier (2016) Sharing reflections on the Sámi University College as a language (re)vitalization center, in J. Olko, T. Wicherkiewicz and R. Borges (eds.) *Integral strategies for language revitalization*. Warsaw: University of Warsaw.

Hancock, A.-M. (2016) *Intersectionality: An intellectual history*. New York: Oxford University Press.

Heikkinen, H. (2003) *Sopeutumisen mallit: Poronhoidon adaptaatio jälkiteolliseen toimintaympäristöön Suomen läntisellä poronhoitoalueella.* [Models of adaptation to post-industrial society in the Western reindeer herding district in Finland]. Helsinki: Suomalaisen Kirjallisuuden Seura.

Hirshberg, D. and A. Petrov (2014) Education and human capital, in J. Larsen and G. Fondahl (eds.) *Arctic human development report: Regional processes and global linkages*. Copenhagen: Nordic Council of Ministers.

Hirvonen, V. (2010) Saamelainen kirjallisuus ja pohjoinen ulottuvuus [Sámi literature and the northern dimension], in E. Rantonen (ed.) *Vähemmistöt ja monikulttuurisuus kirjallisuudessa* [Minorities and multiculturalism in literature] (pp. 71–105). Tampere: Tampere University Press.

Hovland, A. (1996) *Moderne urfolk. Samisk ungdom i bevegelse* [Modern indigenous people: Sami youth in motion]. Oslo: Cappelen Akademisk Forlag.

Hyvärinen, M. (2006). *Kertomuksen tutkimus* [Researching narratives] [online], https://docplayer.fi/412868-Kertomuksen-tutkimus-matti-hyvarinen.html.

International Centre for Reindeer Husbandry (2018). *Sámi & Finns – Finland* [online], https://reindeerherding.org/sami-finns-finland.0

Keskitalo, P. (2019a) Nomadic narratives of Sámi people's migration in historic and modern times, in S. Uusiautti and N. Yeasmin (eds.) *Human migration in the Arctic: The past, present, and future* (pp. 31–65). Singapore: Palgrave.

Keskitalo, P. (2019b). Saamelaisten kertomuksia muuttamisesta kaupunkeihin [The Sámi people's narratives of migration], *Siirtolaisuus Migration* 3: 14–17.

Keskitalo, P., V.-P. Lehtola and M. Paksuniemi (eds.) (2014a) *Saamelaisten kansanopetuksen ja koulunkäynnin historia Suomessa* [Sámi education history in Finland]. Turku: Migration Institute.

Keskitalo, P., V.-P. Lehtola and M. Paksuniemi (2014b) Johdatus saamelaisten kansanopetuksen ja koulunkäynnin historiaan [Introduction to the history of education of the Sámi people in Finland], in P. Keskitalo, V.-P. Lehtola and M. Paksuniemi (eds.) *Saamelaisten kansanopetuksen ja koulunkäynnin historia Suomessa* [Sámi education history in Finland] (pp. 13–28). Turku: Migration Institute.

Keskitalo P. and E. Sarivaara (2016) The definition and task of mediating Sámi research, in S. Uusiautti and K. Määttä (eds.) *The basics of caring research: Bold visions in educational research* (pp. 119–133). Rotterdam: Sense Publishers.

Korkiasaari, J. and K. Tarkiainen (2000) Suomalaiset Ruotsissa [Finns in Sweden]. *Suomalaisen siirtolaisuuden historia 3*. Turku: Siirtolaisinstituutti.

Kortesalmi, J. (2008) *Poronhoidon synty ja kehitys Suomessa* [Reindeer herding and its development in Finland]. Helsinki: Suomalaisen Kirjallisuuden Seura.

Latomaa, S. (2010) "Hänellä ei ole kieltä missä hän voisi elää"—kirjallisuus kielipolitiikan ilmentäjänä ["He has no language where he could live"—literature as an expression of language policy], in E. Rantonen (ed.) *Vähemmistöt ja monikulttuurisuus kirjallisuudessa* [Minorities and multiculturalism in literature] (pp. 40–68). Tampere: Tampere University Press.

Lehtola, V.-P. (2005) *The Sámi people: Traditions in transition* (translated by L. Weber Müller-Wille). Fairbanks: University of Alaska Press.

Lehtola, V.-P. (2014) Saamen kielen lehtoraatista Giellagas-instituutiksi [From Sámi language lecturerhood to the Giellagas institute], in P. Keskitalo, V.-P. Lehtola and M. Paksuniemi (eds.) *Saamelaisten kansanopetuksen ja koulunkäynnin historia Suomessa* [Sámi education history in Finland] (pp. 315–319). Turku: Migration Institute.

Lindgren, A.-R. (2000) *Helsingin saamelaiset ja oma kieli* [The Sámi in Helsinki and their own language]. Helsinki: Suomalaisen Kirjallisuuden Seura.

Linkola, M. (ed.) (1967) *Entinen Kemijoki* [Former Kemi River]. Helsinki: Weilin+Göös Ab.

Lähteenmäki, M. (2014) Northern border regions on focus, *Nordia Geographical Publications* 43(1): 1–6.

Nystad, I. (2003) *Mannen mellom myte og modernitet* [Man between myth and modernity]. Nesbru: Vett & Viten.

Peltola, M., P. Keskitalo and R. Äärelä-Vihriälä (eds.) (2019) *Saamelainen varhaiskasvatus nyt – arvot, käytänteet ja osallisuus arjessa* [Present Sámi early childhood education – values, practices and participation in everyday life], *Acta Universitatis Ouluensis F Scripta Academica 13*. Oulun: Oulun Yliopisto.

Petrov, A. and T. Vlasova (2010) Migration and socio-economic well-being in the Russian North: interrelations, regional differentiation, recent trends and emerging issues, in L. Huskey and C. Southcott (eds.) *Migration in the circumpolar north: New concepts and patterns* (pp. 163–192). Edmonton: Canadian Circumpolar Institute Press.

Rahko-Ravantti, R. (2016) *Saamelaisopetus Suomessa: Tutkimus saamelaisopettajien opetustyöstä suomalaiskouluissa* [Sámi teaching in Finland: research about Sámi teachers' work at Finnish schools]. Rovaniemi: Lapland University Press.

Rantala, L. (2014) Saamen kielen opetus Lapin yliopistossa lukuvuosina 1983–2010 [Sámi language teaching in Lapland at the University during the academic years 1983–2010], in P. Keskitalo, V.-P. Lehtola and M. Paksuniemi (eds.) *Saamelaisten kansanopetuksen ja koulunkäynnin historia Suomessa* [Sámi education history in Finland] (pp. 313–314). Turku: Migration Institute.

Rautio, A., B. Poppel and K. Young (2014) Human health and well-being, in J. Nymand and G. Fondahl (eds.) *Arctic human development report: Regional processes and global linkages* (pp. 299–348). Copenhagen: Nordic Council of Ministers.

Sámi Parliament (2006) *Saamelaisten kestävän kehityksen ohjelma 2006* [Programme for sustainable development of the Sámi people]. Inari: Sámi Parliament.

Sanders, D. (1999). Indigenous people: Issues of definition, *International Journal of Cultural Property* 8: 4–13.

Sarivaara, E. and P. Keskitalo (2019) Sámi language for all: Transformed futures through mediative education, in E. McKinley and L. Smith (eds.) *Handbook of indigenous education* [online]. Singapore: Springer.

Schweitzer, P., P. Sköld and O. Ulturgasheva (2014) Culture and identities, in J. Larsen and G. Fondahl (eds.) *Arctic human development report: Regional processes and global linkages.* Copenhagen: Nordic Council of Ministers.

Seurujärvi-Kari, I. (2011) "We are no longer prepared to be silent." The making of Sámi indigenous identity in an international context, *Suomen Antropologi* 35(4): 5–25.

Seurujärvi-Kari, I. (2014a) Saamentutkimus, saamen kielen ja kulttuurin opetus Helsingin yliopistossa [Sámi research: teaching of the Sámi language and culture at the University of Helsinki], in P. Keskitalo, V.-P. Lehtola and M. Paksuniemi (eds.) *Saamelaisten kansanopetuksen ja koulunkäynnin historia Suomessa* [Sámi education history in Finland] (pp. 308–312). Turku: Migration Institute.

Seurujärvi-Kari, I. (2014b) *Saamentutkimus* [Sámi research] [online], https://saamelaisensyklopedia.fi/wiki/Saamentutkimus.

United Nations (2008) *Urban indigenous people and migration* [online], http://www.un.org/en/events/indigenousday/pdf/factsheet_migration_final.pdf.

Voswinkel, S. (2012) *Survey of Yukon's knowledge sector: Results and recommendations.* Whitehorse: Ylynx Management Consulting, Inc. and Yukon Research Centre.

Wahlbeck, Ö. (2016) True Finns and non-true Finns: The minority rights discourse of populist politics in Finland, *Journal of Intercultural Studies* 37(6): 574–588

Chapter 10

Getting to university
Experiences of students from rural areas in South Africa

Lisa Lucas, Kibbie Naidoo and Sue Timmis

Introduction

Access to higher education in South Africa has for a long time been high on the policy agenda but despite significant investment and policy initiatives, there continues to be unequal access for students from historically under-represented backgrounds, particularly the majority black population which has the lowest participation rates (Cooper, 2015; Leibowitz and Bozalek, 2014). Furthermore, students from rural backgrounds are even less likely to attend or successfully complete higher education. Students from rural backgrounds are more likely to have experienced disadvantages of poverty and poor schooling. National testing results continue to show rural schools at a disadvantage, including final examination rates (Leibowitz and Bozalek, 2014; Mdepa and Tshiwula, 2012). This provides some explanation for why student representation in universities is highly unequal in terms of demographics and geography, with students from rural areas particularly under-represented (Czerniewicz and Brown, 2014).

This chapter provides evidence from the SARiHE (Southern African Rurality in Higher Education) project. This collaborative project involving South African and United Kingdom (UK) partners investigates how rural students in South Africa negotiate the transition to university and how prior cultural and educational experiences influence their higher education trajectories. The SARiHE project addresses a knowledge gap, as expressed by Mgqwashu (2016) that, despite being one of the most marginalised groups, there is relatively little research on students from rural areas in South Africa and limited literature in South Africa on the influence of rurality on students' achievement and participation in higher education. This has been discussed more recently in relation to higher education institutions themselves (Leibowitz et al., 2015, Walker and Mathebula, 2020). An influential study of 'disadvantaged' students in higher education in South Africa found that a multiplicity of factors effect transitions from rural areas, including geography, financial resources, schooling, language and 'other socio-cultural factors' (Jones et al., 2008). Although students from rural contexts in South Africa can certainly be seen as 'marginalised', it is important also to problematise this concept and consider in a more nuanced way, how it might illuminate these students' experiences and their sense of place within their communities as well as within higher education institutions. In addition, it is important not to conceptualise the experiences of a rural background only in terms of a deficit but to consider a dynamic understanding of rurality that explores the plurality of lived experiences and individual and collective agency in transforming contexts (Balfour et al., 2012).

The project employs a participatory methodology where students are co-researchers who generate data about their lives and their experiences at university. The study utilises student co-researcher narratives and multimodal accounts to understand their negotiations of identity and explore their transitions into and through university. The specific focus in this chapter is to look in detail at the experiences of the student co-researchers prior to attending university to understand what influenced their ideas about going on to higher education and also what enabled or hindered their ambitions to attend university and also to take the practical steps to make it a reality.

This chapter explores the experiences and challenges of student co-researchers from three South African universities of going to university and the ways in which they were able to learn about higher education, make applications and ultimately gain a place at university. How was this journey enabled and what were the challenges faced by these student co-researchers? It focuses on student co-researchers' ideas about the value of higher education, access to information for applying to university, the importance of role models (which include teachers, church elders, university graduates and community and family members) and access to technology. Furthermore, it addresses how student co-researchers from rural contexts come to know about studying at university, get access to information and the role of the schools as well as outreach programmes and community organisations.

Rurality in South Africa and inequities of access to higher education

South Africa has a history of marginalisation and exclusion based on race, land possession and a domination of imperialist economic power through seizures of mineral wealth (Oyedemi, 2020). In South Africa, space is a deeply political matter due to the displacement effects of apartheid; 'rurality as a concept reflects the broader history of colonialism and dispossession' (Walker and Mathebula, 2020, p. 3). The relationship between race, geography, land and rurality is further underscored by Gordon (2015, p. 163) who refers to a 'geography of race' in which 'white populations have more geographical space than people of colour'. One of the social categories most marginalised and affected by historical inadequacies is that of rurality, especially as it interrelates with race and ethnicity, both in South Africa and in other Southern African countries. However, rurality is difficult to conceptualise. It is spatial and contextual (Green and Reid, 2014), may be demographic, geographic and cultural (Roberts and Green, 2013), or may be defined 'empirically' as having sparsely populated areas and ontologically as 'a category and set of experiences' (Moreland et al., 2003, p. 56).

Students from rural contexts are one of the historically under-represented groups entering higher education, who have experienced unique forms of disadvantage as a direct result of coloniality and the continuing legacy of apartheid. Widening participation has been a major and ongoing concern in South Africa subsequent to the democratisation in 1994 but the adequacy of the widening access process in numeric terms has been challenged (Cooper, 2015; Leibowitz and Bozalek, 2014). It is difficult to locate clear statistics for the number of students from rural areas in higher education in South Africa as they tend to be grouped together with disadvantaged students (Czerniewicz and Brown, 2014). They are, however, disproportionately represented, i.e. the numbers are fewer than they should be.

Rural contexts are diverse with different and evolving features and should not be essentialised and homogenised (Roberts and Green, 2013). Ideas of rurality are typically concerned with deprivation and deficiency including, among others, isolation, poverty, disease and neglect. These perceptions, however, do not reflect accurately heterogeneous experiences of rurality and the multiple ruralities that exist. For South Africa, Leibowitz (2017) draws attention to the need to also consider the interrelatedness of urban and rural areas in defining rurality as a construct for research in terms of the implications of how people understand their own identities and affiliations, as rural, urban or as both intersecting. Fataar and Fillies (2016), writing about rural working-class students in South Africa, challenge the conceptions that they lack the necessary cultural capital for educational success, showing how learners maximise their family and community resources in their quest for success. 'The point is that students are not passive spectators or "deficient rural students" – they have assets that they might mobilise if the conditions of possibility allow' (Walker and Mathebula, 2020, p. 5). Therefore, the potential for agency of the student co-researchers in this study are explored.

A 2018 World Bank report on South Africa showed that whilst access to higher education and stable labour market income appear key to individual households achieving economic security over time, there is wide differentiation between rural and urban areas. 'Poverty is higher in rural than in urban areas, and the gap between rural and urban poverty rates widened between 2006 and 2015' (Sulla and Zikhali, 2018, p. 10). Walker and Mathebula (2020) highlight that South Africa has a long history of migrant labour into towns and cities, but for young people, the most common reason for rural-urban migration is education. It is normally imperative for students to migrate long distances to attend university as these are located predominantly in urban areas though some are located in smaller towns but still very far from rural areas.

A study by Maila and Ross (2018) shows that despite the challenges students face as a result of lack of resources and information they are still prepared to travel long distances into towns and urban areas to go to university.

A strong impetus for going to university is the expectation of a better job after completing their degree. However, it does mean that students are usually very far from home in unfamiliar urban settings where they are likely to have no family or support network and have to make major adjustments to cope with city life and adapt to very different cultural circumstances.

Figured worlds, transition and agency: challenging marginalisation

Marginalisation is often understood as social exclusion from key institutions, services and activities within society but as Mowat (2015) highlights, it is important to think about what it means to be marginalised not only in terms of populations or groups but 'by looking at the experiences of individuals' (p. 456). It is important also to consider the diversity of experiences of people who may be perceived as marginalised rather than to see them as a homogenised group. Furthermore, marginalisation should not be seen as a fixed state but through subjective agency having also the potential for change:

> My starting point would be to question the notion of a "marginalised group". The difficulty with this conceptualisation is that it equates marginalisation with a global and stable state, inherent within a given population, presenting people as victims of their own fate over which they have little agency, the solution invested in the actions of the state and others. It also takes away any sense of the subjective experience of the individual and confers upon them the identity of "other"
> (Mowat, 2015, p. 457).

It is possible to think of students from rural contexts in South Africa as marginalised in the ways described in the previous section and in particular, in their relative lack of access to higher education. However, for those who have made that transition and gained access to higher education, it is important to understand how this was enabled as well as the challenges along the way. The work of Dorothy Holland et al. (1998) in *Identity and Agency in Cultural Worlds* has been utilised to help understand the idea of transitions between different worlds and trajectories through life worlds and the relationship these have with identity making and agency. Holland et al. (1998) posit the theoretical construct of *figured world*, which can be understood as social encounters in which the positions of those taking part matter, they are socially organised and located at particular times and places. They are also cultural worlds where significance is assigned to certain acts and particular value positions are held. A rural community, a learning environment or a university can be considered as figured worlds. Through our encounters with different figured worlds over time, we gain new or changing identities 'through continued participation in the positions defined by the social organisation of those worlds' activity' (Holland et al., 1998, p. 41). Therefore, identities are not fixed. Rather, how we act when encountering new figured worlds gives rise to and shapes our identities. Instead of seeing identity in essentialist terms, we consider identity dynamically as the 'self in practice' (Holland et al., 1998, p. 31).

The focus of this chapter is on the period of transition when students from rural contexts are applying to higher education and explores their experiences. What are the conditions of possibility both structural and cultural in the figured world of their rural home communities that can enable and enhance their trajectories into higher education or potentially make their transition more difficult? How does the enactment of agency in making the transition towards a new figured world of higher education influence their self-identity? Before addressing these questions, the methodology of the study will be explained.

The research study

A participatory methodology was employed, where student co-researchers participated in researching their own lives and contributed to shaping the direction of the research. The study drew on the principles of participatory research and co-operative inquiry and so worked directly with students as co-producers of knowledge. This approach aspires to work towards a 'decolonizing' mode (Bozalek and Biersteker, 2010), by aiming to avoid a deficit positioning of students as participants or subjects within the study and instead of researching *on* them, to research *with* them. However, despite trying to ensure a certain level of equity and participation in the research, it is important to acknowledge continuing power differentials that exist within all research and acknowledge the limitations for student co-researchers in being able to shape the aims and direction of the research.

Second year undergraduates from rural backgrounds were recruited as co-researchers, developing a model based on previous research in the UK (Timmis et al., 2016) and in South Africa (Rohleder and Thesen, 2012; Leibowitz et al., 2012). Fieldwork was conducted at three universities. These were 'Urban', a 'comprehensive' university with a balanced focus on research, teaching and technology; 'Town', a rural, research-led and 'previously advantaged' university; and 'Local' (a rural, teaching-led and 'previously disadvantaged[1]' university). These institutions were chosen to represent different types of universities where students from rural contexts are strongly represented and are in different geographical parts of South Africa.

There were 24 co-researchers from each of the three institutions, with a balanced number recruited from both STEM and Humanities programmes. There were 72 student co-researchers from the outset and 64 student co-researchers continued to the end of the project. The majority were born in South Africa with one from Lesotho, a neighbouring Southern African country. There was a need to acknowledge the complexities of rurality and what 'coming from a rural background' actually means. The categories provided by the South African Statistics Agency, specifically from their publication investigating appropriate definitions of urban and rural areas (Statistics South Africa, 2003), were used to inform the research. We adopted the categories of 'formal rural' and 'tribal area[2]' to differentiate the types of rural areas and obtain a balanced sample of those from formal rural and tribal area backgrounds. Rurality is both spatial and non-spatial, as explained earlier in the chapter, and so we conducted sampling using both types of indicators. For example – we defined a rural area in terms of low population density but also in terms of the civic and commercial amenities available, including schools. This is because some areas, particularly tribal areas, may have an equivalent population density to some urban areas in South Africa so population density is not sufficient to determine a rural area or background (Laldaparsad, 2006). We aimed for students who had lived and attended school in a rural area (formal rural or tribal area) for at least the first sixteen years of their lives.

Data were generated by the student co-researchers who participated in seven face-to-face workshops over approximately nine months. These workshops included group discussions and activities such as drawings of their educational journeys and mapping their learning lives. Each student co-researcher was given an iPad and they created longitudinal, personal accounts and representations of everyday practices in their rural communities and in their university academic and social lives by collecting a series of digital artefacts using an App called Evernote (or in some cases Google Docs). These included diary entries, audio recordings, drawings, photographs and other artefacts, chosen by co-researchers to represent their lives. It can be argued that multimodal methods can be helpful in reducing reliance on writing and language, especially in a second language (Rohleder and Thesen, 2012). Co-researchers received initial training and were supported throughout the data collection period, creating composite narratives of their trajectories in the final session. They subsequently participated in preliminary data analysis workshops, discussions and networking between the co-researchers from the three universities.

The qualitative data set includes over 72 discussion workshop transcripts, digital documentaries (collections of artefacts) and composite narratives created by student co-researchers. A systematic thematic and multimodal analysis of all data types was conducted by members across the project team, which produced a total of 60 themes (Ritchie and Spencer, 1994). Thematic analyses continued through an ongoing, iterative process involving whole team sessions including one with student co-researchers. Sessions with the team and co-researchers facilitated deeper, theoretically informed and multi-layered interpretations of the data (Pink, 2013).

Ethical mindfulness was central to considering the rights and responsibilities of all members of the research team, including co-researchers. Ethical approval was granted at all institutions and consent was sought from all student co-researchers in using their data. Pseudonyms are used to protect confidentiality.

Transitions from rural contexts to university

The challenges faced by students from rural contexts throughout the education system have been well documented and this has been supported by evidence from student co-researchers in this project. Lack of resources in schools and teacher absence as well as a restricted curriculum are just some of the issues faced by student co-researchers in this study. Successfully navigating compulsory schooling can be a challenge so going on to higher education is even more so (Fataar and Fillies, 2016). Given this was a large study, it is not possible to consider all aspects of the educational and cultural background of student co-researchers here, so this chapter will focus on those aspects that were important in enabling as well as setting up challenges for co-researchers in accessing higher education. Further aspects of the educational and cultural background of the student co-researchers in our study are reported in Timmis et al. (2019) and Timmis and Muhuro (2019). Three key areas will be explored relating to: firstly, the perceived value of higher education and the beliefs within the community about accessing higher education, secondly, how students got to know about university and were able to first consider the idea of applying to university and also how to do this and finally, their experiences of the application process and some of the challenges faced.

Value of higher education and community cultures

The social and cultural rural worlds that the student co-researchers come from are important in understanding their early experiences and the values they are imbued with from their family, schools and community. In rural areas, communitarian values tend to nurture greater community cohesion and collective responsibility (Masinire and Maringe, 2014; Odora-Hoppers, 2004). Thus, decision-making around going to university is not only an individual or even sometimes a family choice, but can involve the wider community.

There is much evidence of a high value placed on education and the idea of going to university. Student co-researchers were often encouraged by their family, school teachers and friends to apply to study at university:

> In the following picture, the class that is next to the two chairs was a Grade 9 class [...] I used to sit there on the chairs or inside with 3 of my fellow matriculants who were older than me. While we were playing Jazz music, they would tell me that I have the potential of going to university so I should not play but instead focus on my studies.
>
> (Evernote, Urban, 1st August 2017, Male)

Going to university is also valued as a way to escape poverty and as a route to a better life not only for the student but also for the potential benefits to the family. There is also often a financial imperative that young people if successful can provide financial support for the family and community:

> In my village it's the same thing because most of the families are poor so the parents are looking for their children to finish matric maybe go to varsity (university) and then their situation might change
> (Discussion group, Urban, 7th September 2017, Female)

However, the value placed on a university education was complex. Some student co-researchers explained that some members of the community, particularly elders may perceive university education as being for only more privileged people who are financially better off and are more likely to be white.

> Yah I would say when it comes to education it's not that much valued because the elders in the rural areas they are not familiar with education and they don't know the benefits of education like to them it's something that is for whites it's not for the community so I cannot say it's valued in the rural area where I come from.
> (Discussion group, Urban, 7th September 2017, Male)

> Many of us if you guys agree we have heard the word university and the concept thereof but there was that mentality especially if you are from

the rural areas that the children who go to universities are those ones who have cash in their families and that stuff, so even though we heard of it because of our financial status we were like no that is not for us.
(Discussion group, Urban, 17th August 2017, Male)

Student co-researchers present a complex picture of the role that families and communities play in their decisions to study at university. While in some instances rural community members place a high value on higher education and directly support them in getting to university, there are others, predominantly some elders, who do not necessarily place the same high value on higher education. Furthermore, it may be perceived by some in the figured world of the rural community that education might result in destroying rural cultural values. In addition, as a result of resource constraints some family members who may place a high value on education and may want to support young people in getting to university but do not have the resources to do so and may be concerned about the viability of this ambition given the hardships that might be faced and the financial challenges. Furthermore, as Maila and Ross (2018) argue there is often a high expectation that students from low-income families will leave school and be able to contribute financially to the family. Within the figured world of the community and the family, therefore, there is often enormous support and pride taken to encourage students into higher education but pressures for these students to contribute to the financial security of the family or a concern about the financial costs of attending university may mean that this support is not always forthcoming and students may have to look elsewhere to gain the information and support needed.

Getting to know about university

My story started in 2005 when I heard about university and in 2007 I kept on hearing it on the radio, 2010 [...] that's when I had to read through a magazine about university [...] then 2011 I was encouraged by my English teacher. She gave me newspapers and told me about people who were passing [exams].
(Discussion group, Urban, 17th August 2017, Female)

This quotation demonstrates the multiplicity of sources of information and support that the student co-researchers talked about in enabling them to learn about universities and to help them to see that this was something that could be aspired to and how to think about making it possible. Access to computers and broadband technology is extremely limited in rural areas in South Africa (Chothia, 2017) and so radio and television can be important media for getting information. Although access to technology is highly differentiated and unequal across many parts of South Africa, those living in rural areas are likely to be the most disadvantaged where it can be extremely difficult to get access, often involving travel outside of the home village and at significant cost (Timmis and Muhuro, 2019):

> I used to listen to the radio, so my listening to Xhosa Radio gave me that information about universities that were open for applying.
> (Discussion group, Town, 22nd July 2017, Male)

> Usually before the year ends most colleges advertise themselves on television for the coming year in order to attract upcoming college students. Also during television news, they broadcast activities such as student protests, graduation days, funerals of highly recognized noble persons and also student performances during festivals.
> (Discussion group, Local, 8th October 2017, Female)

The student co-researchers did also hear about university at school where the idea was introduced. However, this could also be countered by concerns about going to university not being a realistic aspiration for someone from a rural context:

> From lower grades I heard about university but I wasn't interested about it because I thought it's a place that I will never be in and I had this thing in my mind that it is only for children from rich families.
> (Discussion group, Local, 8th October 2017, Male)

> I had no dream about my future [...] Even the time I was doing grade 10, I had no vision seeing myself at varsity. I just told myself that if I pass grade 12, I will just apply to be a policeman. If that fails, I'll go to Gauteng to dig for gold. But at grade 12 level, my principal used to motivate us and tell us about life, but unfortunately I never, ever met someone who was able to tell me about the varsity life, so I heard that thing of going to the varsity it's too much cost to me, I'll be a fool following others, but now I'm not following others.
> (Discussion group, Local, 1st June 2017, Male)

For the student co-researchers the idea of going to university is clearly not an assumed one and indeed there is significant doubt about the possibility given the challenges involved. The student co-researchers in this study represent a minority that are successful in getting to university but there are many for whom this is not the case (Czerniewicz and Brown, 2014). The importance of key individuals was crucial in enabling this success and there are many accounts of the variety of people who helped student co-researchers to think about going to university, including family and friends. Information broadcast through different forms of media, including newspapers and television, are important. However, most crucial seems to be the support and encouragement given in schools. This was certainly not uniform and there were different and diverse experiences. However, for some of the student co-researchers the encouragement and advice given in school was very important in achieving their trajectory to university:

> University, through media [...] which is the television, newspapers and even like other people, family, friends, so I think they are the people who mostly introduced me to how university life works, and how do you enter university. The qualifications and all things that I needed for you to enter university and especially in the media, the radio they were really inspiring us to study hard so that we could meet the requirements for university.
> (Discussion group, Local, 1st June 2017, Female)

> This [picture above] is my home school and this always connects me back home and in my transition to university I had so much support in school were by they always bring motivational speakers and other students from university who passed their matric or grade 12 back home to share the experience with us and what could be done for us to be prepared for the world [...] the teachers always wanted us to work hard by rewarding us every time we do well. I could say I was really motivated by the school, teachers and my peers.
> (Evernote, Urban, 3rd August 2017, Female)

There was also specific support available to high achieving students through special education centres. Through such centres, extra support could be given on specific subjects but could also enable the student co-researchers to think more concretely about going to university and what it would be like at university:

> [Centre] for Maths and Sciences. It's a centre that collects hardworking learners from different schools and gives them extra lessons based on the subject they do or major in. It's a very useful program. I made it to varsity [...] because of it.
> (Evernote, Urban, 1st August 2017, Male)

There were also specific activities that were more focused on thinking about a career and encouraging students to aspire to going to university:

> This are one of the certificates that always inspired me in my transition to university. These were basically the certificate in participating in the career building academy that helps students from the village to know more about the universities in the urban area, how to apply, what to expect when you go to a new environment. In short could say this was one of the projects at home that really had more influence in my transition to university.
> (Evernote, Urban, 3rd August 2017, Female)

There were concerns expressed by some of the co-researchers about whether university would be the right choice for them. However, there were at least for some student co-researchers support and encouragement available from family, friends and the local community. The support and advice in schools and in additional extracurricular educational support was clearly crucial. This was critical in enabling the student co-researchers to begin to see going to university as a realistic option and for them to take steps in trying to achieve this, including additional support in key subjects. The ambitions of the students even when supported by the family and community can be thwarted without the structural guidance and systematic support necessary at school to develop skills and confidence in students. Some form of mentorship within schools is necessary to enable students to understand the idea of going onto higher education and to see it as something that is possible for them (Maila and Ross, 2018). However, making that a reality has significant challenges not least in the process of application, which is discussed in the next section.

Experiences of applying to university

Technology was an important consideration in finding out about universities and similarly technology was extremely vital for being able to complete online applications. Friends, family, teachers and church leaders frequently encouraged co-researchers to consider applying and helped in deciphering the requirements of online applications. There were many examples where co-researchers highlighted the importance of the Internet for finding out about the process and applying to university and access to technological resources for most was extremely limited and presented a huge challenge. In rural areas, Internet access is far more limited than in metropolitan and urban areas and the 2017 South African General Household Survey found that whilst 61.8% of households had at least one member who had access to, or used the Internet either at home, work, place of study or Internet cafés, only one-tenth of South African households had access to the Internet at home, reducing to 1% in the most rural regions (Statistics South Africa, 2018). Furthermore, the high cost of data, only available through limited outlets in rural areas increases the difficulties, including students applying to and engaging in higher education (Chothia, 2017):

> I think technology played like a huge role in actually coming here because I don't think anyone would have applied and gotten like the right information to get here, so like laptops and getting information from internet cafes [...] But I think the internet it's like the biggest resource that we used.
> (Discussion group, Town, 22nd July 2017, Female)

> Digital technology [radio] did play a very crucial role because speakers from different institutions were talking about applying to the Universities, not only one but for many Universities so as to be able to be in a good position to decide which institution do you prefer to attend when they have all admitted me, and advertisements also provided with more information about bursary opportunities that were available.
> (Discussion group, Urban, 8th October 2017, Male)

> I had no phone and I didn't even know internet and google, even a computer. I saw one when I went to apply [to university] [...] when you get to the internet café, you ask strangers to assist you.
> (Discussion group, Town, 22nd July 2017, Female)

Furthermore, once access to technology and online applications is achieved, understanding how to access forms and what is needed in an application, can also present problems:

> Even a way of finding the forms, they can say forms you can go and find or else even if you don't know where to go to find the forms, when they tell you forms are there, you don't know [how to use the] internet. Most of the time you are in the rural area, you don't know about internet you don't know about the fact that you can ask someone to fax you, or email you.
> (Discussion group, Local, 1st June 2017, Male)

Sometimes, completing the application form online is impossible and so making the trip to the university to be a 'walk in' registration becomes the only option. This does not guarantee students access as limited number of spaces in higher education results in few students being admitted as 'walk ins':

> After I passed my grade 12 I decided to come here, I didn't apply because you see I'm from a rural area I didn't have time to come to town so I could print out an application form so I waited to pass my grade 12 then after that I was a walk in at [Local] I came here looking for a school I was lucky I got it.
> (Discussion group, Local, 29th July 2017, Female)

For many students the knowledge of the process and technology required for applying to university was too complex and challenging. Oftentimes, they were reliant on the help of others. Seeking help locally from extended family members, teachers or church leaders and going to libraries and Internet cafes mediated the challenges faced. In referring to a picture of his former teacher, this student commented:

> She was the reason for me to be at [Urban] in the first place she helped me apply using her device and her money to buy airtime for data.
> (Evernote, Urban, 3rd August 2017, Male)

Although most of the student co-researchers did use some form of technology to make an application, this was not always straightforward in contexts without electricity or Internet connectivity. Sometimes the challenges were too much and support was needed from a school teacher or someone in an official capacity to help complete the application on behalf of the student.

> Unable to attach documents to university application form [...] it was so difficult everything was just so electronic, to the point that my dean had to enrol me.
> (Discussion group, Town, 25th March 2017, gender not recorded)

Whilst there were examples of universities going out to rural schools to promote their courses and universities, student co-researchers did not include discussion of help from the universities in supporting students from rural areas with their applications. This suggests a system that does not recognise the challenges of applying online in rural areas, although, at Local, they do not (yet) require all students to apply online. The different universities all offer helplines and applicants can phone for help but when applying using a phone, as many students reported they did, then it is impossible to manage the dual processing on one device.

The evidence from student co-researchers suggests that when applying to university from a rural community, there were numerous technological and technocratic barriers, particularly through the admissions processes. Universities tend to universalise their technocratic systems and processes and students' prior digital experiences and access limitations were not always acknowledged or accounted for (Timmis and Muhuro, 2019). These technocratic systems required specialised knowledges and rationalistic processes that excluded and thus reinforced marginalisation and inequalities (Danforth, 2016). Students were expected to decode or figure out systems in order to apply or engage with university processes (Timmis and Muhuro, 2019). However, it is clear from their accounts that student co-researchers used their own agency and were proactive in seeking help and working with key mentors and supportive school teachers to overcome their disadvantaged positioning. It was imperative for them to be creative and through improvisations enable them to seek solutions to the challenges they faced.

Another important consideration is funding and financial support and information on this can also be elusive and something that was relatively unknown to student co-researchers:

> We also do not know that there are so many bursaries, yah, if we finish our Matric we like we have no funding and that's it but we have bursaries out there that are willing to fund us and go to these universities, which we don't know.
> (Discussion group, Local, 1st June 2017, Female)

Knowledge about the possibilities for funding was obviously crucial for student co-researchers to see the viability of them going to university but getting knowledge and an understanding of what was available was not straightforward. Difficulties of accessing funds was something that continued to be challenging throughout their time at university (Timmis et al., 2019). Knowledge about the funding available was obviously crucial in enabling student co-researchers to see university as a viable option. However, the need for better funding and a more coherent system of funding is still being called for as part of the '#feesmustfall' movement (Maila and Ross, 2018)

Discussion and conclusions

The chapter illustrates the challenges that student co-researchers face in getting to university, but also explores the ways in which they were supported and enabled to see university as a possibility for them and to be able to make an application. It is important to re-iterate that the experiences of the student co-researchers are those for whom success has been possible. For the majority of students from rural backgrounds this success is not achieved and so it is important to understand not only the challenges faced but also what can enable success. The complexities of how student co-researchers navigate cultural and structural shifts in order to transition into higher education are important in understanding how these students, despite being amongst the most marginalised, are able to exercise agency and draw on relationships and community networks to access higher education. However, their experiences demonstrate the challenges of navigating different cultural values within the figured world of their rural communities and that of higher education. Their experiences also demonstrate the crucial role that schools can play in helping to develop the skills and confidence needed to take the required steps. Schools can provide the necessary pivot on which they can experiences themselves and their changing sense of identity as possible future students in the somewhat unknown figured world of higher education (Holland et al., 1998).

The role of the family and community was vital in supporting student co-researchers to aspire to go to university and often in giving practical help as well as emotional support. However, as shown by the experiences of some student co-researchers, the need for financial security for the family for which they were expected to contribute and also concerns about the costs of higher education and the families' inability to meet them, meant that there was a mix of experience of encouragement, but also concern and discouragement in some cases. The sense of identity rooted in their communities that student co-researchers felt was also significant in raising doubts about whether university was for them, which continues to be questioned as students in higher education challenge the system and call for it to be decolonised (Mampane et al., 2018).

The importance of the role of teachers and schools in enabling access to higher education is clear. They help the students to envisage the potential of higher education and to help them begin to see the possibility for them of making this transition. They offer insights into the application process and give the practical help needed to begin the process of accessing higher education and in some instances are essential for ensuring the student can make the application. In particular, the provision of additional tuition and special centres of expertise to help those high performing students to excel further and support their route to higher education. However, this kind of additional support may only be available for the few. Much more widespread and systematic support would be needed within a school system that is severely underfunded if the statistics on access to higher education for students from rural areas were to be significantly improved. Mentoring from teachers but also peers, particularly those who are currently at university, can also help (Malia and Ross, 2019)

Access to technology was clearly a significant barrier to students in finding out about university and in making applications. There are no easy answers to this dilemma given the scale of lack of resources in many rural communities and also in many rural schools (Malia and Ross, 2019). However, universities need to have a better understanding of the severe limitations of digital access and in rural areas and help to mitigate these constraints where possible. Existing outreach initiatives do play a role in preparing students for thinking about higher education but perhaps could be expanded and do more to give the necessary information, skills and technology to make this possible.

Marginalisation and the experiences of exclusion that it implies are clearly relevant in thinking about the experiences of these student co-researchers from rural background in South Africa. However, the processes and particularly the experiences of marginalisation are not uniform and must be understood in context and related to strategies and practices that people might take as well as the values that underpin them (McAllister, 2008). This chapter has attempted to show how the student co-researchers, despite enormous disadvantage utilised their agency in overcoming the challenges to be able to go to university but the structural constraints, including the lack of financial and technological resources, must change if more students can be enabled to follow them.

Acknowledgements

The SARiHE project is undertaken by Principal Investigators Dr Sue Timmis and Professor Thea de Wet with Co-Investigators Professor Sheila Trahar, Professor Emmanuel Mgqwashu, Dr Lisa Lucas, Kibbie Naidoo, Dr Patricia Muhuro and Professor Gina Wisker. We were accompanied on this project by 72 student co-researchers and ten institutional researchers. We fully acknowledge their contributions. This work was supported by the Newton Fund, the Economic and Social Research Council (UK) and the National Research Foundation (South Africa) [ES/P002072/1].

Notes

1 During apartheid higher education institutions were separated along racial lines with significantly fewer resources allocated to institutions designated for black (African, coloured and Indian) South Africans. By 1994, of the 36 higher education institutions there were ten historically disadvantaged universities and seven historically disadvantaged technikons designated for the use of black South Africans (Bunting, 2006). This terminology of 'previously advantaged' or 'previously disadvantaged' is in regular use to acknowledge these differences.
2 The Apartheid government introduced a Bantustan or homeland system through a series of legislations and policies including the Land Acts of 1913 and 1936. The homelands were separated along tribal lines and fell under traditional leaderships (Human Sciences Research Council, 2005). Many of these tribal areas are classified as rural.

References

Balfour, R., N. de Lange and M. Khau (2012) Editorial. Rural education and rural realities: The politics and possibilities of rural research in southern Africa, *Perspectives in Education* 30(1): i–ix.

Bozalek, V. and L. Biersteker (2010) Exploring power and privilege using participatory learning and action techniques, *Social Work Education* 29(5): 551–572.

Bunting I. (2006) The higher education landscape under apartheid, in N. Cloete, P. Maassen R. Fehnel, T. Moja, T. Gibbon and H. Perold (eds.) *Transformation in higher education: Global pressures and local realities* (pp. 35–52). Dordrecht: Springer.

Chothia, A. (2017) For SA's Rural Residents the Data Struggle Is Real, *IOL News* [online],https://www.iol.co.za/news/south-africa/for-sas-rural-residents-the-data-struggle-is-real-7399832.

Cooper, D. (2015) Social justice and South African university student enrolment data by 'race', 1998–2012: From 'skewed revolution' to 'stalled revolution', *Higher Education Quarterly* 69(3): 237–262.

Czerniewicz, L. and C. Brown (2014) The habitus and technological practices of rural students: A case study, *South African Journal of Education* [online] 34(1).

Danforth, S. (2016) Social justice and technocracy: Tracing the narratives of inclusive education in the USA, *Discourse: Studies in the Cultural Politics of Education* 37(4): 582–599.

Fataar, A. and H. Fillies (2016) Die leerpraktykvorming van hoerskoolleerders op 'n plattelandse werkersklasdorp [The learning practice formation of high school learners in a rural working class town], *Litnet Akademies* 13(2): 377–402.

Gordon, L. (2015) Race and justice in higher education: Some global challenges with attention to the South African context, in P. Tabensky and S. Matthews (eds.) *Being at home: Race, institutional culture and transformation at South African higher education institutions* (pp. 157–183). Pietermaritzburg: University of KwaZulu-Natal Press.

Green, B. and J. Reid (2014) Social cartography and rural education: Researching space(s) and place(s), in S. White and M. Corbett (eds.) *Doing educational research in rural settings: Methodological issues, international perspectives and practical solutions* (pp. 26–40). Abingdon: Routledge.

Holland, D., W. Lachicotte, D. Skinner and C. Cain (1998) *Identity and agency in cultural worlds.* Cambridge: Harvard University Press.

Jones, B., G. Coetzee, T. Bailey and S. Wickham (2008) *Factors that facilitate success for disadvantaged higher education students: An investigation into approaches used by REAP, NSFAS and selected higher education institutions.* Athlone: Rural Education Access Programme.

Laldaparsad, S. (2006) Statistical approaches for classifying and defining areas in South Africa as "urban" and "rural". Unpublished master's research report, University of Witwatersrand.

Leibowitz, B. (2017) Cognitive justice and the higher education curriculum, *Journal of Education* 68: 93–111.

Leibowitz, B. and V. Bozalek (2014) Access to higher education in South Africa, *Widening Participation and Lifelong Learning* 16(1): 91–109.

Leibowitz, B., V. Bozalek, S. van Schalkwyk and C. Winberg (2015) Institutional context matters: The professional development of academics as teachers in South African higher education, *Higher Education* 69(2): 315–330.

Leibowitz, B., L. Swartz, V. Bozalek, R. Carolissen, L. Nicholls and P. Rohleder (2012) *Community, self and identity: Educating South African university students for citizenship.* Cape Town: HSRC Press.

Maila, P. and E. Ross (2018) Perceptions of disadvantaged rural matriculants regarding factors facilitating and constraining their transition to tertiary education, *South African Journal of Education* [online] 38(1).

Mampane, R., M. Omidire and F. Aluko (2018) Decolonising higher education in Africa: Arriving at a glocal solution, *South African Journal of Education* [online] 38(4).

Masinire, A. and F. Maringe (2014) Education for rural development: Embedding rural dimensions in initial teacher preparation, *Perspectives in Education* 32(3): 146–159.

McAllister, P. (2008) Are concepts such as 'margins' and 'marginalisation' useful for analysing rural life in the Eastern Cape Province, South Africa?, *Development Southern Africa* 25(2): 169–179.

Mdepa, W. and L. Tshiwula (2012) Student diversity in South African higher education, *Widening Participation and Lifelong Learning* 13(1): 19–34.

Mgqwashu, E. (2016) Education can't be for 'the public good' if universities ignore rural life, *The Conversation* [online], https://theconversation.com/education-cant-be-for-the-public-good-if-universities-ignore-rural-life-56214.

Moreland, N., J. Chamberlain and K. Artaraz (2003) Rurality and higher education: A conceptual analysis, in M. Slowey and D. Watson (eds.) *Higher education and the lifecourse* (pp. 51–66). Maidenhead: Open University Press/Society for Research into Higher Education.

Mowat, J. (2015) Towards a new conceptualisation of marginalisation, *European Educational Research Journal* 14(5): 454–476.

Odora-Hoppers, C. (2004) The cause, the object, the citizen: Rural school learners in the void of intersecting policies and traditions of thought, *Quarterly of Education and Training in South Africa* 11(3): 17–22.

Oyedemi, T. (2020) (De)coloniality and South African academe, *Critical Studies in Education* 61(4): 399–415.

Pink, S. (2013) *Doing visual ethnography* (3rd edition). London: Sage Publications.

Ritchie, J. and L. Spencer (1994) Qualitative data analysis for applied policy research, in A. Bryman and R. Burgess (ed.) *Analyzing qualitative data* (pp. 173–194). Abingdon: Routledge.

Roberts, P. and B. Green (2013) Researching rural places: On social justice and education, *Qualitative Enquiry* 19(10): 765–774.

Rohleder, P. and L. Thesen (2012) Interpreting drawings: Reading the racialised politics of space, in B. Leibowitz, L. Swartz, V. Bozalek, R. Carolissen, L. Nicholls and P. Rohleder (eds.) *Community, self and identity: Educating South African university students for citizenship* (pp. 87–96). Cape Town: HSRC Press.

Statistics South Africa (2003) *Census 2001: Investigation into appropriate definitions of urban and rural areas for South Africa: Discussion document*. Pretoria: Statistics South Africa.

Statistics South Africa (2018) *General Household Survey 2017*. Pretoria: Statistics South Africa.

Sulla, V. and P. Zikhali (2018) *Overcoming poverty and inequality in South Africa: An assessment of drivers, constraints and opportunities*. Washington: World Bank.

Timmis, S., E. Mgqwashu, K. Naidoo, P. Muhuro, S. Trahar, L. Lucas, G. Wisker and T. de Wet (2019) Encounters with coloniality: Students' experiences of transitions from rural contexts into higher education in South Africa, *Critical Studies in Learning and Teaching* 7(1): 76–101.

Timmis, S. and P. Muhuro (2019) De-coding or de-colonising the technocratic university? Rural students' digital transitions to South African higher education, *Learning Media and Technology* 44(3): 252–266.

Timmis, S., W. Yee and E. Bent (2016) Digital diversity and belonging in higher education: A social justice proposition, in E. Brown, A. Krasteva and M. Ranieri (eds.) *E-learning & social media: education and citizenship for the digital 21st Century* (pp.297–320). Charlotte: Information Age Publishing.

Walker, M. and M. Mathebula (2020) Low-income rural youth migrating to urban universities in South Africa: Opportunities and inequalities, *Compare* 50(8): 1193–1209.

Section III

Indigeneity

Chapter 11

Improving higher education success for Australian Indigenous peoples
Examples of promising practice

Kim Robertson, James A. Smith and Steven Larkin

Introduction

Aboriginal and Torres Strait Islander Australians have historically been excluded from higher education in Australia. It took a national Referendum in 1967 to change the Constitution to allow the Commonwealth Government to make laws in relation to Aboriginal peoples. Prior to that (and with the exception of the Australian Territories), the lives of Indigenous[1] Australians were heavily regulated by State Governments, and in many cases closely controlled Indigenous peoples' access to their own resources and those of the nation state, including education at all levels.

The first recorded university graduations of Aboriginal Australians were Ms Margaret Weir with a Diploma from the University of Melbourne in 1959 (Ewen and Hanrahan, n.d.) and Mr Charles Perkins who graduated with a Bachelor of Arts from the University of Sydney in 1966 (University of Sydney, n.d.). Not surprisingly, these achievements occurred at a time of significant sociopolitical change in Australia, including the first explicit public policy efforts by the Australian Government to increase Indigenous participation in tertiary education, through financial support.

It is now 50 years since the Aboriginal Study Grants Scheme (precursor to the current Abstudy Scheme) was introduced in 1969 as part of a Gorton Government 'commitment to implement special measures to assist Australian Aboriginal and Torres Strait Islander people to achieve their educational, social and economic objectives through financial assistance to study' (Department of Social Services, 2018, p. 6). Indigenous Australians welcomed the opportunities, and despite the many and varied hurdles to academic success, enrolment numbers and completions have steadily increased over this time. However, data shows that Indigenous students still have lower access, participation and completion rates compared with non-Indigenous students (Moore et al., 2018; Pollard, 2018; Shalley et al., 2019; Smith et al., 2018a). Indigenous students from regional and remote areas face additional challenges and barriers in accessing and participating in higher education and are further under-represented in the national Indigenous higher education student population. They are likely to belong to multiple equity groups, attracting significant educational disadvantage.

Improving Indigenous education outcomes is now a key focus of many national and global education policies (Smith et al., 2018a; Street et al., 2018). The need to improve Aboriginal and Torres Strait Islander student access to, and participation and success in, post-compulsory education is therefore well documented (Behrendt et al., 2012; Bradley et al., 2008; Frawley, Smith and Larkin, 2015a; Rigney, 2011). Yet there remains a need for more research and evaluation that adopts an Indigenist methodological approach (Rigney, 2017), acknowledging the value of the voices of Aboriginal and Torres Strait Islander student, staff and researcher perspectives about enablers and barriers of completing a higher education degree (Frawley, Smith and Larkin, 2015a).

The focus of this chapter is to highlight where Indigenous higher education strategies and their implementation are showing signs of success and to outline where further investment is required to ensure Indigenous students in Australia are supported to achieve improved higher education outcomes. We primarily draw examples of promising practice from three existing peer-reviewed academic publications alongside the empirical findings from a regional university case study from a recent cross-jurisdictional nationally-funded research grant from the Commonwealth Office of Learning and Teaching (OLT). All publications and research have focused on ways of building and strengthening Indigenous pathways, participation and achievement in higher education. In using these evidence sources, we have deliberately adopted a strength-based narrative throughout this chapter. This is consistent with calls from Indigenous scholars to explicitly shift away from deficit discourses, particularly in health and education sectors (Fogarty et al., 2018; Vass, 2013; Wilson et al., 2017).

The primary evidence sources we have used include the following:

- A book chapter entitled 'Indigenous pathways and transitions into higher education: an introduction' (Frawley, Larkin and Smith, 2017a);
- A report entitled '"Can't be what you can't see": the transition of Aboriginal and Torres Strait Islander students into higher education' (Kinnane et al., 2014);
- A 2015 special issue of *Learning Communities: International Journal of Learning in Social Contexts* journal entitled 'Indigenous pathways and transitions into higher education' (Frawley et al., 2015b);
- A consultation paper entitled 'Accelerating Indigenous higher education' and published by the National Aboriginal and Torres Strait Islander Higher Education Consortium (NATSIHEC, 2018)[2]; and
- An empirical case study from an unpublished report entitled 'Addressing the gap between policy and implementation: strategies for improving educational outcomes of Indigenous students' (Fredericks et al., 2019).

Our analysis is framed against the recommendations of the watershed report into Indigenous higher education in Australia – the 'Review of higher education access and outcomes for Aboriginal and Torres Strait Islander people' (Behrendt et al., 2012) commonly known, and hereafter referred to, as the Behrendt Review. Specifically, we have grouped these recommendations under the following three key themes:

- the involvement of Indigenous people in university leadership and governance;
- the provision of appropriate support services provided across the entire university; and
- collaborative approaches with local communities, relevant professional organizations and employers.

Our overarching question was 'what are the emerging promising practices (including strategies, activities and policy guidelines) likely to improve Indigenous higher education outcomes as benchmarked against the Behrendt Review (2012) recommendations?'

Theme A: the involvement of Indigenous people in university leadership and governance

University strategic planning and Indigenous strategies

A scan of university websites shows that many universities in Australia make public reference to Indigenous education within their strategic aspirations, and some have articulated this into their corporate documents, governance structures and executive level positions. This is a relatively recent occurrence. The University of Sydney, Australia's oldest university, developed its first ever Aboriginal and Torres Strait Islander integrated strategy in 2012 (Sherwood and Russell-Mundine, 2017, p. 133). The Behrendt Review (2012) highlights the need for universities to demonstrate such inclusion within the policies and the processes of university governance at the highest levels. This is strongly supported by the NATSIHEC report (2018), which recommends that universities define the commitment to Aboriginal and Torres Strait Islander higher education across all areas of university strategic plans, not just in equity/widening participation strategies or the introduction/opening statements of strategic plans (Recommendation 2). It further suggests strong accountability measures in the planning, recommending that universities 'develop KPIs in core areas of the university with accountability linked to the vice-chancellor and the deputy vice-chancellor in the related core area' (p. 15).

As an example, one regional university studied in Fredericks et al. (2019), acknowledges the importance of Indigenous knowledge systems and reflects a desire to create an environment which is respectful of, and celebrates, Indigenous peoples' culture and knowledge systems, through a specific high-level policy document (Charles Darwin University [CDU], 2015; Street et al., 2017). This document has been in place for some time and it identifies the senior staff who hold accountabilities for implementing policies and provides some guiding principles. The University's ten-year Strategic Plan (CDU, 2019) also includes a focus on Indigenous education and leadership as one of five pillars. Indigenous education interests are therefore articulated as strategically important as other university core business areas; teaching and learning, research, internationalization and engagement. Priorities are identified as appointment of Indigenous staff and capacity building of Indigenous staff, improved outcomes in teaching, learning, research and engagement (with targets) and supporting the aspirations of Indigenous peoples through tailored programs and improving cultural competency across the organization. An important achievement has been the endorsement of an Indigenous-specific whole-of-university strategy which aligns with the ten-year Strategic Plan (CDU, 2019). The Indigenous strategy identifies priority projects and senior managers responsible for actions and includes some targets, with more to be identified by proposed intra-university working groups. Though there is no explicit strategy to increase the number of Indigenous people in senior management positions, since the Behrendt Review (2012) at least one additional fixed-term executive (director) level position was established. Additionally, the Indigenous Pro Vice Chancellor position is part of the Executive Leadership Group and reports directly to the Vice Chancellor. There are currently no Indigenous identified positions on Council or high-level committees, other than those occupied by the Indigenous Pro Vice Chancellor. It is implicit that senior managers contribute to achieving parity targets, as outlined in the Strategic Plan and Indigenous Strategy, though there is an Indigenous Advisory Council that was established prior to the Behrendt Review (2012) to provide strategic, culturally-relevant advice and guidance.

Theme B: the provision of appropriate support services provided *across* the entire university

Indigenous student services and Commonwealth funding programs

All Australian universities have Indigenous-specific student centers designed to increase access and participation. These centers, known generically as Indigenous Education Units (IEUs) units provide support to Aboriginal and Torres Strait Islander students, create a network of Aboriginal and Torres Strait Islander students/academics and provide an Indigenous presence on all Australian university campuses (NATSIHEC, 2018). The Commonwealth Government provides funding to universities explicitly for this purpose through a range of funding grants which are administered by different Government departments. Contracts are negotiated separately with each institution.

Universities provide Indigenous student services, some through multiple centers, and Frawley et al. (2015) provides many examples of this. They offer regional outreach and engagement for all Indigenous students, including regular phone calls and face-to-face contact. Services include tutorial and academic support, Indigenous scholarships, funding for students to travel away from home base to attend lectures and placements, academic skills workshops, advocacy and referral services (see, for example, Fredericks et al., 2015; Hall and Wilkes, 2015). Some co-ordinate dedicated valedictory ceremonies for all graduating Indigenous students and many institutions have created unique Indigenous-designed stoles for use in formal graduations. The IEUs have continued to deliver tutorial support (previously the Indigenous Tutorial Assistance Scheme [ITAS]), which is now administered through the Indigenous Advancement Strategy alongside the Indigenous Student Success Program (ISSP) funding scheme (Smith et al., 2017a). The funding model is now performance based, placing a much sharper focus on participation and completion. This presents different challenges for different IEUs as some have direct responsibility for teaching and research delivery and outcomes, whereas others have responsibility for support services only.

One of the regional universities studied (Fredericks et al., 2019) has developed a leading model for student support through a dedicated Indigenous accommodation space at the on-campus residential facility for students which is co-managed by the IEU staff and the University facilities management team and prioritizes room bookings for Indigenous students attending programs on campus who are funded through the Away From Base (AFB) program. AFB provides funding assistance for Indigenous students who are undertaking an approved course by distance education, to access compulsory course elements (e.g. intensive teaching sessions, assessments and fieldwork) in a location away from their permanent home, for short periods of time (National Indigenous Australians Agency, n.d.; Smith et al., 2017). The University initiated and developed its own administrative and data systems and processes to successfully administer the AFB program. This has received national interest and attention to guide sector-wide change. The IEU team has also played a significant role in developing a whole-of-university approach to Indigenous scholarship administration at the University and has created a position of 'assistant manager of grants and scholarships' to assist with this task.

Reconciliation

Australian universities are increasingly committing to reconciliation with Aboriginal and Torres Strait Islander peoples through the development and implementation of Reconciliation Action Plans (RAPs). RAPs are an initiative of Reconciliation Australia[3] (RA) and in 2019, there are over 1,000 organizations across Australia that have RAPs. Over 1.5 million Australians study or work in an organization with a RAP.

Gunstone (2019) presented on his recent research into RAPs in Australian universities and highlights some critical issues including the need for better measurement of RAPs and their impact on transforming their organization. Swinburne University conducted an electronic survey with all staff, asking what RAP events or activities (such as cultural competency training) they engaged in over the last three years, and to rate their own personal level, and Swinburne's level, of cultural competency and whether this has changed since the RAP process. A high response rate of around 25% was received and additional methods are being undertaken to broaden the research and develop improved measurement of RAP outcomes. Gunstone summarizes as follows:

> RAPs with their requirements for measurable actions and targets, offer organisations a mechanism to deal with the long-standing failure to addressing substantive reconciliation in their organisation. However, organisations need to also more significantly engage with a number of critical issues such as; Indigenous rights, self-determination, deficit discourse, governance, culture, white fragility, white privilege, employment and institutional and individual racism, to genuinely make more meaningful impact in their organisation and to contribute to a more meaningful national reconciliation environment.
>
> (Gunstone, 2019, n.p.)

The inaugural RAP Conference was held in 2018 in partnership with Swinburne University, with a second in 2019 in partnership between RA and Curtin University. Despite some of the challenges and constraints identified, the NATSIHEC report (2018) supports the inclusion of RAPs as potentially useful tools that can complement a wider university approach and recommends that universities 'implement reconciliation action plans and plans that complement wider university strategies and University Australia's Indigenous Strategy 2017–2020, and that act to change the culture of institutions and naturalize the teaching of Aboriginal and Torres Strait Islander science' (NATSIHEC, 2018, p. 15).

The research currently underway into meaningful RAP evaluations will provide much needed guidance on their specific impacts for universities, and for Indigenous student success.

Teaching, learning and research

Universities commonly articulate their Learning and Teaching Plans as key corporate documents, with a small percentage of universities also developing Indigenous-specific Learning and Teaching Plans.

The Behrendt Review (2012) states that 'Indigenous knowledge, translated into practical curriculum, teaching practices and graduate attributes makes important contributions to helping professionals meet the needs of Indigenous communities' (p. 94). Frawley (2017) purports that, though to a certain extent Australian universities have heeded these calls, the presence of Indigenous knowledges and Indigenous-specific graduate attributes in the academy presents some tensions.

One university reviewed in the Fredericks et al. (2019) study had an Indigenous Learning and Teaching Plan, and this has again been identified as a priority in the new Indigenous strategy. The University also has a distinctive graduate attribute that states that graduates are expected to gain an appreciation and understanding of Indigenous Australians. An online resource called the 'Indigenous research resource centre' has been developed and includes a unit about supervising students researching in Indigenous spaces. The University commits to strengthening their Indigenous research focus; developing an industry engagement strategy with Indigenous organizations and partners to align research priorities and developing an Indigenous higher degree research cohort program and have identified the need to increase the numbers of Indigenous research students and academics.

Further investment in this area is highly desirable, particularly where universities conduct a large percentage of research about Aboriginal and Torres Strait Islander peoples, and/or their professional graduates (especially in health and education) will be expected to work with Indigenous Australians.

Contributions to Indigenous higher education research and evaluation

Recent years have seen significant contributions to building an evidence-base about ways to strengthen Indigenous higher education in Australia. Researchers from one regional university from the Fredericks et al. (2019) have led, or contributed to, nearly $8.5 million in Indigenous higher education research and evaluation projects over the past four years (2014–2018). Many of these projects have been completed in collaboration with other higher education institutions, peak bodies/networks and national centers, such as NATSIHEC, the National Indigenous Research and Knowledges Network and the National Centre for Student Equity in Higher Education (NCSEHE).

Rigney (2017) outlines a design and evaluation framework for Indigenisation of Australian universities and analyses the development and implementation of the University of Adelaide's whole of institution Indigenous Education Strategy between 2012 and 2014. The case study indicates that university-wide approaches can be implemented to good effect using the following enablers:

> leadership, resources to support enactment, well-trained high-quality staff, supportive environments to resolve challenges, collaborative staff learning and teacher training, inter-cultural competency, a positive

institutional culture, a capable and culturally-responsive organisation, and ensuring that Indigenous success drives all actors and actions.

(Rigney, 2017, p. 59)

There have been successive calls for the development of a national monitoring and evaluation framework/strategy to assist in improving Indigenous higher education outcomes in Australia (Smith et al., 2017b). To date, the Australian Government has failed to adequately respond to these calls. This is disappointing given that strategies for strengthening evaluation in Indigenous higher education contexts in Australia have been clearly documented (Smith et al., 2017b, 2018b; Smith and Robertson, 2020). Importantly, this evaluation research has deliberately privileged the voices of Indigenous scholars. In addition, NCSEHE (2018) hosted a legacy and capacity building workshop on evaluation and Indigenous data sovereignty in April 2018, which identified a series of principles that can underpin Indigenous higher education evaluation work (Smith and Robertson, 2020). Again, this privileged Indigenous perspectives.

University preparation programs

The Behrendt Review (2012) noted that in 2010 over half of the Indigenous students entered university via university preparation (or enabling) programs compared with only 17% of non-Indigenous students.

Enabling programs support Indigenous students to access education, and through education attain better economic and socio-economic futures for themselves and their families, and Fredericks et al. (2017) provide evidence of the multi-layered benefits of such programs through a qualitative study across three Australian universities. Key findings suggest that the development of a best-practice framework for Indigenous enabling programs should consider the following:

- Pedagogy, curriculum and mode of delivery;
- The framework of the institution ethos and drivers for implementation;
- Understanding local, regional and national Indigenous perspectives; and
- Support structures for staff and their professional development needs.

The study mentioned above surmised that;

> the strengthening of enabling education for Indigenous Australians is regarded as an excellent platform for offering Indigenous students the best chance of "success", with "success" having a multi-layered interpretation that includes impacts on participation (for the institution), reaffirming personal identity and confidence (for the learner) and broader community and indirect benefits.
>
> (Fredericks et al., 2017, pp. 130–131)

Theme C: collaborative approaches with local communities, relevant professional organizations and employers

Indigenous workforce strategies and agreements

Statistics show that, despite growing Indigenous student enrolments, the numbers of Indigenous staff in universities are relatively low (NATSIHEC, 2018). The low numbers of Indigenous people in academic positions are particularly concerning, especially when linked to the identified enabling practices of embedding Indigenous knowledges into teaching, learning and research. In addition, increasing the Indigenous workforce is perceived to help in combatting individual and institutional racism experienced in universities. Figure 11.1 indicates some alarming results from the National Tertiary Education Union's (NTEU) second report into the levels of racial discrimination, cultural respect and lateral violence in both society and the workplace (NTEU, 2018). This project was undertaken as a follow-up to the earlier '*I'm not a racist, but…*' report (NTEU, 2011), to gauge the levels of racism, discrimination and lateral violence amongst Aboriginal and Torres Strait Islander union members today and to compare findings from the 2011 report to the 2018 survey findings.

The report shows some improvements in the numbers of anti-discrimination policies and workplace training throughout Australian universities. However, according to members, the implementation and the usefulness of these in ameliorating incidents of discrimination against Indigenous staff have decreased since 2011.

The NATSIHEC Consultation Paper (2018) revealed that current proportion of the Indigenous academic workforce is 0.82% and, as of 2015, falls well short of the target parity rate of 2.7%. Indeed, to meet the parity target,

---

Racial discrimination in the workplace

- Racial discrimination in the workplace has not reduced since 2011. Respondents to the member survey expressed a 13.1 % increase in Aboriginal and Torres Strait Islander staff often experiencing racial discrimination.
- 47.7 % of survey responses expressed that colleagues are the main perpetrators of racial discrimination in the workplace.
- In attempting to address issues of racial discrimination in the workplace, survey respondents indicated that little action is being undertaken. Only 21.7 % of respondents stated that action was taken, 12.2 % indicated positive action was instigated yet only 11.6 % of survey respondents stated that the action taken by their university was successful in addressing issues of racial discrimination in the workplace.

Figure 11.1 Racial discrimination in the workplace (Source: NTEU, 2018).

> **Successful innovations**
>
> - The University of Newcastle has a program called Indigenous New Career Academics (INCAs), wherein participants spend one-third of their time on each of PhD studies, teaching and research, over a three-year, full-time contract. Some INCAs are attached to the Wollotuka Institute and some are located in faculties and disciplines.
> - Charles Sturt University's program includes a four-year contract comprising 75% PhD work, 20% teaching and 5% administration. Participants are mentored to move to an ongoing position within the university.
> - Murdoch University has a similar program to Charles Sturt University, with 20% teaching and the remaining workload comprising PhD completion.
> - The Sydney University Leadership program is for 5 years with 1 day a week teaching and the rest PhD. There is also the Breadwinners programme for undergraduates with family responsibilities. These programs are successful because they focus on the core business of completing a PhD, teaching and research.

Figure 11.2 Successful innovations (Source: NATSIHEC, 2018).

set for 2015, would have required a further 816 Indigenous academics to be employed in Australian universities. It was also noted that a much smaller proportion of Indigenous academics work in the higher levels of employment in universities than non-Indigenous academics. This needs to change.

Notwithstanding such limitations, the available data suggest that the Indigenous academic workforce is slowly growing but at a much lower rate than the non-Indigenous workforce. The NATSIHEC Consultation Paper (2018) provides a comprehensive and systemic range of recommendations targeted at institutions, Government and the higher education sector to improve the numbers of Indigenous academic workforce, and includes some examples of promising employment practices in recruiting and retaining Indigenous staff in universities, where the institutions operate programs designed to 'grow their own' academic staff (see Figure 11.2).

Additional enabling factors in the recruitment and retention of Indigenous staff were identified as; affirmative action in recruitment, national networks, setting employment targets, supporting staff and formally acknowledging Indigenous staff contributions (NATSIHEC, 2018, p. 149).

Cultural competency

In Australia, the concept of cultural competency, especially when applied to the education sector, is not simply a matter of responding to cultural or ethnic difference. Rather the cultural incompetence of schooling and post-schooling institutions has its foundations in the historical exclusion and discrimination experienced by Indigenous peoples in education (Sherwood and Russell-Mundine, 2017). The legacy of that past is still evident in our present. It should not be surprising then, that the Behrendt Review (2012, p. 24) Recommendation 32 reads:

> That universities continue to develop and implement a range of strategies to improve the cultural understanding and awareness of staff, students and researchers within their institution, including the provision of cultural competency training.

The ongoing importance of this is reiterated through the Universities Australia commitment to cultural competence and the NATSIHEC Report (2018, pp. 15–16) Recommendation 4:

> That universities develop and implement facilitation procedures for embedding cultural programs across the university that result in a culturally safe and responsive environment for the entire university community, including [six specific actions].

The National Centre for Cultural Competence (NCCC) was established in 2014 at the University of Sydney as a joint venture between the Australian Government and the university. Their mission is to be a major contributor – through collaboration and partnerships with diverse individuals, communities and organizations – at the interface between cultural competence and Aboriginal and Torres Strait Islander peoples, and aligns with their whole-of-university Indigenous strategy. The NCCC's vision is long-term, as they state:

> We develop knowledge and build capacity in cultural competence across a range of social domains. The NCCC has initially prioritised the growth of student, staff and community cultural competence. Our broader perspective is forming national and international partnerships, initiating dialogues and implementing initiatives to improve educational, economic, cultural and social outcomes throughout society.
>
> (NCCC, n.d., n.p.)

The NCCC recently compiled an open access book on the topic of cultural competence in higher education that provides unique perspectives about strategies being adopted, or that could be adopted, in Australia (Frawley et al., 2020). At the institutional level, an increasing number of universities have mandated induction training for staff to attend a short (one or two days) cultural awareness training session, usually delivered by a local Aboriginal academic or consultant. Many universities host an Academic/ Elder-in-Residence, some of whom are located within the IEU. Building cultural competence through Indigenous knowledges into curriculum and pedagogy has also been a focus of some academics.

As will be highlighted later through the qualitative interviews, these types of strategies and practices are important to Indigenous staff and students, and an evaluation of their effectiveness deserves more attention (Smith and Robertson, 2020).

Indigenous identity

There is limited evidence of universities having an explicit strategy to encourage Aboriginal and Torres Strait Islander students to identify their Aboriginal and/or Torres Strait Islander heritage, although it is usually an option on the standard university enrolment forms. In addition, the scope of services offered to Indigenous students through the designated IEUs is actively promoted across the university and in the community, to encourage Indigenous students to utilize the services on offer. To access some of the funding, services and scholarships, Indigenous students are required to provide written verification of their Indigenous heritage.

Social marketing approaches that profile existing Indigenous staff and students, and the reasons they choose to identify, could have a twofold impact. It could increase levels of identification; and it could potentially acknowledge and celebrate the achievements of existing Indigenous students and staff. The University of Saskatchewan in Canada has adopted this approach (Smith et al., 2018b), and James Cook University has also used this approach through online marketing strategies (Frawley, Ober et al., 2017b).

To summarize, the results of the policy analysis are mixed, and the various university examples demonstrate that the elements of best-practice have been championed at different universities across the sector including the large established institutions and smaller, regional universities with significantly different profiles. The above analytical review of strategic policies and practices has been triangulated with qualitative data in the form of one-on-one interviews with fifteen staff and Indigenous students from one regional university with a high level of Indigenous enrolments. This is supported by growing national and international commentary about privileging Indigenous narratives, and associated epistemologies and ontologies, in discussions about Indigenous higher education. It also aligns with contemporary discourses about Indigenous data sovereignty (Smith et al., 2018b; Wilks et al., 2018). The voices of those interviewed are highlighted next.

Findings: interviews

The findings presented below provide a snapshot of the enabling practices and barriers identified by both the students and staff from one regional university involved in the OLT research project mentioned above (Pollard et al., 2017). The findings are presented separately to allow comparisons and differences in opinions between these two groups.

Perspectives from Indigenous students about their success in higher education: enablers

Indigenous students identified a range of enablers that supported them to participate in, and succeed at, university. One spoke about accessing basic infrastructure to support their studies, stating: 'It was great having access to the Indigenous computer lab, access to the computer, printer, and internet on campus' (Student 8).

However, the majority of students spoke about the importance of social support received through Indigenous colleagues and staff and that of their own family. This is consistent with recent scholarship about self-efficacy among Indigenous students (Frawley, Ober et al., 2017b). As one student commented,

> I know everyone and I'm friendly with most of the people [at University] but at the end of the day, I just know I am more comfortable around Indigenous people [...] I feel like I know that they [non-Indigenous people] are always going to be thinking, "You're Indigenous. You're getting everything because you are". I just know.
>
> (Student 3)

Some participants indicated that it was not just the social support within itself, but the level and intensity of social support provided. For example, 'there was a lot more support that I received than I thought I would, especially from lecturers and other students' (Student 6).

One student suggested that the level of direct support offered by the university – as a regional university – was perceived to be greater than that provided at larger institutions, where their needs may get lost. As one student, suggested,

> The lecturers from what I understand, you can get it more one-on-one with them and the major universities you can't really, there's so many (students), it's very hard.
>
> (Student 9)

Academic support was also perceived to be important among Indigenous students,

> ...my tutor. The factor is tutor support. I feel like I have an amazing tutor [...] she's just really great.
>
> (Student 4)

Students frequently spoke about both the pastoral support provided through the Indigenous services center. It was the safe space provided through the center that was considered to be most important:

It just feels that sometimes people just don't know how to handle me, they don't want to deal with me, but here [Indigenous Student Services] is a very, very, very, very safe space for me.

(Student 7)

Perspectives from Indigenous students about their success in higher education: barriers

For many Indigenous students, it appears that university is a great unknown. This can be a deterrent if students are not fully prepared or adequately supported as they enter a higher education context. As one participant simply stated, 'I didn't really have a view of how it [University] would be' (Student 6).

Some students were concerned about their own previous educational experiences: 'I thought I was going to be in strife because I didn't do very well at school' (Student 7). Whereas other students were confronted about the delivery of education:

What didn't meet my expectation coming into my higher education degree was sitting and listening to a lecturer for two hours, not asking questions, not the group discussions or activities, anything.

(Student 8)

Students also expressed dissatisfaction in the skill level of tutors and lack of communication between schools, colleges and the tutorial service:

I've been [...] offered tutors who aren't skilled in the area, and I can't understand why there's not much communication between my School (College) and the tutorial service.

(Student 9)

Other students also raised concerns about the cultural appropriateness of some services offered through other areas of the University. For example, one female student mentioned, 'I went to a writing course at the library and it's just one-to-one with a guy, like it's so culturally unsafe' (Student 4).

Personal motivation was articulated as a critical element of Indigenous student success. One interviewee talking about another student who had recently withdrawn from study, stated, 'You can't force someone to do something if their heart's not in it' (Student 3).

The discussion below provides a more expansive account of the various enablers and barriers discussed by participants throughout the interviews. Overall, Indigenous students identified more enablers than barriers, indicating significant potential for positive change and the adoption of a strengths-based approach to better support Indigenous student achievement.

Perspectives from staff about Indigenous student success in higher education: enablers

In speaking about the importance of IT resources, one staff member stated, 'we use technology as much as we can, I think that's a big benefit these days' (Staff 5). This is an important concept within the context of this university, which has had an increased focus on online learning over the past few years. This has meant that nearly half of the Indigenous students enrolled in higher education, are doing so through online course delivery. This includes a significant proportion in metropolitan areas of Australia.

Staff also emphasized the importance of creating culturally-safe spaces. This was often articulated in relation to having an increased number of Indigenous staff within the university 'I think it's very important as an Aboriginal space, that we do have Aboriginal faces' (Staff 1).

The motivation level of students was also perceived as an enabler. One staff member indicated that they were more inclined to support a student if they could see that the student had a good level of motivation to complete the task at hand, 'sometimes it's really about how badly you want to get it done and are you ready to spend much more time and effort to do that' (Staff 6). Most staff recognized that student success was highly dependent upon (Indigenous) students having the capability to become proficient in academic English. Indigenous students that developed their proficiency in academic English throughout their university journey were often perceived by staff as having the greatest potential to achieve 'success':

> As they [students] progress on their study trajectory, as they gain more and more familiarity with reading academic works [...] and the way English is used in an academic sense, and just through practice, people are able to take on that dialect.
>
> (Staff 2)

Conversely, those students who struggled with academic writing and were perceived to be 'at-risk' of not completing, were perceived by staff to benefit from targeted tutorial assistance:

> With these identified [at-risk] students, where we could be wrapping more support, especially tutorial support trying to increase hours for them [...] and definitely working with the academic support officers, and hopefully there's some liaison with the lecturers.
>
> (Staff 1)

This indicates that the role of Indigenous tutorial assistance cannot be underestimated and was succinctly summarized by one staff member who said, 'having tutorial support is major with our students, especially in that first year' (Staff 1).

Perspectives from staff about Indigenous student success in higher education: barriers

Whilst most staff generally believed that there was a benefit in having dedicated academic and support services tailored for the needs of Indigenous students, some staff also indicated that such services could be better aligned with teaching activities. As one staff member commented, 'I believe there's a real disconnect between [Indigenous student services] and the lecturers' (Staff 1).

Some staff reported that a few Indigenous students did not have a good grasp on what university was likely to constitute and suggested this was one reason that these students are likely to withdraw from their studies: 'I don't believe they've [Indigenous students] got a very well-developed idea of what a university is' (Staff 2). Other staff members recognized that the potential lack of understanding about expectations at university related to the fact that many Indigenous students were first-in-family to complete high school and therefore have the opportunity to attend university:

> Non-Indigenous students they may have some role model, or example in their family or someone they know who has actually achieved it [...] whereas for people from an Indigenous background they may be the first person [in their family] to ever finish high school.
>
> (Staff 5)

Whilst academic English was perceived as an enabler, it was also perceived as a barrier if the basics could not be mastered. This was often highlighted in the context of providing adequate support for regional and remote students that may have English as an Additional Language or Dialect. As one staff member stated, 'academic English [...] just about all the assessments are based on your fluency with that dialect and that's generally a barrier' (Staff 2).

Although, the real barrier was not necessarily perceived to be the learner's ability to achieve proficiency in academic English, more-so that there is a lack of tailored support services for Indigenous students in comparison to migrant populations, captured by one staff member who stated, 'Indigenous students in Australia [...] don't have any access to any English as a second language programs, because we are Australian citizens' (Staff 4).

Finally, the perceived lack of suitable financial support to Indigenous students was also frequently cited as a barrier to success: 'I think what we could do is provide a little more financial support for students' (Staff 5).

Discussion

This section brings together the promising practice examples in relation to Behrendt Review (2012) recommendations; and the analysis of interviews with Indigenous students, and current staff, at a regional Australian university. We discuss the common enabling practices and barriers in the context of the research findings. Our analysis has shown that key practices that enable and support Indigenous participation and completion at university include:

- The promotion and provision of study pathways with clear career prospects;
- The provision of support from their employer which came in a range of forms – financial, paid release from work, opportunities for work-related study projects and scheduled study time;
- Access to, and the provision of, quality pastoral care (reported to be most successful when delivered by Indigenous staff, and when student needs were considered holistically and from a cultural standpoint);
- The provision of a dedicated Indigenous student facility and services including study spaces, places to network and build relationships with peers, and with staff;
- The provision of culturally safe environments, though this meant different things to different people. It included engaging with culturally-competent staff (both non-Indigenous and Indigenous), the presence and valuing of Indigenous staff, the provision of a specific student facility (mentioned above), visual acknowledgement of local Indigenous languages and history, Indigenous artwork and signage, individually-tailored study environments and programs and events that engage Indigenous families and the broader Indigenous community;
- Access to adequate academic tutorial support (i.e. ITAS/ISSP) was deemed to be critically important;
- The provision of culturally-responsive enabling programs to facilitate entry into undergraduate education courses for Indigenous students of all ages;
- The provision of flexible scholarships, including scholarships for part-time students, to reduce financial stress. This was also emphasized as important in the Indigenous component of the internal evaluation of the university's targeted student recruitment program; and
- A high level of personal resilience and self-determination. This was often accompanied by a goal-oriented approach to higher education.

Conversely, this analysis also identified barriers or practices which prevent or hinder Indigenous participation and completion at university, including the following:

- Insufficient student preparation prior to, and upon entry into, university;
- Unrealistic or indifferent student expectations in comparison to those set by the university and its staff;
- Financial stress in relation to both course costs and daily-living expenses, particularly for those supporting their families (including extended families), and particularly relevant in the rural and remote Australia where living costs are high;

- The challenges of juggling work/life/study commitments can be onerous. Study is usually the first priority to be dropped if things get unmanageable, or where study deadlines are inflexible;
- The rigidity of higher education delivery was raised repeatedly. This was particularly important for full-time workers and/or mature age students that already had substantial life experience with demonstrated time management and multitasking capabilities. A more flexible and individually co-ordinated approach to study load negotiated in the context of all course requirements (across a semester), rather than just individual unit requirements, could be beneficial;
- The academic language and literacy expectations of higher education were considered to be daunting for some Indigenous students, particularly those transitioning from VET. This has also been identified through previous research (Smith et al., 2017a; Frawley, Smith et al., 2017c).
- The English language, literacy and numeracy standard of Indigenous students can be a barrier, particularly among regional and remote students. This has been identified previously as a key policy issue in the Northern Territory, which requires urgent attention (Language, Literacy and Numeracy Action Network, 2017; Shalley and Stewart, 2017).
- Additional support mechanisms such as formalized peer-support networks are required for students 'at-risk' of withdrawing from study.
- There are inevitably individual lecturers at university that lack the cultural competence to teach effectively, or even worse, exhibit blatantly racist behaviors. More concerted disciplinary and/or corrective action should be put in place when such instances are raised by Indigenous students, staff and observers.

Additional issues, as outlined below, have been identified throughout this research:

- Many students perceived that regional universities were less confronting than larger universities and provided a deeper level of one-on-one support. This is consistent with the recent work on remote students generally (Pollard, 2018). It is also important within the context of the recent 'Independent Review into Regional, Rural and Remote Education' in Australia (Halsey, 2018);
- Turnover of key Indigenous leadership roles, such as the Indigenous Pro Vice Chancellor (or equivalent positions), has been problematic for some universities. This is especially impactful in a context that requires advocacy, strong leadership and sustained action;
- Increasing numbers of students are studying at university through online platforms, and this trend is the same for Indigenous students. Yet, a paucity of research examines this impact. Given that the online learning environment has changed rapidly since the Behrendt Review (2012) particularly during the COVID-19 global pandemic where Indigenous

and equity groups were required to study online without necessarily having the infrastructure, resources or capacity to do so, this area urgently requires more nuanced research.
- There was minimal evidence of Australian universities investing in the evaluation of Indigenous-focused higher education program and policy initiatives, despite the importance of such work for guiding quality improvement (Smith et al., 2018b; Smith and Robertson, 2020). A refresh of the *On Stony Ground* report (Moreton-Robinson et al., 2011) is urgently required. It is also noted that Smith et al. (2018b, p. 8) have recently recommended that a 'meta-analysis of Australian research studies and evaluation reports examining Indigenous student and staff perspectives about pathways, transitions, participation, success and achievement in higher education' is needed;
- Little research has examined the impact of undergraduate studies on the employability of Indigenous students, although this surfaced as an important issue for retaining Indigenous students;
- Indigenous higher education scholarship is increasingly demanding that universities acknowledge the impact of colonization, and the restraints of Western power and privilege, in promoting Indigenous student achievement (Moreton-Robinson et al., 2011; Smith et al., 2018b). We recommend this is more explicitly incorporated into Indigenous higher education strategy development, and practice; and
- Further evaluation and research into the substantial investments made by some universities into the delivery of Indigenous-focused public events and participation in local Indigenous festivals, would also be beneficial.

Conclusion

This chapter has provided an overview of promising practices aimed at improving Indigenous student pathways, participation and achievement in higher education within Australia universities. This has been complemented by empirical research with Indigenous students. We have compared these findings with national recommendations from the Behrendt Review (2012) and the NATSIHEC Report (2018). We acknowledge this is only one way to frame a strength-based discussion about Indigenous higher education and trust it will be a useful contribution to compare and contrast with other similar analyses as they emerge. Attention now needs to turn to the effective implementation and evaluation of these strategies for the retention of current and future Indigenous students, and their aspirations for success.

We also highlighted a series of enabling practices and barriers specific to one regional Australian university context. Continued investment in Indigenous student-centered services has been emphasized, with a greater need for Indigenous-focused outreach and preparatory activities with prospective students and their families. Additionally, the provision of a culturally-safe environment, focused on delivering high quality education to Indigenous students, is essential. We highlight where further nuanced research would be beneficial.

Not all investments required are financially onerous – much of the recent research points to organizational culture and embedding systemic values in institutions which can withstand the tides of national policy change in higher education, including those relating to Indigenous higher education, equity and higher education, and the other economic challenges which the sector faces. Whilst smaller, regionally-based universities may be more vulnerable to such external factors, research highlights they may also be better placed to demonstrate innovative, relationship-based solutions for Indigenous students due to their proximity to Aboriginal communities and potential for agile responses to policy and regulatory changes. We trust this chapter has provided a useful overview of the systems changes and strategies required to further improve Indigenous Australian student outcomes over the ensuing years.

Acknowledgements

We would like to thank Ms Charmaine Woods and Dr Kellie Pollard for assisting with the policy review and interviews presented in this chapter, and all of the key informants for volunteering their time to participate and share their voices.

Notes

1 The term Indigenous is used interchangeably in this chapter to refer to Aboriginal and/or Torres Strait Islander peoples of Australia. The term is used for brevity. The authors acknowledge the diversity of views with regard to preferences for these terms.
2 NATSIHEC (AC) (www.natsihec.edu.au) and its antecedent group has advocated for Aboriginal and Torres Strait Islander access, scholarship and research in the higher education sector since the early 1990s and is a key advisor to the Federal Minister for Education and Training for Aboriginal and Torres Strait Islander Higher Education. Membership to the Consortium is open to Aboriginal and Torres Strait Islander people working in higher education.
3 Reconciliation Australia (www.reconciliation.org.au) was established in 2001 as the national expert body on reconciliation in Australia. It is an independent, not-for-profit organisation whose vision is for a just, equitable and reconciled Australia.

References

Behrendt, L., S. Larkin, R. Griew and P. Kelly (2012) *Review of higher education access and outcomes for Aboriginal and Torres Strait Islander people: Final report.* Canberra: Australian Government.

Bradley, D., P. Noonan, H. Nugent and B. Scales (2008) *Review of Australian higher education: Final report*. Canberra: Australian Government.

Charles Darwin University (2015) *Connect discover grow: Strategic plan 2015–2025*. Darwin: Charles Darwin University.

Charles Darwin University (2019) *Indigenous leadership strategy 2019–2021*. Darwin: Charles Darwin University.

Department of Social Services (2018) *ABSTUDY policy manual* (1st May 2018 update). Canberra: Australian Government.

Ewen, S. and D. Hanrahan (n.d.) *The unique value of indigenous knowledge* [online], https://pursuit.unimelb.edu.au/articles/the-unique-value-of-indigenous-knowledge.

Fogarty, W., M. Lovell, J. Langenberg and M.-J. Heron (2018) *Deficit discourse and strengths-based approaches: Changing the narrative of Aboriginal and Torres Strait Islander health and wellbeing*. Melbourne: Lowitja Institute.

Frawley, J. (2017). Indigenous knowledges, graduate attributes, and recognition of prior learning for advanced standing: tensions within the academy, in J. Frawley, S. Larkin and J. Smith (eds.) *Indigenous pathways, transitions and participation in higher education: From policy to practice* (pp. 65–80). Singapore: Springer Nature.

Frawley, J., S. Larkin and J. Smith (2017a) Indigenous pathways and transitions into higher education: An introduction, in J. Frawley, S. Larkin and J. Smith (eds.) *Indigenous pathways, transitions and participation in higher education: From policy to practice* (pp. 3–14). Singapore: Springer Nature.

Frawley, J., R. Ober, M. Olcay and J. Smith (2017b) *Indigenous achievement in higher education and the role of self-efficacy: Rippling stories of success*. Perth: National Centre for Student Equity in Higher Education.

Frawley, J., G. Russell and J. Sherwood (eds.) (2020) *Cultural competence and the higher education sector: Australian perspectives, policies and practice*. Singapore, Springer Nature.

Frawley, J., J. Smith, A. Gunstone, E. Pechenkina, W. Ludwig and A. Stewart (2017c) Indigenous VET to higher education pathway and transitions: A literature review, *International Studies in Widening Participation* 4(1): 34–54.

Frawley, J., J. Smith and S. Larkin (2015a) Beyond Bradley and Behrendt: Building a stronger evidence-base about Indigenous pathways and transitions into higher education, *Learning Communities: International Journal of Learning in Social Contexts* 17: 8–11.

Frawley, J., J. Smith, S. Larkin and M. Christie (eds.) (2015b) Indigenous pathways and transitions into higher education, *Learning Communities: International Journal of Learning in Social Contexts* 17 (special issue).

Fredericks, B., S. Kinnear, C. Daniels, P. Croft-Warcon and J. Mann (2017) Perspectives on enabling education for Indigenous students at three comprehensive universities in regional Australia, in J. Frawley, S. Larkin and J. Smith (eds.) *Indigenous pathways, transitions and participation in higher education: From policy to practice* (pp. 119–132). Singapore: Springer Nature.

Fredericks, B., T. Lamey, M. Mikecz and F. Santamaria (2015) Enabling people to 'see what they can be': The Community Aspiration Program (CAP-ED), *Learning Communities: International Journal of Learning in Social Contexts* 17: 54–63.

Fredericks, B., D. Wood, J. Smith, L.-I. Rigney, M. Grupetta, J. May, F. Watkin Lui, S. Larkin and J. Judd (2019) Addressing the gap between policy and implementation: Strategies for improving educational outcomes of Indigenous students. Unpublished report.

Gunstone, A. (2019) Substantive reconciliation: The impact of Reconciliation Action Plans, *AIATSIS National Indigenous Research Conference*, 3rd July, Brisbane.

Hall, L. and M. Wilkes (2015) "It's a safe environment for us Indigenous students." Creating a culturally safe learning space for Indigenous pre-tertiary students, *Learning Communities: International Journal of Learning in Social Contexts* 17: 112–122.

Halsey, J. (2018) *Independent review into regional, rural and remote education: Final report*. Adelaide: Commonwealth of Australia.

Kinnane, S., J. Wilks, K. Wilson, T. Hughes, S. Thomas, N. Drew, K. McNaught and K. Watson (2014) *'Can't be what you can't see': The transition of Aboriginal and Torres Strait Islander students into higher education*. Sydney: Department of Education.

Language, Literacy and Numeracy Action Network (2017) *Updated action statement on Aboriginal adult English LLN in the Northern Territory*. Darwin: Charles Darwin University.

Moore, T., J. Smith and K. Robertson (2018) *Whole of Community Engagement Initiative: Evidence based actions to support remote Indigenous participation in higher education*. Darwin: Charles Darwin University.

Moreton-Robinson, A., M. Walter, D. Singh and M. Kimber (2011) *On stony ground: Governance and Aboriginal and Torres Strait Islander participation in Australian universities*. Canberra: Department of Education, Employment and Workplace Relations.

National Aboriginal and Torres Strait Islander Higher Education Consortium (2018) *Accelerating Indigenous higher education: Consultation paper*. Adelaide: National Aboriginal and Torres Strait Islander Higher Education Consortium.

National Centre for Cultural Competence (n.d.) *About us* [online], https://www.sydney.edu.au/nccc/about-us.html.

National Centre for Student Equity in Higher Education (2018) *Building legacy and capacity workshop three: Indigenous perspectives on evaluation in Indigenous higher education*. Perth: National Centre for Student Equity in Higher Education.

National Indigenous Australians Agency (n.d.) *Away-from-base mixed-mode program* [online], https://www.niaa.gov.au/indigenous-affairs/education/away-base-mixed-mode-program-afb.

National Tertiary Education Union (2011) *I'm not a racist, but…: report on cultural respect, racial discrimination, lateral violence and related policy at Australia's universities*. Melbourne: National Tertiary Education Union.

National Tertiary Education Union (2018) *I'm still not a racist, but…: 2nd report on cultural respect, racial discrimination, lateral violence and related policy at Australia's universities*. Melbourne: National Tertiary Education Union.

Pollard, K., C. Woods and J. Smith (2017) *Analysis of Charles Darwin University policies pertaining to Indigenous students and staff*. Darwin: Charles Darwin University.

Pollard, L. (2018) *Remote student university success: An analysis of policy and practice*. Perth: National Centre for Student Equity in Higher Education.

Rigney, L. (2011) *Indigenous higher education reform and Indigenous knowledges*. Adelaide: University of Adelaide.

Rigney, L. (2017) A design and evaluation framework for Indigenisation of Australian universities, in J. Frawley, S. Larkin and J. Smith (eds.) *Indigenous pathways, transitions and participation in higher education: From policy to practice* (pp. 45–64). Singapore: Springer Nature.

Shalley, F. and A. Stewart (2017) *Aboriginal adult English language, literacy and numeracy in the Northern Territory: A statistical overview*. Darwin: Charles Darwin University.

Shalley, F., J. Smith, D. Wood, B. Fredericks and K. Robertson (2019) *Understanding completion rates of Indigenous higher education students from two regional universities: A cohort analysis*. Perth: National Centre for Student Equity in Higher Education.

Sherwood, J. and G. Russell-Mundine (2017). How do we do business: Setting the agenda for cultural competence at the University of Sydney, in J. Frawley, S. Larkin and J. Smith (eds.) *Indigenous pathways, transitions and participation in higher education: from policy to practice* (pp. 133–150). Singapore: Springer Nature.

Smith, J., J. Frawley, E. Pechenkina, W. Ludwig, C. Robertson, A. Gunstone and S. Larkin (2017a) *Identifying strategies for promoting VET to higher education transitions for Indigenous learners*. Perth: National Centre for Student Equity in Higher Education.

Smith, J., M. Bullot, V. Kerr, D. Yibarbuk, M. Olcay and F. Shalley (2018a) Maintaining connection to family, culture and community: Implications for remote Aboriginal and Torres Strait Islander pathways into higher education, *Rural Society* 27(2): 108–124.

Smith, J., K. Pollard, K. Robertson and F. Shalley (2018b) *Strengthening evaluation in Indigenous higher education contexts in Australia: Equity Fellowship report*. Perth: National Centre for Student Equity in Higher Education.

Smith, J., K. Pollard, K. Robertson and S. Trinidad (2017b) What do we know about evaluation in Indigenous higher education contexts in Australia? *International Studies in Widening Participation* 4(2): 18–31.

Smith, JA, Robertson, K (2020) Evaluating cultural competence in indigenous higher education contexts in Australia: A challenge for change. In: Frawley, J, Russell, G, Sherwood, J (eds) *Cultural Competence and the Higher Education Sector: Australian Perspectives, Policies and Practice*. Singapore: Springer, 117–135.

Street, C., J. Guenther, J. Smith, K. Robertson, S. Motlap, W. Ludwig and R. Ober (2017) The evolution of Indigenous higher education in Northern Territory, Australia: A chronological review of policy, *International Studies in Widening Participation* 4(2): 32–51.

Street, C., J. Guenther, J. Smith, K. Robertson, S. Motlap, W. Ludwig and K. Gillan (2018) A historical overview of responses to Indigenous higher education policy in the Northern Territory: Progress or procrastination? *Australian Universities' Review* 60(2): 38–48.

University of Sydney (n.d.) *A history of thinking forward* [online], https://sydney.edu.au/about-us/our-story/australias-first-university.html.

Vass, G. (2013) 'So, what is wrong with indigenous education?' Perspective, position and power beyond a deficit discourse, *Australian Journal of Indigenous Education* 41(2): 85–96.

Wilks, J., G. Kennedy, N. Drew and K. Wilson (2018) Indigenous data sovereignty in higher education: towards a decolonised data quality framework, *Australian Universities' Review* 60(2): 4–14.

Wilson, B., B. Fogarty, M. Dodson, S. Gorringe, L. Waller and K. McCallum (2017) Deficit discourse in Indigenous education, *AIATSIS National Indigenous Research Conference*, 21st March, Canberra.

Chapter 12

The Orang Asli and higher education access in Malaysia

Realising the dream

Graeme Atherton

Introduction

Malaysia is one of, if not *the,* leading nations in the south East Asian region where the development of its higher education system is concerned. It is a hub for international students attracting nearly twice the number of students than the rest of the countries in the ASEAN[1] region (Atherton et al., 2018). Over the period from 2002 to 2014 the number of higher education students expanded by nearly 70% (Ministry of Education, 2015). However, despite the overall progress being made in terms of the growing student numbers, there are still parts of the Malaysian population where for the vast majority, higher education remains a distant dream. This chapter will focus on the indigenous Orang Asli people of Malaysia and their access to higher education. As will be outlined below, the Orang Asli endure a range of educational and social challenges many of which originate in discrimination and prejudice. They are also at the forefront of the impact of climate change in the region. In this context what is being done at present to support greater progression in compulsory and higher education will be explored and the implications of the Orang Asli experience for our understanding of how the most marginalised populations in the world can access higher education.

The Orang Asli

The Orang Asli are the oldest populations of Malaysia living in the main rural and village communities. Orang Asli communities have descendants that can traced back to tribes that have lived in Peninsular Malaysia as early as 11,000 BC (Shah et al., 2018). The Orang Asli is in fact a term used to describe a heterogeneous group of eighteen groups living in Peninsular Malaysia. In terms of the groups that make up the Orang Asli overall, Figure 12.1 shows how they are divided into three main groups.

The groups described in Figure 12.1 differ significantly in size. The Negrito Orang Asli tribes are the smallest group representing only around 3% of the whole population. It is also the oldest of the recognised groups. The largest of the three broad groups in Figure 12.1 is the Senoi Orang Asli who constitute 54% of the total population of Orang Asli in Peninsular

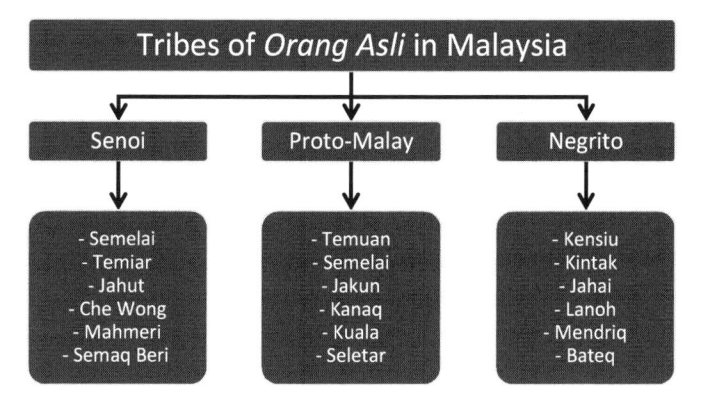

```
Tribes of Orang Asli in Malaysia
    │              │              │
   Senoi       Proto-Malay      Negrito
    │              │              │
 - Semelai      - Temuan       - Kensiu
 - Temiar       - Semelai      - Kintak
 - Jahut        - Jakun        - Jahai
 - Che Wong     - Kanaq        - Lanoh
 - Mahmeri      - Kuala        - Mendriq
 - Semaq Beri   - Seletar      - Bateq
```

Figure 12.1 Tribes of Orang Asli in Malaysia.

Malaysia (Jabatan Hal Ehwal Orang Asli [JHEOA], 2002; Nicholas, 2000). As Shah et al. (2018, p. 1157) state, 'there are small physical differences between the Senois and Negritos which are the slightly taller physical stature, lighter skinned and wavy hair without curls'. Senois are proficient hunters and foragers. Descending from the Polynesian Malay group, the Proto-Malay group are around 43% of the total Orang Asli population in Peninsular Malaysia (JHEOA, 2002; Nicholas, 2000).

While Figure 12.1 appears to delineate clearly the Orang Asli peoples into eighteen groups within three strands, the reality is far more complex than this. Within these tribes there are over 90 different communities. As with other indigenous communities around the world, the term, 'the Orang Asli', was introduced for administrative reasons in order to classify the range of rural indigenous minority peoples. As Masron et al. (2013, p. 79) state, before 1960 'the communities in the Peninsular did not see themselves as a homogenous group, nor did they consciously adopt common ethnic markers to differentiate themselves from the dominant population'.

The diversity within the Orang Asli reflects the preciously held identities, beliefs and lifestyles of the different communities and their geography. Their lifestyles and sources of income differ. In Peninsular Malaysia, the Orang Laut, Orang Seletar and Mahmerior live by the coast and, in the main, fish to survive. Other communities such as the Temuan, Jakun and Semai people own rubber, oil palm or cocoa farms while about 40% are resident within forest regions. A small minority of the communities are nomadic or semi-nomadic.

Ethnicity in Malaysia

Accepting the differences within the Orang Asli community, overall the population of Orang Asli represents less than 1% of the total population of around 30 million people in Malaysia (Shah et al., 2018). As a whole, the country is characterised by ethnic and religious division. The Bumiputera or Malay people represent 61.8% of the population (Malaysian Government, 2016). While often described as indigenous the Malaysian constitution defines Malay 'as a person who professes the religion of Islam, habitually speaks Malay, conforms to Malay customs and is the child of a Malaysian parent' (Barnard, 2003).

The constitution does not actually use the term Bumiputera. The term has developed over the last 40 years as a way of describing 'natives' of Malaysia including Malay people (defined more by religion) and also other indigenous peoples of east Malaysia. The Orang Asli are included in this definition at particular times, but also are seen as separate at others. The malleability of the term Bumiputera with regard to the Orang Asli provides the opportunity for policy interventions which are targeted at their particular needs at times, but also to ignore these needs at other times under blanket policies for all of those who are Bumiputera. The remaining 40% of the population are split between those who are Chinese Malaysian at just over 20% and then Indian at nearly 7%. The Chinese Malaysian group are the most economically powerful in the country. Over 75% of the bottom 50% of earners in 2014 were Bumiputera as opposed to 16% of the Chinese population (Abdul Khalid and Yang, 2019). Chinese Malaysians do, though, also experience challenges as a result of positive discrimination in favour of the Bumiputera in the fields of housing, finance, governance and also education. These affirmative actions were implemented in the 1970s in order to defuse inter-ethnic tensions following riots and disorder after the 1969 national elections which had led many Malays, already marginalised economically, to feel excluded from public life as well. As is outlined below, the New Economic Policy which included these affirmative action policies, implemented from the 1970s to the 1990s, had profound implications for the development of the Malaysian higher education system.

Orang Asli and socio-economic life

As a group, the Orang Asli experience poverty, poor health outcomes and low levels of life expectancy (Rusaslina, 2010). The numbers of Orang Asli experiencing poverty and a detailed explanation of the nature of this poverty are very hard to obtain. Reporting on his visit to Malaysia, Professor Philip Alston, United Nations Special Rapporteur on extreme poverty and human rights, was scathing in his assessment of the way in which data on poverty were collected in the country:

> Malaysian officials consistently say that poverty has been virtually eliminated, with only "pockets" remaining. That claim, however, is based on a statistical sleight of hand which has had nefarious consequences.

The use of a very low and highly unrealistic poverty line obscures the more troubling reality that millions of families scrape by on very low incomes and there is significant hardship in urban as well as rural areas.
(Office of the United Nations High Commissioner for Human Rights, 2019, n.p.)

Building an accurate picture of the economic and social circumstances of the Orang Asli is especially difficult. As senior economist for the World Bank Kenneth Simler stated in 2019, 'the Household Income Survey (HIS) that is used as the basis for poverty measurement excludes Orang Asli settlements, foreign workers and refugees' (Simler, 2019, n.p.).

Data assembled in 2015 by the United Nations as part of an assessment of the progress against the United Nations Millennium Development Goals (United Nations Malaysia, 2015) suggested that around 35% of Orang Asli were living in poverty (Economic Planning Unit [EPU], 2015). However, one of the major issues with understanding poverty in Malaysia identified by Philip Alston in his report quoted above and by the World Bank was the poverty line measure used in the country which is unrealistically low. Given this and the lack of data it is fair to assume that more Orang Asli are living in poverty or at least on very low incomes close to subsistence. These income levels, while they may be low, may be just enough to enable Orang Asli to survive in a way of life consistent with their traditional customs and the operations of their local economies. However, they may not be enough to be consistent with educational progression of young people from the community through the education system up to higher education. Data from the same report does show however the importance of education to addressing poverty. As Table 12.2 below shows the incidence of poverty falls remarkably for those with post-secondary education to less than 2% from over 46% for those with secondary education.

Table 12.2 The relationship between poverty and education in Malaysia

Education of household head	Incidence of poverty %			
	2004	2007	2009	2014
Primary or less	10.0	6.9	7.9	1.8
Secondary	3.9	2.7	2.8	0.6
Post-secondary or tertiary	0.5	0.3	0.2	0.0
	Proportion of poor households %			
Primary or less	67.0	61.9	61.2	51.9
Secondary	31.6	36.5	37.6	46.2
Post-secondary or tertiary	1.4	1.6	1.3	1.9

Source: EPU, 2015

The Orang Asli and education

The levels of educational attainment and progression for Orang Asli children are far below the Malaysian average (Wahab et al., 2016). As with information on the economic circumstances of the Orang Asli population up to date data that captures the experiences of the whole community is an area for development, but what data is available suggests that the point of transition to secondary education is particularly important. While enrolment in primary school is good, with United Nations Malaysia (2015) estimating it at close to 100%, drop out entering and over the secondary phase is very high. The report estimates that only half of those who entered secondary school actually complete their studies.

The reasons given for the high levels of drop out from secondary education are varied. To an extent it is argued it reflects both practical and cultural concerns Orang Asli parents hold regarding the participation of their children in education (Abdullah et al., 2013, Mustapha, 2013). Given the nature of the local Orang Asli economies detailed above, the rationale for children staying in education beyond the level where they have developed basic literacy skills is apparently questioned by many of their parents. They may also be required as workers within these economies. Alongside these cultural barriers, there are practical ones in particular the distance some children have to travel to actually undertake secondary school study. For some children this can involve up to and over two hours travelling per day.

Provision has been made for Orang Asli young people to stay in residential secondary schools in the week, returning to their families at the weekends. However, such schools are not ideal and many parents are unhappy about their children being away from home at such a young age. There have been high profile incidents in recent years where Orang Asli children have died trying to escape these schools (Palansamy, 2019). The role of such schools as productive ways of facilitating greater engagement by indigenous people's children in formal education has been widely questioned. Staffed often by teachers who themselves are not there by choice, they have been accused of trying to force Orang Asli children to surrender their culture and identities (Rabahi et al., 2015).

The failures of the education system to understand the needs of Orang Asli communities and also to be a site of active prejudice against children from these communities are cited as the other major contributing factor to poor attainment and drop out. Evidence suggests that instances of teachers referring to Orang Asli children as animals or routinely subjecting them to discriminatory treatment are too common. As one student stated in a 2017 article: 'In schools, students and even the teachers call us dirty. They call us pigs, they call us dogs' (Study International, 2017, n.p).

There is also research that calls into question the assumption that Orang Asli parents do not, for whatever reason, want their children to do well in school. Ethnographic work looking at the relationship between education and Orang Asli culture, done with albeit a small number of Orang Asli families, suggested that 'the emerging grounded theory of Orang Asli parents leading learning illuminates the [parental interest] that happened at home, which is not visible to the educators in the school, thus the common perception of the lack of Orang Asli [parental interest]' (Rabahi et al., 2015, p. 101).

The research argues that while as with other low income groups across the world engagement with school is a challenge, this does not mean parents do not hold educational aspirations for their children. The other key point to emerge from this work is how the role of parents is conceived. As Rabahi et al. (2015, p. 100) state:

> the role of parents in the learning system of the Orang Asli households is a shared responsibility. The conceptual role of parents includes mothers, mothers [sic], grandparents, older siblings, aunts, uncles and older relatives.

The Malaysian higher education system

The first university in the country, the University of Malaya, was founded in 1949. Reflecting the colonial status of the country at the time the University was created in the image of British universities. Further universities were not introduced until the 1970s with four more public universities and then a further two in the 1980s. There are now twenty public universities in Malaysia. According to Wan et al. (2015, p. 267), 'these Malaysian public universities continued to be predominantly "Western" with a combination of British legacy, American influence, and indigenization of the local culture'. In the mid-1990s and through the introduction of the Private Higher Education Institutions Act in 1996, a large number of private universities were formed in Malaysia. By 2019 there were nearly 500 private higher learning institutions (Hamisah binti Tapsir, 2019).

The majority of these institutions are small specialist institutions but there are 33 fully fledged private universities. The two different types of higher education are quite contrasting in a number of ways. Private universities were introduced to undertake a more vocational and economic function while as Wan et al. (2015, p. 269) state 'public universities have been viewed to fulfil the developmental and nation-building purposes'. Private higher education institutions were also a means of enabling and expanding access to those in society who could not enter public universities (Tham, 2011).

As the demand for higher education increased with an expanding Malaysian population, as with many developing world countries, they turned to the private sector to meet this demand. In doing so, though, this leads to different types of higher education on offer. The focus in the public universities is predominantly on Bachelor level qualifications, while in the private sector over 50% are pursuing sub-degree level courses. In terms of financing, public universities are heavily subsidised by the state meaning that they are able to offer very low fees in comparison to private universities that have to be self-sustaining. Hence, private universities have to be both responsive to student demand and innovative in how they offer their courses in order to survive. They have grown strongly however, and include a strong international element with a number of branch campuses of leading western universities. In 2018 the division between students in Malaysian higher education was close to 50:50 with 500,000 students enrolled in the twenty public universities and more than 600,000 in the nearly 500 strong private learning institutes (Hamisah binti Tapsir, 2019).

While the differences between public and private universities outlined above are similar to those found in other developing higher education systems, the distinctiveness in the Malaysian case is found in who progresses to public and who to private universities.

Prior to the disorder following the 1969 general elections described above, Chinese students occupied the majority of the places in public universities. One of the results of the 'New Economic Policy' that followed this disorder was a huge shift in the composition of public universities as a result of positive discrimination policies in favour of Bumiputera students via a quota system. The quota system pushed many Malaysian students to study overseas meaning that by 1985 only 15,000 Malaysian students were studying in local higher education institutions, compared with 68,000 studying overseas through their private funds, especially in the United Kingdom, the United States and Australia (Tan, 2002).

The introduction of private universities in the 1990s provided a domestic option for non-Bumiputera students in particular and this form of provision expanded radically. In 2002 the quota was removed and a policy of meritocracy was introduced (Wan, 2007). However, the divisions in participation in higher education by sector between different ethnic groups in Malaysia remain. One of the main reasons for the remaining division is the system of entry into higher education in Malaysia. There are two routes into higher education in Malaysia – via the matriculation and STPM[2] programmes. The former is shorter at one year and the latter takes two years, being modelled on the British 'A-Level' system. The matriculation route was introduced in 1998 and was reserved for Bumiputera students. It provides an almost guaranteed route into lower cost – and still seen as more prestigious – public universities. Despite some recent attempts to open up more places on the matriculation route for non-Bumiputera students in 2018 when the programme was expanded to accept 40,000 students instead of 25,000, the 90:10 quota was kept in place. In 2018–19 over 20,040 applications were received from non-Bumiputera students but only 4,068 were eventually accepted (Tho, 2019).

The Orang Asli and higher education

The picture where Orang Asli students and higher education progression are concerned is one of individual students overcoming the cultural and structural barriers described above in the context of a system already divided along ethnic lines. Data on the exact numbers of Orang Asli students studying in the Malaysian higher education system is hard to obtain. The data that are available appear to show some significant increases over the early 2000s. From 2009 to 2016 the number of Orang Asli students in higher education increased from 75 to nearly 600. Reports since then suggest it has further increased, with the Minister for Education stating that there were 767 Orang Asli students in the system in 2016 (Malay Mail, 2017). The distribution of these students across the higher education system in Malaysia is uneven though. Data from 2015 showed that nearly half were attending one university – Universiti Teknologi MARA (known as UiTM) (Abdullah 2017).

The government of Malaysia has attempted to address the economic and educational inequalities facing the Orang Asli while also maintaining a commitment to extending access to higher education. In the Tenth Malaysian Plan (2011–2015), targets were set to reduce the incidence of poverty among Orang Asli from 50% to 25%. On access to higher education, the Malaysian Higher Education Blueprint from 2015 to 2025 makes continued references to improving equity in the system, although the detail is light:

> Data is not yet available to accurately assess socio-economic equity in the Malaysian higher education system. As such [...] the Ministry will commence regular data collection to allow the measurement and comparison of student outcomes from various demographic groups. The Ministry [...] is committed to improving the enrolment rate and completion rate of students from socio-economically disadvantaged backgrounds and communities.
>
> (Ministry of Education, 2015, p. C-4)

The goals in access per se are ambitious – with a goal of 70% of young people entering higher education by 2025. In terms of specifically higher education progression there have been attempts to offer additional support to support potential Orang Asli students. In the early 2010s, special entry programmes into higher education were introduced for Orang Asli students (Division of Student Admission, 2011). More recently a programme called the 'special lane initiative' has been undertaken by the government to enable greater higher education progression for Orang Asli students (Malay Mail, 2019).

Enabling progression to higher education for Orang Asli students

Some efforts are clearly underway in Malaysia to support greater progression and success in higher education for those from Orang Asli communities and there does appear to be some progress being made.

However, any such efforts are occurring in the context of a group in Malaysian society who have been and remain extremely marginalised. They are also being attempted at the same time as other long standing inequalities in the Malaysian higher education system remain unaddressed. But even given these inequalities, there is an awareness of issues of equity in higher education participation and high-level policy commitments to addressing such issues which is comparatively rare globally, aside from in what is still a developing country. The picture where Orang Asli students and higher education progression is concerned is one of individual students overcoming the huge barriers described above. The extremely low numbers make it hard to develop an understanding of what progression and success could look like at the collective or group level.

The engagement of universities in helping better understand the educational and other social and political challenges the Orang Asli face is a way to build a relationship between the communities and higher education. A range of other examples exist of university-led research working with Orang Asli communities. Looking at the Australian experience, where there is an active academic engagement with the experiences of indigenous people, may be instructive here. There are significantly higher levels of participation in higher education by indigenous communities in Australia (Abdullah, 2017). The contexts are very different across countries and comparisons very difficult but the implication is that potential to make progress in Malaysia exists. Academic engagement via research and scholarship is not the same as pursuing an active policy agenda at the political and institutional level to increase access. The latter requires a much greater level of investment, in particular by universities. But it can be part of a broader agenda that frames the relationship between higher education and the Orang Asli in a more reciprocal way that rejects the acculturation which has defined their past relationship with the school system.

This rejection of the acculturation approach should be central to informing attempts to increase opportunities to access higher education for the Orang Asli people. It involves moving away from the deficit approach that has characterised much of how schooling for the Orang Asli and other indigenous people has been framed. Instead the starting point for this access agenda should be recognising the unique relationship that Orang Asli have with education and the strengths this can bring. As Nicholas (2006) argues with relation to schooling, education to an Orang Asli is about being a good person as much as it is about economic progression. Integrating such an understanding into how universities may engage with Orang Asli communities is a challenge but there are examples of Orang Asli students themselves shaping the pedagogical narrative. For example, the Faculty of Law of the National University of Malaysia, popularly known as Universiti Kebangsaan Malaysia (UKM), organised a motivational programme for Orang Asli students in 2014. The programme was facilitated by Orang Asli 'Student Icons' – twelve Orang Asli students representing various faculties in UKM (Nordin et al., 2018).

Without an improvement in completion and attainment in schooling for Orang Asli children, the numbers who can take advantage of any preferential admissions arrangements will be inevitably limited. There is a further risk of replicating what has happened in India where quotas are in place to enable progression to higher education for lower caste groups, but there are not enough learners from these groups to fill them (Navani, 2016).

What this engagement between schools and universities looks like also needs to be defined and then developed. Despite its public commitment to extending equitable access to higher education, which is rare in the vast majority of countries in the world, including those in southeast Asia, there is no systematic programme/policy to enable systematic collaborative working between schools and universities focused on raising the attainment of learners from groups under-represented in higher education and marginalised in society. Such work is found only in handful of countries (Atherton, 2016). The work in these countries offers some pointers, in particular with respect to indigenous communities in Australia and Canada, but needs to be redefined in the context of the specific Orang Asli experience.

The Orang Asli and the higher education system

In order to make such progress deeper, more fundamental questions regarding the position of the Orang Asli in 21st century Malaysia need to be confronted. Ethnic identity continues to shape the political landscape in contemporary Malaysia with, it is argued, the present affirmative action for Bumiputera both failing the poorest and skewing political decisions (Nair, 2020). The fact the Orang Asli community represent only around 1% of the Malaysian population within this broader landscape will always represent a challenge in terms of getting traction around the needs of the Orang Asli people. Again, though, this may be where higher education can contribute via gathering data and offering advocacy on Orang Asli issues. Such a role for higher education in Malaysia, though, may not be a natural one. Both private and public universities depend heavily in different ways on political support. There is not the history of higher education via institutions or students acting as political actors in Malaysia or most Asian countries that exists in South America or to an extent in Europe, for example. It is possible, though, to continue to push for higher education equity to be part of the overall Orang Asli agenda and, reciprocally, Orang Asli needs being part of the higher education equity agenda. In this reciprocity there is more chance of stronger connections between the compulsory and tertiary education systems.

Creating specific admission routes into higher education for Orang Asli students, such as the 'special lanes' described above, is welcome but it can only go so far in extending access into higher education for the community.

Finally, the uniqueness of the Malaysian system offers another set of challenges and opportunities where the progression of learners from Orang Asli communities is concerned. The private higher education sector across the world has been accused of offering provision of a variable quality, but it has offered routes into higher education for learners from more diverse backgrounds and a broader range of qualifications. There are also a number of strong private higher education providers in Malaysia. However, routes into such providers may be financially prohibitive for Orang Asli students. Entering public universities may be more feasible then in Malaysia, but this would require these older, more academic universities to accommodate the needs of Orang Asli. There are some advantages to the divisions in the Malaysian system. In most countries the tendency is to assume that those from low income, rural or other marginalised backgrounds should naturally pursue more vocational courses and/or focus on shorter higher education qualifications. This assumption comes from a combination of the perceived preferences of the groups themselves and also reflects taken-for-granted power relationships. These preferences are usually borne of a lack of understanding of the characteristics of more academic subjects and a risk aversion therefore to these subjects.

There is an interesting potential opportunity to subvert this relationship and move away from an assumption that students from marginalised backgrounds should automatically be steered towards more vocational subjects. However, the absence of the private sector from the higher education of Orang Asli also presents more issues to address, not least the matter of where any provision could be located. The strong ties the Orang Asli people have to their lands need to be acknowledged. These ties have significant implications for education (Noor, 2012).

If there are to be significant increases in progression into higher education for the Orang Asli, the delivery of it where the community lives will need to be considered. It would not necessarily benefit the Orang Asli community if increased higher education progression represents a form of 'brain drain' with students being compelled to leave the community.

Moving forward

The challenges faced in enabling greater higher education progression for Orang Asli people are in many ways similar to those faced in supporting the progression of other indigenous people from across the world. The physical and cultural distance between the communities and the education system create an interlocking set of challenges that will need to be addressed at the broader political level as much as in the education system. Layered on top of this in Malaysia is a higher education system that is divided by ethnicity in ways that present unique challenges and opportunities for higher education progression. On the basis of the evidence presented in this chapter though, there are a number of potential ways in which researchers, activists and policymakers could look to advance higher education progression for the Orang Asli communities in Malaysia.

Notes

1 Association of Southeast Asian Nations.
2 Malaysian Higher School Certificate.

References

Abdullah, R., W. Mamat, W. Zal and A. Ibrahim (2013) Teaching and learning problems of the Orang Asli education: Students' perspective, *Asian Social Science* 9(12): 118–124.

Abdullah, Y. (2017) *Participation of Indigenous students in higher education: An overview on Australia and Malaysia*, Bulletin of Higher Education Research: IPPTN

Abdul Khalid, A. and L. Yang (2019) *Income inequality among different ethnic groups: the case of Malaysia*, [online], https://blogs.lse.ac.uk/businessreview/2019/09/11/income-inequality-among-different-ethnic-groups-the-case-of-malaysia.

Atherton, G. (ed.) (2016) *Access to higher education: Understanding global inequalities*. London: Macmillan.

Atherton, G., S. Azizan, M. Shuib and G. Crosling (2018) *The shape of global higher education: Understanding the ASEAN region*. London: British Council.

Barnard, T. (ed.) (2003). *Contesting Malayness: Malay identity across boundaries*. Singapore: Singapore University Press.

Division of Student Admission (2011) *Peluang pengajian tinggi melalui UPU: Sesi Akademik 2012/2013* [Opportunities for higher education through UPU: Academic Session 2012/2013]. Putrajaya: Unit Pengambilan Universiti [Division of Student Admission].

Economic Planning Unit (2015) *Elevating B40 households towards a middle-class society: Strategy paper 2*. Putrajaya: Economic Planning Unit.

Hamisah binti Tapsir, S. (2019) Harmonising public and private higher education, *New Straits Times* [online], https://www.nst.com.my/opinion/columnists/2019/05/488452/harmonising-public-and-private-higher-education.

Jabatan Hal Ehwal Orang Asli (2002) *Kehidupan, budaya dan pantang larang Orang Asli* [Life, culture and taboos of the Orang Asli]. Kuala Lumpur: Jabatan Hal Ehwal Orang Asli.

Malay Mail (2017) Najib: govt to provide special additional aid to Orang Asli students, *Malay Mail* [online], https://www.malaymail.com/news/malaysia/2017/09/23/najib-govt-to-provide-special-additional-aid-to-orang-asli-students/1471497.

Malay Mail (2019) Maszlee: Education Ministry to set up special committee on education needs of Orang Asli, *Malay Mail* [online], https://www.malaymail.com/news/malaysia/2019/09/24/maszlee-education-ministry-to-set-up-special-committee-on-education-needs-o/1793807.

Malaysian Government (2016) *Demography of population* [online], https://www.malaysia.gov.my/portal/content/30114.

Masron, T., F. Masami and N. Ismail (2013) Orang Asli in Peninsular Malaysia: Population, spatial distribution and socio-economic condition, *Journal of Ritsumeikan Social Sciences and Humanities* 6: 75–115.

Ministry of Education (2015) *Transformation of Malaysia's higher education system: Malaysia education blueprint (2015–2025)*. Putrajaya: Ministry of Education.

Mustapha, R. (2013) Attributes that affect self-efficacy and career development of Orang Asli youth in Peninsular Malaysia, *Journal of Southeast Asian Education* 6(1): 1–24.

Nair, C. (2020) Malaysia's 'Malay first' malaise, *The Diplomat* [online], https://thediplomat.com/2020/03/malaysias-malay-first-malaise.

Nicholas, C. (2000) *The Orang Asli and the contest for resources: Indigenous politics, development and identity in Peninsular Malaysia*. Subang Jaya: Centre for Orang Asli Concerns.

Nicholas, C. (2006) *The state of Orang Asli education and its root problems*. Subang Jaya: Centre for Orang Asli Concerns.

Noor, M (2012) Advancing the Orang Asli through Malaysia's Clusters of Excellence policy, *Journal of International and Comparative Education* 1(2): 90–103.

Nordin, R., M. Sayuti bin Hassan and I. Danjuma (2018) Orang Asli student icons: An innovative teaching method for Orang Asli students, *Pertanika Journal of Social Science & Humanities* 26(1): 219–238.

Office of the United Nations High Commissioner for Human Rights (2019) *Statement by Professor Philip Alston, United Nations Special Rapporteur on extreme poverty and human rights, on his visit to Malaysia*, 13-23 August 2019 [online], https://www.ohchr.org/en/NewsEvents/Pages/DisplayNews.aspx?NewsID=24912.

Palansamy, Y. (2019) After Pos Tohoi deaths, where is Education Ministry's promised cultural sensitisation policy for teachers? *Malay Mail* [online], https://www.malaymail.com/news/malaysia/2019/07/28/after-pos-tohoi-deaths-where-is-education-ministrys-promised-cultural-sensi/1775363.

Rabahi, M., H. Yusof and M. Awang (2015) Leading learning: A grounded theory perspective of Orang Asli parental involvement and engagement, *Procedia: Social and Behavioral Sciences* 211: 94–103.

Rusaslina, I. (2010) *Basic rights for the Orang Asli*. Singapore: Institute of South East Asia Studies.

Shah, N., R. Rus, R. Mustapha, M. Hussain and N. Wahab (2018). The Orang Asli profile in Peninsular Malaysia: Background & challenges, *International Journal of Academic Research in Business and Social Sciences* 8(7): 1157–1164.

Simler, K. (2019) An idea whose time has come: Increasing Malaysia's poverty line, *World Bank Blogs* [online], https://blogs.worldbank.org/eastasiapacific/idea-whose-time-has-come-increasing-malaysias-poverty-line.

Study International (2017) *Indigenous tribe members called 'pigs', 'dogs' in Malaysian schools* [online], https://www.studyinternational.com/news/orang-asli-malaysia-school.

Tan, A.M. (2002) *Malaysian private higher education: Globalisation, privatisation, marketization, transformation and market places*. London: ASEAN Academic Press.

Tham, S.Y. (2011) *Exploring access and equity in Malaysia's private higher education*. Tokyo: Asian Development Bank Institute.

Tho, X.Y. (2019) Outcry over retaining ethnic quota for pre-university admission in Malaysia, *Channel News Asia* [online], https://www.channelnewsasia.com/news/asia/malaysia-outcry-ethnic-quota-matriculation-admission-11514578.

United Nations Malaysia (2015) *Malaysia millennium development goals report*. Kuala Lumpur: United Nations Malaysia.

Wahab, N., R. Mustapha and A. Ahmad (2016) The roles of administrators in aboriginal schools: A case study in a Malaysian state, *International Journal of Social Science and Humanity* 6(5): 370–374.

Wan, C.D. (2007) Public and private higher education institutions in Malaysia: Competing, complementary or crossbreeds as education providers, *Kajian Malaysia* 25(1): 1–14.

Wan, C.D., M. Sirat and D. Razak (2015) The idea of a university: Rethinking the Malaysian context, *Humanities* 4(3): 266–282.

Chapter 13

Higher education and disadvantaged groups in India

N.V. Varghese

Introduction

Inequalities in India are widening. The increasing inequalities indicate the need for progressive public policies and state actions to mitigate them. The logic of affirmative actions stems from this premise. The objective of affirmative actions is to extenuate disadvantages derived from socio-historical processes. An affirmative action is a measure aimed at minimizing, if not eliminating, discrimination and deprivation of the disadvantaged groups. The disadvantaged groups in India are broadly classified into four categories: Scheduled Castes (SCs), Scheduled Tribes (STs), Other Backward Classes (OBCs) and Economically Weaker Sections (EWSs).

The argument for special treatment of these groups is that they have faced social and economic discrimination in the past and have severely been under-represented in public life. Therefore, the Constitution of India enjoins the state to ensure equality of opportunity, disapproves any form of discrimination and includes special provisions for the socially and educationally disadvantaged classes. The affirmative actions in practice include reservation of places for the disadvantaged groups in educational institutions, in employment market and provision of scholarships, grants and other student support measures. This chapter analyses issues related to inequalities in access to and success in education of the disadvantaged groups in India.

Inequalities, education and inclusive development

The world is growing unequal. The world was more equal when most people were poor. It became more unequal when some became rich and others did not. The variations in the rates of growth increased economic distances between countries and between people within the same country. In other words, the economic growth in the recent decades is accompanied by widening of income inequalities in most countries.

The between-country inequalities were on the increase in the past century. In the post-2000 decades the within-country inequalities have been increasing. Thus global inequalities in income growth are driven by strong forces of convergence between countries and divergence within countries (Roser, 2013). The global top 1% income share increased from 16% in 1980 to 20% by 2015. The market-led economic growth has resulted in higher growth in income for the upper income groups than the lower income groups contributing to a widening of inequalities in most countries.

Inequalities in India are widening. Recent estimates for India (Chancel and Piketty, 2017) indicate that the top 1% accounts for 22% of the national income; the top 10% accounts for 56% of the national income and the bottom 50% is left with around 16% of the national income. The inequalities between the rich and the rest continue to grow in India. Income inequality in India has reached historically high levels.

The increasing inequalities indicate that one cannot rely on 'trickle-down effect' to share benefits of growth equally (Atkinson, 2008). One needs to rely more on public policies to fight against poverty and inequality. A good policy and a democratic approach can make a difference to compact inequality. 'Inequalities in any society can be seen as the cumulative result of unjust policies and misguided priorities' (Stiglitz, 2015, p. 3). Countries need committed public policy reforms to reverse the trend of economic inequality and promote conditions for broad-based prosperity.

The inequalities in the present have implications for the next generation. More unequal countries, in general, are prone to hand over poverty and disadvantage to their children. Those excluded in the present may continue to remain marginalized in the process of development. They are denied rights to resources in the present and opportunities to progress in the future. Marginalization of any group goes against the objective of inclusive development. Faster progress by the deprived groups is necessary to level-off the differences among social groups.

How to ensure faster progress of the deprived groups is the challenge in moving toward an inclusive society. Two strategies that have worked in many countries are as follows: a) increased social spending and b) ensured education of every child. First, when incomes are more equally distributed and in countries where social spending is high, fewer people remain poor. It is observed that social mobility is higher in countries with lower income inequality. In those developed countries which experience relatively more equality, the governments have been taxing more and increasing social spending to offset inequalities (Organisation for Economic Cooperation and Development, 2008). What matters is equity in opportunities and increased social spending which play an important role in building inclusive societies.

Second, while land and physical capital were the sources of economic growth, personal income and inequalities in the past, education has emerged as the major source in the recent past. Education plays an important role in promoting growth in national income and an equally important role in the sharing (distribution) of national income through employment and earnings. When educational opportunities and attainment are unequally distributed, they become an important source of inequalities and it requires corrective public policies. It is in this context that an active state intervention is sought.

It is now recognized that equality of educational opportunities is a necessary condition to promote economic and social equity (World Bank, 2018).

Public provision or funding of education in particular may increase social mobility, reduce poverty and hasten the process toward constructing inclusive societies. Public spending is a substitute for parental inputs of low income groups to invest in their children's education. The move toward the Right to Education Act in 2009 in India was a serious effort to equalize educational opportunities at the bottom of the pyramid to promote an inclusive development.

Strategies to improve access to education of disadvantaged groups

One of the strategies adopted in several countries to address issues related to the disadvantaged is affirmative action. In education, especially higher education, these measures may be reflected in terms of reservation policies or quota system in admission to educational institutions. India has adopted policies to ensure admission of disadvantaged groups into higher education.

The first step followed in India was to identify the disadvantaged to target them in the process of development. The disadvantaged groups in India are broadly classified into four categories as laid out in the introduction to this chapter. The non-disadvantaged social groups are termed as general category. In 1950 the Constitution of India recognized the SCs and STs as the two most disadvantaged groups needing special protection. A number of provisions have been made in the Constitution with a view to abolish all forms of discrimination and put these groups at par with others.

The Constitution of India guaranteed 15% reservation in admissions to higher education and in employment for the SCs and 7.5% for the STs in 1950. In 1987 an additional quota of 27% was extended to OBCs in jobs and in government and government aided higher education institutions. Apart from reservation, there is also relaxation in the minimum qualifying marks for admission in educational institutions. The reservation is granted to these groups on the basis of the argument that they have faced social and economic discrimination in the past and have severely been under-represented in public life.

Among these groups, the STs remain in remote rural areas and they face exclusion as part of a spatial marginalization process in development in addition to the social disadvantage they experience along with SCs. It needs to be mentioned that most of the families belonging to the SC and ST groups are poor and economic marginalization is common among these two disadvantaged groups. However, they are included in the category of caste-based reservation, although the government very recently introduced reservation based on the economic status to other groups.

According to the 103rd Constitutional Amendment Act 2019, 10% of all government jobs and seats in higher educational institutions in India are reserved for the EWSs within the general category. The reservation will be in addition to the existing 49.5% reservation in favor of the SCs, STs and OBCs.

In other words, the reservation or the quota of seats will now cover nearly 59.5% of the admissions in institutions of higher education. It needs to be added that some of the state governments follow quota systems in admissions to higher education institutions and in the labor market which exceed this level.

The University Grants Commission (UGC) has issued instruction to strictly adhere to the reservation policies in all public institutions of higher education. The UGC has a dedicated SC/ST/OBC section in the Commission to monitor effective implementation of the reservation policy as per the constitutional provisions. The government (both central and provincial) has introduced scholarships to the students belonging to the disadvantaged groups to financially enable them to participate in education. The scholarships are also provided at the school level and at post-secondary levels including study in premier educational institutions in India and abroad.

The disadvantaged groups are also given hostel facilities in the universities. Some of the universities and colleges have special hostels for disadvantaged groups; in other cases, there are quotas for disadvantaged groups in the hostels where all categories of students live. Since the STs live in remote rural areas, the Central Government established 'tribal universities' in India to promote their education. The Indira Gandhi National Tribal University, Amarkantak and Central Tribal University of Andhra Pradesh, Vizianagaram, are examples of special efforts to enroll tribal students, provide them with living facilities and also to promote studies and research on tribal communities in India.

The UGC is implementing several schemes for the benefit of the disadvantaged groups. These schemes include the following: (a) residential coaching academies for minorities/SCs/STs and women, (b) centers in universities for study of social exclusion and inclusive policy, (c) establishment of equal opportunities cells/units in the institutions of higher education and (d) establishment of SC and ST cells/units in the universities.

Among these, the coaching schemes include the following: (i) remedial coaching at the undergraduate and graduate level to reinforce the curriculum transacted in the classrooms, (ii) coaching to appear in the competitive examinations for job selection and (iii) coaching for the 'national eligibility test' – a national competitive examination introduced by the UGC to provide fellowships for the doctoral studies and to decide the eligibility for academic positions in the universities.

The coaching scheme for job selection was introduced with the objective of improving the level playing capacity of the disadvantaged in competitive examinations and success in obtaining good jobs. The coaching is provided for competing for higher level jobs through the competitive examinations conducted by various national and state level recruitment bodies and agencies. The extent of impact of these reservation measures at the entry level and support strategies after the admissions on the educational performance and labor outcomes of the disadvantaged is debatable.

The debate on the effect of reservation policies on the upward mobility of the disadvantaged group centers around the issues of targeting, mismatch and catch-up (Alon and Tienda, 2005). As we will discuss later, the reservation policy, no doubt, has been helpful in addressing issues related to the exclusion of the disadvantaged groups and the marginalized, especially at the ports of entry into the institutions of higher education (Varghese et al., 2019). However, their performance in the studies, learning and employment outcomes need to be examined more closely.

Massification of higher education and disadvantaged groups

Indian higher education system has traditionally been a state controlled and state funded sector. The public policy and the financial health of the state determined the pace of growth of the sector. It has been a sector characterized by slow growth and low gross enrolment ratios (GER). The GER remained at the single digit (8.1%) in the first 50 years of planned development. The scenario changed from the turn of this century.

After a prolonged period of slow growth, the higher education sector in India experienced accelerated growth and massive expansion in this century. The sector experienced two-digit growth rates and the fast expansion of the sector helped India enter into a stage of massification of higher education. According to 2018–19 data (Ministry of Human Resource Development [MHRD], 2019), India has the second largest higher education system in the world with 993 universities, nearly 40,000 colleges, 1.3 million teachers and 37.2 million students accounting for a GER of 26.3% (Table 13.1). The massive expansion is due to the increasing role played by the private higher education institutions. In other words, the higher education sector in India moved away from a predominantly state supported sector to a predominantly private financed sector. At present, more than three-fifths of the enrolment in higher education in India is accounted for by private higher education institutions. The more important question this chapter addresses is to what extent the disadvantaged groups have benefited from massification of higher education?

The empirical evidence on the expansion of higher education in India shows that all groups benefited from expansion. However, the social inequalities in access to higher education continue to persist. Further, some of the

Table 13.1 Higher education expansion in India

Year	Universities	Colleges	Enrolments (in millions)	GER %
1950–51	27	578	0.2	0.7
2000–01	256	12,806	8.4	8.1
2010–11	564	33,023	17.0	20.8
2018–19	993	39,931	37.4	26.3

Source: UGC annual reports and MHRD, 2019

Table 13.2 Enrolment and GER of the SCs and STs

	GER total 2011	GER total 2019	GER SC 2011	GER SC 2019	GER ST 2011	GER ST 2019
GER (%)	20.8	26.3	14.9	23.0	11.0	17.2
Total (millions)	29.2	37.4	3.6	5.6	1.3	2.1

Source: MHRD, 2019

disadvantaged groups benefited more than others. Consequently, some of the disadvantaged still remain far behind (Varghese, 2019a). The persisting inequalities signal that the bottom of the pyramid is less benefited than others from the massification of the higher education sector. At the bottom of the pyramid one finds larger share of the socially and economically disadvantaged groups.

An analysis of the access to higher education indicates that the GER among the disadvantaged groups, in general, is lower than that among the general category. In 2018–19 the GER at the all-India level was 26.3% while that for SC was 23.0% and for ST was 17.2% (Table 13.2). Did the disadvantaged groups benefit from massification of the sector? There are signs of catch-up by the SC and ST groups. For example, while the increase in the total GER between 2011–12 and 2018–19 was around 6% points, that among the SC was 8% points and that among the STs was 6.2% points. It can be argued that between the most disadvantaged groups in India – the SCs – are making faster progress than the STs. All these indicate that the inequalities in enrolment between the disadvantaged and the rest have not widened over time, although they remain significant and high.

While SCs are catching up, the OBCs are moving faster than the SCs to close the gap with the general category. For example, the OBCs increased their share in enrolment from 32.9% in 2014–15 to 36.3% in 2018–19. It is important to note that the share of the general category students in enrolment decreased from 48.8% in 2014–15 to 43.3% in 2018–19. It seems that the single group that benefited the highest from massification of higher education in India is the OBC category (Varghese, 2019b).

It is pertinent to pose a question regarding the effectiveness of the affirmative polices. The increase both in the GER and in the share of enrolment of disadvantaged groups are good signs and indications of the positive effect of the affirmation policies. However, in many states, including some of the larger states, the share of SC and ST students enrolled is less than the expected quota. According to the Census of India 2011, the SC population accounted for 16.6% and the STs formed 8.6%. However, the share of enrolment in higher education in some of the states was less than 20%. Similarly across the prestigious Indian Institutes of Technology (IITs), the SC and ST students accounted for less than 19% and less than 20% in Indian Institutions of Management (IIMs) in 2018–19 (Rukmini, 2019).

These pieces of evidence indicate that despite regulations many regions are not strictly adhering to the quota fixed for the disadvantaged groups in admissions to higher education. This can be an added reason for the continued inequalities in enrolment between the disadvantaged groups and the general category students. The existing inequalities among social groups in access to higher education further marginalize some groups within the disadvantaged groups. There is a need for further strengthening of the implementation of the quota system in admissions to ensure that the share of the disadvantaged is maintained at the constitutionally mandated share and for expanding student support systems in terms of fee concessions, scholarships and hostel accommodation to ensure retention of those enrolled.

The empirical evidence shows that the disadvantaged groups continue to remain at the bottom of the pyramid in India. Although they have benefited from higher education opportunities, their relative disadvantage continues to remain. The affirmative policies have not yet adequately benefited the disadvantaged groups to be equal with others in the social and educational progress. The disadvantaged groups in India, like in other societies, continue to remain at the margin and experience marginalization in the process of educational development.

Now let us consider the inequalities between genders within the disadvantaged groups. One of the unique features of higher education is that unlike school education, gender parity is achieved at lower levels of GER in higher education. In most of the developed countries the GER of females surpasses that of males. India has not yet reached that stage, although in some of the states, female GER is more than that of males. The variations in GER between sexes are the lowest among the general category. The GER of higher-caste women was almost three times that of ST women (Table 13.3). The GER of the women in the general category is almost three times that of ST women, twice that of SC women and 1.5 times that of OBC women. Among the disadvantaged groups the variation in GER between sexes is the highest among ST, followed by OBC and SC.

The gender parity index (GPI) at the national level is 0.86. Women lag behind men in terms of enrolment in higher education among all social groups. The deprivation of women is higher among the disadvantaged and

Table 13.3 GER by Social Groups and Gender in 2014

Social Group	Male	Female	GPI
ST	17.4	13.1	0.75
SC	21.9	18.2	0.83
OBC	29.6	23.1	0.78
Others	37.9	35.4	0.93

Source: Ministry of Statistics and Programme Implementation [MSPI], 2014

lower caste groups. For example, the GPI is 0.93 among the upper caste groups (Table 13.3) while it is 0.75 in case of ST groups. Although the OBCs have made fast progress in enrolment the GPI continues to be low at 0.78. The GPI indicates that the disadvantaged groups experience higher disparities between sexes in enrolment in higher education institutions.

Why do the disadvantaged groups continue to remain at the bottom of the pyramid despite affirmative policies in place? Part of the reason lies in the fact that the disparities reflected in the higher education sector is an extension of those at the school education sector. The opportunity cost of sending children to school is higher among the disadvantaged groups, especially among the SC and ST groups. Given the low level of income and poverty common in their households, children are seen as a source of income to the household since they can earn income by working. This increases the opportunity cost of their education and resultantly only a limited number of children from the disadvantaged families complete secondary levels of education to be qualified to seek admissions in institutions of higher education.

As discussed already, in the case of some of the disadvantaged groups like the STs the social disadvantage intersects with geographical disadvantages. Many of the tribal households are located in remote rural areas where schooling facilities are poor and higher education facilities are almost non-existent. This, combined with the poor financial background of the households, make it easier for them to keep their children away from education. Another equally important reason for low enrolment is the lack of information regarding higher education opportunities and the facilities provided by the government as part of the affirmative measures.

Choice of institutions and programs of study and the disadvantaged

Now let us consider some of the characteristics of those disadvantaged groups who are enrolled in higher education institutions. There are two dimensions to this question – choice of programs of study and institutions of study. The enrolment by study areas is an indication of the future job orientation and hence the extent of marginalization of the disadvantaged in higher education can be better understood, if one considers their areas of specialization in colleges and universities. The SC and ST students are increasingly seen in subject areas such as humanities, science, agriculture and education (Table 13.4). Their share in enrolment in the study areas such as commerce, engineering, management and chartered accountancy is very low. Interestingly, the share of OBCs is more evenly spread across subject areas. It seems that STEM[1] subjects are studied mostly by the privileged students from the OBCs and general categories. The high castes, higher income groups and those mostly residing in urban areas increasingly opt for subject

Table 13.4 Study programs by social groups 2014 (%)

Subjects Being Studied	Social Groups			
	ST	SC	OBC	General
Humanities	8.9	20.3	38.1	32.6
Science	6.5	12.8	48.7	32.0
Commerce	5.7	13.5	37.8	43.1
Medicine	4.5	11.2	40.3	44.0
Engineering	2.7	9.9	47.6	39.7
Agriculture	11.6	20.9	37.7	29.7
Law	5.1	13.3	37.0	44.6
Management	1.9	8.6	39.9	49.6
Education	5.8	18.9	43.1	32.1
Chartered accountancy and similar	2.1	3.6	21.3	72.9
IT/computer courses	4.5	10.9	37.0	47.5
Total	6.7	15.6	41.2	36.6

Source: Varghese et al., 2019

areas which have a higher market premium and students from the disadvantaged and marginalized groups and those residing in rural locations enroll increasingly in study programs of arts and humanities, social sciences and agriculture which have low priority in the employment market.

What about admissions to the prestigious institutions of higher education? The distribution of higher education institutions, in general, is skewed in favor of poor quality ones and the high quality institutions are in short supply. This, in turn, leads to an increase in the demand for admissions to these institutions and for reservation to be adhered to (Basant and Sen, 2010). The Indian IITs and IIMs are considered to be the most prestigious and globally well recognized Indian institutions. Admissions to IITs and IIMs are based on highly competitive examinations. IITs are centrally funded institutions and there are many institutions and admissions to IITs are based on a common entrance examination called Joint Entrance Examination (JEE) conducted by the National Testing Services. Let us consider how the disadvantaged groups fair in these highly competitive entrance tests.

A detailed analysis of those qualified in the JEE (Robles and Krishna, 2011) indicate that SC/ST students account for 22% of those in the lowest decile and 3% at the top decile. Almost 80% of the students in the top decile come from the general category. Although affirmative policies adopted to promote enrolment of the disadvantaged groups were helpful, the fact remains that inequalities in access to prestigious higher education institutions still persist.

Privatization and the exclusion of disadvantaged groups

With the adoption of economic reforms in India in the 1990s, the role of the private sector in higher education has significantly increased and it also resulted in reducing the State's commitment toward the social sector under the pretext of fiscal discipline (Khan, 2018). The private institutions are established mostly in the domains of technical courses like engineering, professional courses like medical, nursing and management. Private higher education is expensive and the students from the disadvantaged groups may find it difficult to afford their education in private universities. The private and self-financing institutions do not always follow the reservation policies adhered to in student admissions in public higher education institutions. This results in under-representation of disadvantaged groups in professional and technical courses as seen in Table 13.4.

The fast expansion of private higher education also leads an urban bias and regional concentration of higher education institutions. For example, in 2018–19 the number of colleges per 100,000 populations varied from seven in Bihar to 53 in Karnataka and 50 in Telengana. The concentration of higher education institutions gives an advantage in the form of 'distance discount' to those living closer to the urban centers. The distance discount is reflected in the form of reduced costs (living expenses) and improved affordability and access. Among the disadvantaged groups, the STs face spatial marginalization and they will be more adversely affected by this pattern of higher education development resulting from concentrated location of institutions in the urban or semi-urban areas. It can be stated that the students from general category and economically better-off families within the disadvantaged groups, especially OBCs, benefited more from the private sector led massification of higher education in India.

Economic status and the exclusion of the disadvantaged

There seems to exist a positive association between household income levels and enrolment in higher education. The National Sample Survey (NSS) data show that the GER of children belonging to the poorest group in the lowest quintile (lowest 20%) increased only from 4% in 2007 to 9.9% in 2014 while that among the privileged belonging to the highest quintile (highest 20%) increased from 47.6% to 73.8% (Varghese, 2019a).

There is an intersection between economic status, social groups and the share in enrolment. More than 68% of the enrolment in general higher education in the general category is from the highest two quintiles (Table 13.5). The corresponding share in the disadvantaged categories of SC and ST is around 46% and that of the OBCs is 56%. The pattern in the share of enrolment changes in case of technical/professional higher education. More than 92% of the enrolment in general category comes from the highest two quintiles. The corresponding figures for the disadvantaged groups are more than 70% for SC and ST groups and more than 80% for the OBCs (Table 13.5). These trends bring out some of the important features related to social class origin of higher education enrolment in India.

First, enrolment is closely associated with economic status of the household. There is a positive association between level of economic group (quintile) and the share of student enrolment from any social category. Second,

Table 13.5 Share of students by social groups and income, 2014 (%)

	Income quintile	ST	SC	OBCs	Others
General higher education	first quintile	7.7	11.6	7.8	4.1
	second quintile	16.4	15.3	13.7	8.3
	third quintile	29.0	24.7	21.9	18.8
	fourth quintile	23.7	21.8	26.4	20.9
	fifth quintile	23.2	26.6	30.1	48.0
	Total	**100**	**100**	**100**	**100**
Technical/ professional	first quintile	7.5	6.1	1.6	0.7
	second quintile	10.8	7.5	5.7	2.2
	third quintile	10.9	16.1	11.2	4.8
	fourth quintile	16.7	17.2	16.6	12.6
	fifth quintile	54.0	53.1	64.8	79.7
	Total	**100**	**100**	**100**	**100**

Source: MSPI, 2014

the positive association between economic status and enrolment becomes stronger among all social categories in technical and professional subject areas than in general higher education. Third, while technical and professional education is an exclusive category of the elites, the general higher education attracts non-elite students from the general category. Fourth, the spread of students across economic categories is more even in case of the disadvantaged categories. This is more so in case of SCs and STs in general higher education where majority of the students are from the lowest three quintiles.

The empirical evidence on the relationship between economic status and enrolment indicates that the massification of the sector benefited more the higher income groups, irrespective of the social background, than the lower income groups. The poor are, in a sense, excluded, from access to higher education. It is still debatable whether or not economic factors are more dominant than social factors in the exclusion of students from access to higher education.

The Indian evidence shows that there is a high correlation between the socially disadvantaged and economically poor categories. Therefore, exclusion of the poor also includes exclusion of the socially disadvantaged categories. It can be reliably argued that the poor belonging to the disadvantaged groups have benefited least from the massification of higher education in India.

The other argument can be that the affirmation policies have played an important and positive role in overcoming economic barriers of the disadvantaged groups in their pursuit for higher education. At the lower end of the economic pyramid (the lowest two quintiles) the share of enrolment of the disadvantaged groups is more than 20% in general higher education against 12.4% in case of general category. Further, 18.3% of the ST students, 13.6% of the SC students and 7.3% of the OBC students in the technical and professional education come from the lowest two quintiles. The corresponding share of the general category students from the lowest two categories is only 2.9% (Table 13.5).

Some of the universities such as Jadavpur University (26%), Jawaharlal Nehru University (24%) and University of Hyderabad (23%) which occupy top positions in the Indian ranking of higher education institutions also have a higher share of SC and ST students than other institutions and more than the mandated share. Of these the Jawaharlal University also has a majority (51%) women (MHRD, 2019). The academic performance of these institutions indicates that they have put in place strategies to address student diversity in the classrooms and in the campuses.

English language and the exclusion of disadvantaged groups

The language of instruction is increasingly becoming a major source of exclusion in India. A majority of school students in India study in local languages. However, the most preferred medium of instruction at the university level is the English language. English is seen as the language of the elite and the most preferred language in the academic discussions in universities. This is true of India and more so in the context of globalization of higher education.

The middle class households in India show a preference of schools which follow English as the medium of instruction. According to the NSS survey of 2014, nearly 72% of the students in unaided private schools followed English as the medium of instruction while the corresponding share in the government institutions is only 34%. Most of this category of schools are in the private sector and are very expensive. What is unsurprising is that the very same households which prefer private English medium schools prefer elite public higher education institutions such as IITs and IIMs at the higher education level. The students from private English medium schools account for a disproportionately higher share in enrolment in the universities and elite higher education institutions. This pattern reinforces the elite nature and exclusionary pattern of higher education development in India.

The SC and ST students are enrolled mostly in government schools where the medium of instruction is the local/state language. Their proficiency in English language remains low when compared to those graduating from private English medium schools. These students face various challenges to compete with others in the competitive selection tests and even after entry into institutions of higher education. This is validated by some of the case studies which showed that all good academic performers from the non-SC/ST category and the SC/ST category come from English medium schools (Dhende, 2017). The lack of proficiency in English language becomes a constraint at the entry level and a bottleneck while pursuing their studies in institutions of higher education in India.

Unequal educational outcomes and disadvantaged groups

The Indian experience shows that the public policies promoting the quota system and student support initiatives helped developing a more inclusive entry conditions into higher education institutions. Did the success in access of the disadvantaged groups translate into their improved learning and employment outcomes?

The affirmative policies have helped enroll larger number of disadvantaged students and it has changed student composition in the campuses. The higher education campuses have become more diverse. However, the administration, institutional mechanisms and the teachers and teaching learning processes remain poorly developed to address diversity at the classroom and campus levels. Studies (e.g. Sabharwal and Malish, 2018) show various forms of exclusionary behavior practiced in the domains of student-teacher interactions, student-administration interactions and student-student interactions in the campuses contribute to the poor learning outcomes of the disadvantaged groups.

Some of the follow-up studies of the disadvantaged students in elite institutions such as Indian Institutes of Technology (e.g. Henry and Ferry, 2017) show that many students from the SC and ST categories did not perform well in their studies. The SC and ST students face several disadvantages after their entry into institutions of higher education resulting in poor academic performance and eventual drop out from institutions of higher education. The limited cultural capital the students bring along with them, a lack of English language proficiency and poor college preparedness are some of the factors affecting their academic performance and social interactions.

It seems the catch up by the SC and ST students is slow and inadequate. The minority and SC and ST students fall behind their peers in selective majors (Robles and Krishna, 2011) in institutions of higher education. At times the disadvantaged students in the selective majors earn less on jobs than their friends with similar social background enrolled in less selective majors. It is also observed that being enrolled in a more selective major increases stress levels and feelings of not belonging among SC/ST students (Alon and Tienda, 2005). This evidence supports the mismatch hypothesis in the efforts by the disadvantaged to compete with the general category students to achieve parity at the outcome levels. In one of the studies in India, Bertrand et al. (2010) empirically validates the mismatch hypothesis. They find that the effect of the quota-based admissions in Indian engineering colleges is positive and they earn more in the labor market. However, their gain is less than what the students they displace lose.

The poor academic performance of the disadvantaged groups also creates barriers to entry into the employment market. The unemployment rate among different social groups indicates that in 2014 it was the highest at 10.5% among SCs followed by 8.9% among STs, 8.2% among OBC and 6.4%

Table 13.6 Unemployment rates among educated social groups

Social Group	Secondary	Higher secondary	Diploma/ certificate	Under- graduate	Post-graduate and above
ST	6.2	6.4	5.5	8.9	8.9
SC	2.6	5.0	12.0	10.5	13.1
OBC	2.7	4.0	10.0	8.2	8.3
Others	2.2	4.5	4.7	6.4	6.1
All	2.7	4.4	8.1	7.6	7.5

Source: Based on MSPI, 2014

among the general (non-disadvantaged) categories (Table 13.6). The unemployment rate among post-graduates is higher than that among the undergraduates. There is a sudden spurt in the rates of unemployment of the SC and ST groups as one moves from secondary school level to higher education level. This positive association between rates of unemployment and level of education is surprising and is despite the extension of the reservation policies to job recruitments.

Concluding observations

The discussions in this chapter indicate several policy measures adopted and strategies relied on to address the concerns of disadvantaged groups, especially the SCs, STs and OBCs in India. The affirmative policies such as the quota system in admissions have, no doubt, helped increase the number of students from the disadvantaged groups in higher education institutions and campuses in India. Further, the provision of residential facilities, scholarships and financial support to the disadvantaged students has helped retaining them in the institutions of higher education. These are areas of success in addressing the challenges posed in extending higher education to the disadvantaged groups.

Unlike in the case of admissions, the success is less pronounced in the area of learning and employment outcomes of the disadvantaged groups. Studies have shown that the disadvantaged students, especially those belonging to the most marginalized groups such as SCs and STs face academic challenges, social isolation and remain less integrated with the campus culture and its social life. There is need for added intervention to evolve strategies and mechanisms to address diversity at the institutional level. It is mandatory to create separate units/cells to address the specific problems faced by the disadvantaged groups in the higher education campuses. Many of these units are already created at the institutional level as per the mandate. However, most of them in many institutions are relatively non-functional or functioning less effectively.

The SC and ST students need academic support and social protection in the campuses. There are several programs designed at the national level which also extend financial support to implement these schemes at the institutional level. Some of the institutions organize compensatory classes, programs for improving performance in competitive examinations in the job market and courses to improve English language proficiency. These programs, if well implemented, are found to be very helpful to improve the academic and employment performance of the disadvantaged students.

The institutional culture needs to respect diversity and students from diverse backgrounds. Diversity is a social reality and is a non-negotiable element when the system transits from an elite stage to a stage of massification. The experience of some of the top ranking institutions such as Jadavpur University, Jawaharlal Nehru University and Hyderabad University in India show that there is no conflict between the twin objectives of promoting student diversity and achieving academic excellence. The institutional failure to address diversity may adversely affect the academic performance and employment outcomes of the disadvantaged groups.

Note

1 Science, Technology, Engineering and Mathematics.

References

Atkinson, A. (2008) *Unequal growth, unequal recession?* OECD Observer [online], https://oecdobserver.org/news/archivestory.php/aid/2751/Unequal_growth,_unequal_recession_.html.

Alon, S. and M. Tienda (2005) Assessing the "Mismatch" hypothesis: Differences in college graduation rates by institutional selectivity, *Sociology of Education* 78(4): 294–315.

Basant, R. and G. Sen (2010) Who participates in higher education in India? Rethinking the role of affirmative action, *Economic and Political Weekly* 45(39): 62–70.

Bertrand, M., R. Hanna, and S. Mullainathan (2010) Affirmative action in education: Evidence from engineering college admissions in India, *Journal of Public Economics* 94(1–2): 16–29.

Chancel, L. and T. Piketty (2017) *Indian income inequality, 1922–2014: From British Raj to billionaire Raj?* World Inequality Database [online], https://wid.world/document/chancelpiketty2017widworld.

Dhende, L. (2017) A study of scheduled caste and higher education scenario in India, *International Journal of Engineering Technology Science and Research* 4(11): 345–351.

Henry, O. and M. Ferry (2017) When cracking the JEE is not enough: Processes of elimination and differentiation, from entry to placement, in the Indian Institutes of Technology (IITs), *South Asia Multidisciplinary Academic Journal* [online] 15: 1–28.

Khan, K. (2018) Access to school and higher education among scheduled castes and scheduled tribes: Changing scenario and policy issues, *Journal of Social Inclusion Studies* 4(2): 234–257.

Ministry of Human Resource Development (2019) *All India survey of higher education*. New Delhi: Department of Education.

Ministry of Statistics and Programme Implementation (2014) *Employment and unemployment situation in India: NSS* 68th round. New Delhi: Ministry of Statistics and Programme Implementation.

Organisation for Economic Cooperation and Development (2008) *Growing unequal? Income distribution and poverty in OECD countries*, Paris: Organisation for Economic Cooperation and Development.

Robles, V. and K. Krishna (2011) *Affirmative action in higher education in India: Targeting, catch up, and mismatch at IIT-Delhi*. Cambridge: National Bureau of Economic Research.

Roser, M. (2013) Global economic inequality, *Our World in Data* [online], https://ourworldindata.org/global-economic-inequality.

Rukmini, S. (2019) India's unequal university system, *LiveMint* [online], https://www.livemint.com/news/india/still-too-few-dalits-in-indian-colleges-1568013598781.html.

Sabharwal, N. and C. Malish (2018) *Student diversity and social inclusion: An empirical analysis of higher education institutions in India*. New Delhi: Centre for Policy Research in Higher Education.

Stiglitz, J. (2015) *The great divide: Unequal societies and what we can do about them*. New York: W.W. Norton.

Varghese, N.V. (2019a) Attainment and inclusion in Indian higher education, in R. Helms, L. Rumbley and L. Brajkovic (eds.) *Attainment and inclusion in higher education: International perspectives (International briefs for higher education leaders no. 8.)* (pp. 10–12). Boston Council for Education and Centre for International Higher Education.

Varghese, N.V. (2019b) Higher education in India: Managing the sector's unprecedented expansion, in *Commonwealth education report 2019* (pp. 60–62). London: Commonwealth Business Communications.

Varghese, N.V., N. Sabharwal and C. Malish (2019) *Equity and inclusion in higher education in India*. New Delhi: Centre for Policy Research in Higher Education.

World Bank (2018) *World Development Report 2018: Learning to realize education's promise*. Washington: World Bank.

Chapter 14

Concluding thoughts
Making meaning from diverse narratives

Neil Harrison and Graeme Atherton

In this book, we set out to provide a space for authors to tell new stories about access to higher education for communities whose narratives have received little or no attention in the past. The twelve chapters that we have included are diverse in terms of the groups focused upon, the methodologies deployed to draw out their stories and the theoretical lenses used to understand them in their wider context. It is important to remember, though, that there are also many other stories that have not been included, either because of the constraints of space in a modest book such as this or because they have not yet received attention from the international research community. New marginalised communities are constantly emerging to demand fair access to higher education, while new forms and expressions of the *process* of marginalisation evolve through worldwide trends of income inequality, conflict, climate change and public health crises, among others (Balarin, 2011). This book can only be a starting point.

For example, this concluding chapter is being written three months into the global Covid-19 pandemic; an event that is disrupting long-held spatial assumptions about higher education, where educators and students are physically co-located for much of the time. The concomitant mass shift to online teaching to provide adequate 'social distancing' places a new premium on internet connectivity and digital skills which are imbued with their own inequalities and dimensions by which individuals and communities are marginalised (Williamson et al., 2020).

Given the disparity stories contained in this book and the constantly shifting terrain, it important to find paths to broader meaning-making that helps us to understand the mechanisms of marginalisation in higher education – and thereby to suggest solutions for policy and practice. If we simply treat every marginalised community as unique and decontextualised, change will be piecemeal, precarious and transient.

With this in mind, the purpose of this final chapter is to take two cross-cutting 'looks' to see what can be learned for the future, using slightly different lenses on the same issue. We first show how Sen and Nussbaum's capabilities approach can be used to identify the 'unfreedoms' – structural constraints on individual agency – that compromise students' ability to engage with higher education. Then, drawing on the normative mission of the capabilities approach, we go on to explore what the unfreedoms contained in the book's narratives of marginalisation can tell us about the *processes* within higher education that *cause* marginalisation to occur. We propose four such dimensions (by society, by systems, by time/space and by relevance) and suggest some of the actions that policymakers and university managers might take to work towards an inclusive future for higher education across the globe.

Using the capabilities approach

In Chapter 6, Stevenson draws on the capabilities approach to conceptualise her data on religious students in the United Kingdom (UK). Developed by Amartya Sen (1993, 2001, 2009) and Martha Nussbaum (2000, 2011), this seeks to provide a normative framework for understanding equality and justice at the level of the individual within society. We believe that this has particularly utility with respect to higher education, where individual institutions have significant autonomy to make meaningful changes to their practices in order to promote inclusion. Indeed, changes to support marginalised groups are likely to have a positive impact on the wider student body, many of whom will be subject to similar inequalities, albeit experienced less profoundly.

The foundation of the capabilities approach is that, as humans, we all have outcomes that we 'value and have reason to value' (Sen, 2001, p. 291). These are embodied in the 'functionings' of our everyday lives; the things that we are able (or forced) to do and to be within the constraints of law, the material resources available, the expectations of society, our own knowledge and access to information and so on. A capability is thus a form of agentic freedom to act to achieve outcomes that we value – one that underpins our wellbeing and flourishing. We can only attain these personalised outcomes if we are able to accumulate the necessary functionings in our own context. National policy and institutional practices can therefore undermine capabilities by preventing certain functionings or they can support them by removing unfreedoms (Sen, 2001).

Achieving a higher education is an outcome that many people have reason to value. Aside from providing access to more lucrative and rewarding work with greater social impact, it has an emancipatory role in allowing people to understand themselves and their place in the world. Learning is an inherently enjoyable activity for many people, a means to an end for others. The capabilities approach makes no supposition that what is valued by some (especially the dominant groups in society) should be valued by all, nor that people's values are fixed in time. Similarly, higher education is a collection of functionings that contribute to learning – engagement with a curriculum, dialogue with a teacher and/or peers, time taken in contemplation and reflection, completion of formative assessment tasks and so on.

Wilson-Strydom (2015, 2016) has recently explored the use of the capabilities approach with respect to the marked inequalities in access to, and student success within, South African higher education. She argues for the importance of 'the relationship between the available resources and the ability of each student to convert these into valued capabilities and then make choices which will inform their actual functionings (outcomes)' that is key to understanding why some students are in a position to thrive in the higher education environment while others are not (Wilson-Strydom, 2015, p. 151). From this, she posits that it is possible to identify a list of core capabilities that underpin equitable participation, suggesting a list of seven; Harrison et al. (2018) add an eighth from their work with low-income students in the UK. The combined list is shown in Table 14.1.

The relevance of this list to the marginalised groups discussed in this book should be readily apparent to the reader. Space precludes a full articulation of the unfreedoms that individuals in these groups might experience when participating in higher education – or attempting to do so – so we will confine ourselves to a few brief illustrations:

- **Example 1:** the care-experienced students featured in Chapter 2 are identified as having issues with academic gaps due to their disrupted schooling (*Capability 2*) and concomitant issues with their confidence as a learner (*Capability 3*). Many have difficulties with their mental health arising from the childhood trauma (*Capability 6*) and may struggle to build strong bonds with others, potentially exacerbated by unstable housing (*Capability 4*).
- **Example 2:** the refugees in Germany in Chapter 7 have been thrust into a new country where their language skills may not be strong (*Capability 7*) and where they have a precarious status in terms of society and official bureaucracy (*Capability 4*). While their desire to learn is demonstrably high, they may have knowledge gaps due to their mobility or different pedagogic norms in their home country (*Capability 2*).
- **Example 3:** the Indigenous peoples in Chapters 10, 11 and 12 share many features in terms of their capabilities. They are subject to a long history of active discrimination from the state and wider society (*Capability 4*) that has, *inter alia*, led to economic marginalisation that makes access to the curriculum challenging, for example, in securing access to the internet (*Capability 8*). Many will also have to experience higher education through a language that is not their own as it is not the dominant language within their own country (*Capability 7*).
- **Example 4:** the legal circumstances of the parolee students discussed in Chapter 3 places constraints on their time and their freedom to use it for learning (*Capability 8*). It also limits their ability to participate in the social learning environment of the university (*Capability 4*) and singles them out as being different (*Capability 5*).

These examples are not intended to be exhaustive and nor are they intended to be read to apply to all members of the groups discussed. Nevertheless, the

Table 14.1 List of capabilities associated with flourishing in higher education

	Capability	Description
1	Practical reason	Being able to make well-reasoned, informed, critical, independent and reflective choices about post-school study and career options.
2	Knowledge and imagination	Having the academic grounding needed to be able to gain knowledge of chosen university subjects, and to develop methods of academic inquiry. Being able to use critical thinking and imagination to identify and comprehend multiple perspectives.
3	Learning disposition	Being able to have curiosity and a desire for learning. Having the learning skills required for university study. Having confidence in one's ability to learn. Being an active inquirer.
4	Social relations and social networks	Being able to participate in a group for learning, working with others to solve problems or tasks. Being able to form networks of friendships and belonging for learning support and leisure. Mutual trust.
5	Respect, dignity and recognition	Being able to have respect for oneself and for others as well as receiving respect from others, being treated with dignity, not being diminished or devalued because of one's gender, social class, religion or race. Valuing other languages, other religions and spiritual practices and human diversity. Being able to show empathy, compassion, fairness and generosity, listening to and considering other persons' points of view in dialogue and debate. Having a voice to participate effectively in learning.
6	Emotional health	Not being subject to anxiety or fear which diminishes learning. Having confidence in one's ability to learn.
7	Language competence and confidence	Being able to understand, read, write and speak confidently in the language of instruction.
8	Autonomous learning	Being able to access the formal curriculum through resources such as books, the internet and specialist equipment, and having sufficient time to do so. Being able to access co-curricular opportunities such as internships and placements.

Note: Adapted from Wilson-Strydom (2016) and Harrison et al. (2018).

lens of capabilities does demonstrate the multiple dimensions along which people experience marginalisation from higher education. Their agentic freedoms are compromised and the set of functionings available to them is smaller than for their more privileged peers in the same institution.

Where does this then leave us? Proponents of the capabilities approach contend that it is not only an analytical tool for identifying the way things *are*, but also a moral framework for defining the way things *should be*. Once one has identified the unfreedoms experienced by an individual or a group of which they are a member, the responsibility is on policymakers and/or practitioners to find ways to remove them. As we have seen in many of the chapters, there has been recent progress for some groups, albeit that success has generally been muted to date – which is why the groups remain marginalised.

We now turn to explore what the unfreedoms identified above tell us more generally about the macro social, economic and political forces through which marginalisation in higher education occurs. This is a stepping stone to better understanding the process of marginalisation itself and therefore offers clues as to how it might be mitigated or avoided through purposeful action.

Dimensions of marginalisation

In the previous section, we explored how the individual and sociocultural circumstances of members of marginalised communities can impact on their capability to engage successfully with higher education. In this next section, we look thematically at *the means* by which their functionings are constrained in an attempt to identify broader realities that can be the focus for systemic changes in policy and/or practice. In essence, our aim is to propose a broad framework for understanding how marginalisation in higher education occurs at the macro level.

Marginalisation by society
Active or tacit stigmatisation or discrimination within wider society

Marginalisation by systems
Dissonance with prevailing bureaucratic or technocratic systems

Marginalisation in time/space
Compromised ability to access traditionally configured learning times and spaces

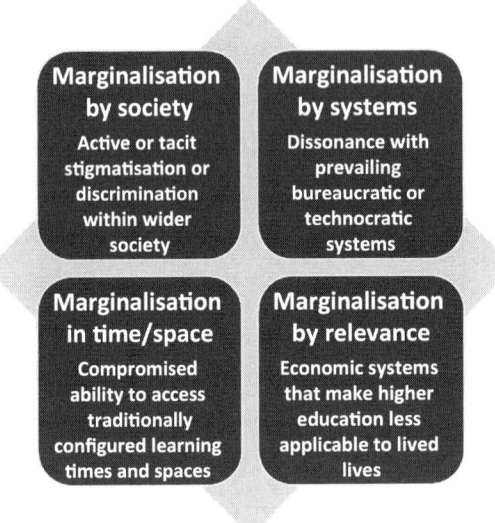

Marginalisation by relevance
Economic systems that make higher education less applicable to lived lives

Figure 14.1 The dimensions of marginalisation.

Based on the chapters in this book, we are proposing that there are four principal dimensions along which this occurs, summarised in Figure 14.1: *by society*, *by systems*, *by time/space* and *by relevance*. Importantly, these are interconnected in different ways and may amplify the marginalisation felt by students. We will briefly explore each of these in turn and suggest how they might assist policymakers and educators in reducing marginalisation within higher education.

Marginalisation by society

This form of marginalisation comes closest to that discussed in our introductory chapter where communities are forced to the edges of mainstream society by its purposeful actions or by the unintended consequences of sociopolitical decisions (Messiou, 2012; Mowat, 2015, Petrou et al., 2009). Historically, many of the communities explored in this book have been subject to deliberate discriminatory practices that have sought to exclude them from educational opportunities, including higher education. The processes by which this occurred are well-known: racist segregation laws, suppression of languages, forced movements, religious and social persecution and criminalisation of traditional lifestyles. Others have been excluded more invidiously through policies that have *de facto* had a similar effect through, for example, the underfunding of schooling in certain locations making progression to higher education effectively impossible. Fair access to education is, for example, one of the demands of the global Black Lives Matter movement, recognising that the very foundation of higher education in many countries is grounded in racism and/or the legacy of colonialism.

What the chapters in this book demonstrate is that the legacy of these practices – whether active or tacit, intended or unintended – remains potent for the affected communities. In many instances, these communities have moved in recent decades from being the subject of societal repression to having strong legal protections and benefiting from government aid programmes designed to support educational engagement (e.g. Chapters 8, 9, 11 and 13). However, as we have seen, actual improvements in access to higher education – in terms of absolute numbers or their likelihood of success – have been slow to materialise. This does not necessarily speak for a reluctance from these communities to take up the opportunities available, but that the building of trust and belonging within an alien institution takes both time and resolute efforts in the face of decades of discrimination and exclusion; programmes predicated on quick turnarounds are likely destined to fail.

Also represented in our chapters are communities that may have never been the subject of formal discrimination with respect to higher education, but who have been the victims of subtler forms of stigmatisation within society, on the basis of negative stereotyping, low expectations, religious intolerance and constructions of 'otherness', including care-experienced (Chapter 2), ex-prisoner (Chapter 3), trans (Chapter 5) and religious (Chapter 6) students. The marginalisation felt by these communities is often harder to counter, embedded as it is in individual and everyday microaggressions enacted by university authorities, educators and/or other students.

Institutions need to holistically consider how they ensure that they are welcoming spaces for communities whose historic experiences of (higher) education have been negative or non-existent. Clear, publicised and enacted equalities policies, targeted outreach and financial access programmes, visual recognitions of student and staff diversity, the provision of (real or virtual) 'safe' spaces, decolonised and culturally-responsive curricula and staff awareness training will all be part of the admixture to realise Gale and Mills' (2013) vision of creating welcoming campuses for marginalised communities.

Marginalisation by systems

A key feature of contemporary society has been the development of bureaucratic and technocratic systems designed to cope with complexity on a massive scale. Higher education has not been immune to this, for example, through the systems that are used to manage university admissions, eligibility for student support or the calculation of degree results. These systems, which are often little more than historical evolutions of happenstance or convenience, make a series of (often unwritten) assumptions and simplifications in order to allocate individuals into convenient boxes based on surface similarities that are important for the decisions that are to be made about them – e.g. applicants with equivalent qualifications.

Another facet of bureaucratic systems is that many were established explicitly to serve the needs of the majority – often to the detriment of others. Indeed, the concept of institutional racism is built on an acknowledgement that systems are rarely neutral in the ways in which they treat the people interacting with them (Law et al., 2004). Whether through deliberate design, an absence of transparency or independent oversight, the law of unintended consequences or implicit biases embedded in decision-making processes, bureaucratic systems are often implicated in the processes of marginalisation.

We have seen how communities can be marginalised by the tacit assumptions that systems within higher education make about students' identities or circumstances. This might be, for example, the assumption that students have ready access to the internet in order to complete forms (Chapter 10) or that their mental health allows them to engage with learning opportunities in the same way as other students (Chapters 2 and 4). This 'systems dissonance' sees them disadvantaged and needing to find workarounds or making repeated requests for special dispensations or consideration outside of the system. Aside from the time-consuming and stressful nature of fighting against an established system, it gives a message to the individual and their community that they are different, inconvenient and potentially unwanted. As we saw in Chapter 7, they can also find themselves caught between multiple bureaucratic systems that take time to adapt to new situations and that are rife with contradictions and inequalities.

Overcoming marginalisation by systems requires a root-and-branch rethink about how key higher education systems operate and particularly in laying bare the assumptions on which they are built. In most instances, these will be predicated on 'traditional' ideas about who students are – generally young, affluent, male, from the dominant sociocultural group, urban, without family commitments and so on. Vitally, those responsible for systems, whether national or institutional, need to actively engage with marginalised communities to understand *how* they experience the system and what steps are needed to remove the systems dissonances that serve to marginalise them (Mowat, 2015).

Marginalisation by time/space

Time enjoys a privileged role in most societies – through wages, it becomes a metric for measuring the contribution that an individual makes, while good timekeeping permeates the professional and personal expectations that we hold about each other. A failure to meet these expectations often sees individuals or communities stigmatised as unproductive, unreliable or disrespectful. Notionally, we all have the same amount of time at our disposal within a given day. However, in reality, our time is constrained in highly individual ways – many of us have much of our day hypothecated before we wake. For some, it might be caring duties, for others it might be time-consuming journeys, frequent medical or legal appointments or religious festivals. Necessary tasks will take some people longer than others, perhaps due to disability or poverty.

Higher education is a time-bound world (see Burke and Manathunga, 2020). Classes are tightly timetabled to maximise the number of students that can pass through buildings, assessments have inflexible deadlines (with punitive procedures for those that miss them) and the timed solo examination remains the norm in most disciplines. Meanwhile, the growth in teaching staff on short-term, part-time and otherwise precarious contracts in many countries means that their availability to students is heavily prescribed to certain time and days (Leathwood and Read, in press). Similarly, the idea of higher education as a physical community of scholars has its roots deep in history. The easy flow of ideas, the maintenance of the teacher-student bond and the accumulation of written texts are all features that have defined universities for centuries; the contemporary campus is simply the latest development of a longstanding idea of how higher learning should be organised.

In most forms of higher education, there is a tacit assumption that students should be physically present at specific times and in specific spaces – and that they have an equal opportunity to do so. This is, of course, not the case. As we have seen, there are many reasons why a student's time and ability to travel may be constrained and in different ways. Some will be generally time-poor due to other commitments (e.g. Chapter 4), while others will have specific times that are unavailable to them for learning or be subject to unpredictable events that impact on their ability to fit reliably into the expectations of higher education (e.g. Chapter 3). Others will be located far from campuses, requiring extensive travel (e.g. Chapter 13). In all of these cases, marginalisation can result as they are effectively excluded from the mainstream educational experience and potentially forced into situations where they fall foul of university expectations or regulations.

It is readily apparent that those undertaking higher education need to have sufficient time available to study and complete the required learning. However, is less clear *when and where* that time needs to be and the extent to which institutions are able to accommodate students constrained in time and space; as, for example, during the Covid-19 pandemic. Institutional flexibility around time has grown in recent years, with, for example, more use of technology-assisted asynchronous teaching (e.g. lecture video capture) and greater understanding around missed assessment deadlines – there is undoubtedly scope for more progress and for existing good practice to be disseminated (Mkwananzi and Mukwanbo, 2019). However, there is perhaps also an opportunity for a wider reconsideration of how time and space *work* within higher education and how it influences the flow of students' learning, especially for those at the margins (Finn and Holton, 2019).

Marginalisation by relevance

The final dimension of marginalisation that we are proposing, like the first, relates to the individual's connection with mainstream society – and hegemonic power within it. However, rather than relating to the sociopolitical environment, discrimination and stigmatisation, its focus is on the prevailing socioeconomic model and the role of higher education within it. This dimension is particularly relevant to those communities who continue to pursue traditional lifestyles and occupy economic niches that are simultaneously culturally important and distant from the mainstream of wider society – especially in its globalised form. Within the chapters in this book, there are examples of hunter-gatherer communities (Chapter 12), those concerned with migratory animal herding (Chapter 9) and those engaged in seasonal agriculture (Chapter 8).

The initial question is the extent to which individuals in these communities view higher education as relevant to their lives – not in terms of whether they will be accepted or supported, but whether it offers something that they have reason to value (in the broadest sense) in their socioeconomic context. For example, is the opportunity for personal emancipation and discovery through mainstream higher education culturally meaningful? Does it provide routes to personal advancement within the community or to increase the capability of the community as a whole, for example, by providing new access to legal, medical or business expertise? The answers to these questions are going to depend to a greater or lesser degree on the community's context, including its epistemic traditions, the prevailing labour markets, pressures from external factors (e.g. climate change or land right conflicts), the cost of study and so on. Indeed, for some individuals, the value of higher education may actually be in offering a route to leave the community by providing a bridge into wider society. As Jensen et al. (2016) note, questions about legitimacy were – and remain – key to post-colonial higher education in many African nations.

This is a difficult form of marginalisation for higher education institutions to address. Most of the chapters in this book are derived from nations with more-or-less free market sectors where the 'numbers game' of student recruitment is vital to their economic survival. This drives organisational behaviour where the courses offered have to have wide appeal in order to be viable and where it is a challenge to offer courses that may have specific appeal to marginalised communities. Even in those nations with greater government intervention or where higher education institutions have more room for manoeuvre, this particular circle will be difficult to square given the sociocultural sensitivities that need to be navigated and the existential risks that higher education potentially poses to some communities.

There are, nevertheless, things that can be done as stepping stones towards increasing the relevance of contemporary higher education to marginalised communities. One is to ensure that the curriculum 'offer' is likely to appeal. This might include purposeful co-construction with the community in question, for example, by focusing courses on the issues facing them (e.g. in engineering or law) or drawing on their cultural traditions as a field of study in its own right (e.g. in the arts). More generally, universities need to find innovative ways of valorising the ontologies, epistemologies and knowledges of those communities – the scope for this will inevitably vary between disciplines, especially for those where the curriculum is heavily prescribed by professional bodies.

Similarly, there is scope to rethink how and where teaching and learning is offered as an antidote to marginalisation (Gale and Mills, 2013). We have briefly explored issues of time and space in the previous section, but there is an additional opportunity to consider provision within the communities themselves. This has the practical impact of making participation simpler and less expensive, but with the additional symbolic meaning vested in higher education being physically *present* within the community it serves.

Conclusion

In conceiving this book, we set out to pull together some of the lesser-heard stories about participation in higher education from across the world – the sort of stories that generally get missed in the broader debates on social justice, equality and social mobility. We felt that students whose experiences were among the most unusual, challenging or even dysfunctional deserved to have the attention afforded by a book and so collected these twelve unique contributions, most of which are from researchers who are blazing a trail and opening up new research spaces.

We were – and remain – hopeful that these would be engaging and inspiring in and of themselves, but that they would also provide insight into wider questions about who is marginalised from higher education, why this occurs, which other groups might be worthy of research attention and what should be done about it. As for any authors or editors, we will leave this to the reader's judgement to decide whether we have been successful in our endeavours!

Our original organising principles of looking at *disadvantage*, *mobility* and *indigeneity* still remain valid, we believe, for thinking about the reasons why communities might be marginalised. In this chapter, we have also explored the insights afforded by Sen and Nussbaum's capabilities approach to social justice, drawing on the unfreedoms identified to suggest four dimensions of marginalisation: *by society, by systems, by time/space* and *by relevance*. These potentially contribute an alternative lens for considering the phenomenon and allowing us to draw parallels between otherwise disparate groups. None of this is new, in the sense that we have largely discussed what universities have, in some instances, been doing for decades. However, we are hopeful that this chapter will provide a binding principle to better understand *how* marginalisation works and what might be built into our higher education systems and institutional architectures in order to provide marginalised communities with the capability to engage fully in learning and flourish. We end with the rejoinder that getting it right for these groups at the fringes of what is generally considered to be the 'mainstream' student experience is likely to lead to improvements in provision for the wider student body too, by promoting openness, diversity and inclusion.

References

Balarin, M. (2011) Global citizenship and marginalisation: Contributions towards a political economy of global citizenship, *Globalisation, Societies and Education* 9(3–4): 355–366.

Burke, P.-J. & C. Manathunga (2020) The timescapes of teaching in Higher Education, *Teaching in Higher Education*, 25:6, 663–668

Finn, K. and M. Holton (2019) *Everyday mobile belonging: Theorising higher education student mobilities.* London: Bloomsbury.

Gale, T. and C. Mills (2013) Creating spaces in higher education for marginalised Australians: Principles for socially Inclusive pedagogies, *Enhancing Learning in the Social Sciences* 5(2): 7–19.

Harrison, N., S. Davies, R. Harris, and R. Waller (2018) Access, participation and capabilities: Theorising the contribution of university bursaries to students well-being flourishing and success, *Cambridge Journal of Education* 48(6): 677–695.

Jensen, S., H. Adriansen and L. Madsen (2016) Do 'African' universities exist? Setting the scene. In H. Adriansen, L. Madsen and S. Jensen (eds.) *Higher education and capacity building in Africa: The geography and power of knowledge under changing conditions* (pp.12–38). Abingdon: Routledge.

Law, I., D. Philips and L. Turney (2004) *Institutional racism in higher education.* Stoke-on-Trent: Trentham Books.

Leathwood, C. and B. Read (in press) Short-term, short-changed? A temporal perspective on the implications of academic casualisation for teaching in higher education, awaiting publication in *Teaching in Higher Education*.

Messiou, K. (2012) *Confronting marginalisation in education: A framework for promoting inclusion*. London: Routledge.

Mkwananzi, F. and P. Mukwanbo (2019) Widening participation in higher education for marginalised migrant youth through flexible teaching and learning mechanisms, *Widening Participation and Lifelong Learning* 21(2): 100–119.

Mowat, J. (2015) Towards a new conceptualisation of marginalisation, *European Educational Research Journal* 14(5): 454–476.

Nussbaum, M. (2000) *Women and human development: The capabilities approach*. Cambridge: Cambridge University Press.

Nussbaum, M. (2011) *Creating capabilities: The human development approach*. Cambridge: Harvard University Press.

Petrou, A., P. Angelides and J. Leigh (2009) Beyond the difference: From the margins to inclusion, *International Journal of Inclusive Education* 13(5): 439–448.

Sen, A. (1993) Capability and well-being, in M. Nussbaum & A. Sen (eds.) *The quality of life* (pp. 30–53). New York: Routledge.

Sen, A. (2001) *Development as freedom*. Oxford: Oxford University Press.

Sen, A. (2009) *The idea of justice*. Cambridge: Harvard University Press.

Williamson, B., R. Eynon and J. Potter (2020) Pandemic politics, pedagogies and practices: Digital technologies and distance education during the coronavirus emergency, *Learning, Media and Technology* 45(2): 107–114.

Wilson-Strydom, M. (2015) University access and theories of social justice: Contributions of the capabilities approach, *Higher Education* 69(1): 143–155.

Wilson-Strydom, M. (2016) A capabilities list for equitable transitions to university: A top-down and bottom-up approach. *Journal of Human Development and Capabilities* 17(2): 145–160.

Index

Page numbers in *italics* refer to figures; **bold** refer to tables; n refer to endnote.

Aboriginal Australians 9, 179–198, 234; first graduations 179; involvement in university leadership 181–182
Aboriginal Australians (collaborative approaches) 181, 187–190; cultural competency 188–190; Indigenous identity 190; indigenous workforce strategies and agreements 187–188; racial discrimination in workplace 187; successful innovations 188
Aboriginal Australians (provision of university support services) 181–186; Commonwealth funding programmes 182–183; contributions to HE research and evaluation projects 185–186; Indigenous student services 182–183; reconciliation 183–184; teaching, learning, research 184–185; university preparation programmes 186
Aboriginal Study Grants Scheme (1969–) 179
accommodation 17, 19, 26, 68, 113, 234; availability, appropriateness, security 27–29, 32; summer disruption 28; summer (parental-home assumption) 26; year-round 26
accountability 181–182
acculturation 7, 60, 210
Action Plan for Traveller Participation in HE 2019–21 (HEA, 2019) 132–133
Adult Dependants' Grant 48
advocacy 18, 25, 33, 73
affirmative action 188, 204, 208, 211; effectiveness (discussed) 221–222; India 216–230

age 38, 50, 60–61
agency 10, 52, 158–160, 170–172, 232–233, 235
Ainscow, M. 4
Alsop, R. 49
Alston, P. 204–205
American Psychological Association 65
Anderson, T. 100, 112
apartheid 157–158, 172n1, 172n2
applying to university 167–171
ASEAN 202, 213n1
assimilation 8, 144–145, 147
assimilationism 121, 129
asylum-seekers (Germany) 98–99, 108
Atheist Societies 86
Atherton, G. vii, viii, 1–10, 202–213, 232–242
austerity years (2008–) 123
Australia 99–100, 208, 210–211; constitutional referendum (1967) 179; improving HE access for Indigenous peoples 9, 179–198; racial discrimination in workplace 187; university strategic planning and Indigenous strategies 181–182; *see also* Australia
autonomous learning (capability) 234, **235**
Away From Base (AFB) programme 183

Bantustans 172n2
Barker, E. 80
Becker, S. 49
Behrendt Review 181–182, 184–186, 189, 194, 196–197
Berg, J. viii, 7, 97–114

Bertrand, M. 228
best practice vii, 19, 38, 186, 190
Bihar 225
Bilge, S. 50
Billson, J. 80
biographical narrative interviews 52
Black Lives Matter 237
Booth, T. 4
boundary positions (Luhmann) 102
Boyd, J. 87
Boyle, A. 130
brain drain 151, 212
British Social Attitudes annual survey 80
Brück, L. 100
Bruton, R. 133
Buddhism 80–81
Bumiputera 204, 208, 211
Bundesausbildungsförderungsgesetz (BAföG) 108, 115n1, 115n4
bursaries 19–20, 32, 51, 56–57, 133, 135n10, 168, 170
By Degrees project 17

Cameron, C. 32, 34
Canada 99–100, 112, 211
capabilities 7, 79, 81–85, 90–91, 232–236, 242; associated with flourishing in HE **235**
Carabez, R. 65
care: context (UK) 48–49; 'life-course' approach 50
Care Act (2014) 48
Care Experienced Governance Group (Scotland) 21
care-experienced students: academic challenges and adaptation 31–32; aftercare services (Scotland) 19–20; definition 15; demographic profile **22**; disability, mental health, emotional well-being 29–30, 32; discussion 32–33; England and Scotland 6, 15–35, 234, 237–238; financial support 25–27, 32; Harrison study (2017) 21–23, 34; housing 27–29, 32–33; intersectionality 32; O'Neill study (2019) 21–23, 35; parents themselves 28, 30, 33; pathways through care 16–17; pathways into HE 17–187; policy context (England) 18–19, 32; policy context (Scotland) 19–21, 32; support services and trusted individuals 24–25, 33; transitions (managed and unmanaged) 23–24, 32

Care Leaver Covenant 19
care leavers 15, 17–19, 32, 33n1
carers 4, 239; number (2011 UK census) 49; official UK definition (2018) 48–49
Carer's Allowance 48
Carers' Trust 49
care status (contact from university staff) 23–24
caring responsibilities, gendered expectations 60
Case, J. M. vii
caste system (India) 9, 216–230
Cathedrals Group of universities 81, **84**, 86, 91n3
censuses: (1981) 121; (2002) 120–121, 135n2; (2006) 120; (2011) 120, **125**, 128; (2016) 120, 126; (2021) 135n2; India (2011) 221; Ireland (1812) 120; UK (2011) 49, 79–80
Central Tribal University of Andhra Pradesh (Vizianagaram) 219
Charity Commission 88
Charles Darwin University (CDU) 182
Charles Sturt University 188
child abuse 6, 15, 17, 29, 32
children 148, 150
Children and Young People (Scotland) Act (2014) 19–21
Children and Young Persons Act (2008) 18
Chinese cultural context 64–65
Chinese Malaysians 9, 204, 208
Christianity 6–7, 69, 81, 89
church leaders 157, 167, 169
Clark, D. 82
codes of ethics 73
cognitive behavioural therapy 53
college experiences: collateral impact of post-prison supervision (US) 6, 36–45
Collins, P. 50
colonialism 1, 3, 237
Commission on Itinerancy report (GoI, 1963) 120–121, **122**, 128–129
Commission on Widening Access: *Blueprint for Fairness* (2016) 20, 34
Common European Framework 98
Commonwealth funding services 182–183
Commonwealth Government 182
Commonwealth Office of Learning and Teaching (OLT, Australia) 180, 190

Commonwealth Reconstruction Training Scheme 1
communication (Luhmann) 101–102
community corrections officers 37–38
community cultures (SA) 162–164
community sanctions 44; rationale 38
community support 157–158, 164, 167
compulsory schooling 8–9, 16, 119–120, 126–127, 130, 132, 162, 180, 211
computers 164, 168, 191
conditional programmes (Luhmann) 102
conflicts 102
Confucianism 6–7, 69
Connelly, G. viii, 6, 15–35
Constitution of India (1950) 216, 218; 103rd Constitutional Amendment Act (2019) 218
corporate parent 15, 33n1
Cotton, D. 18, 34
Council of Professional Conduct in Education (HK) 72
counselling 24, 65, 71, 73–74, 97, 109
Counter Terrorism and Security Act (2015) 87
Covid-19 pandemic 7, 196, 232, 239
Cultural Awareness Training (Australia) 189
cultural capital 158, 228
cultural competence 182, 184, 188–190, 195–196
curfew restrictions 38, 40, 42–44
curriculum 'offer' 241
Curtin University 184

Deutscher Akademischer Austauschdienst 99
development (inclusive) 216–218
disabilities 2, 23–24, 29–30, 32, 71, 71, 239
disabled parents 48
disadvantage 5–7, 13, 15–34, 36–45, 48–61, 64–74, 79–91, 242; care-experienced students (England and Scotland) 15–35; genderism and trans students (HK) 64–74; marginalisation of religious students (UK) 79–91; post-prison supervision (US) 36–45; student carers' narratives (UK) 48–61
disadvantaged groups (India) 9, 216–230, 239; access to education 218–220; economic status and exclusion of 225–227; English language and exclusion of 227; excluded from prestigious HE institutions 224; gender inequalities 222; massification of HE and 220–223, 230; privatisation of HE and exclusion of 224–225; programmes of study 223–224; share in HE enrolment 225, **226**; subjects studied at university (low priority in employment market, 2014) **224**; unemployment rates 228–229, **229**; unequal educational outcomes 228–230
discourses 101, 103–104, 111–112, 114; international students 113
discrimination 2–3, 5, 8–9, 67–70, 87–88, 202, 216, 218, 234, 237
distance discount (India) 225
distance learning 146, 150–151; *see also* online learning
diversification 106, 110–114
Driscoll, J. 18, 34
Dublin City University 132
Dugan, J. 68
Dyson, A. 4
dyspraxia 53

Economically Weaker Sections (India) 216, 218
economic status (India) 225–227
education: role in development 216–218
educational disruption 16–17–18, 31
education participation 36–37
Eleventh of September attacks (2001) 83, 87
elites 1–2, 124, 226–227, 230
Ellis, K. 32, 34
emotional health (capability) 234, **235**
emotional well-being 29–30, 33
employability 126, 197
employment 39–41–45, 146, 151, 159, 218; coaching for competitive examinations 219
employment progress 36–37
employment status 128
England 6; care-experienced students 6, 15–35; care experienced students (policy context) 18–19; further education colleges 21, 33n3; YiPPEE project 17–18
English Civic University movement 85
English language 227–228, 230

Enlightenment 85, 91
environment (of system) 101–102
Equality Act (UK, 2010) 88, 91n7
Equal Opportunities Commission (HK) 73
equity groups (Ireland) 126, 128, 135n6
Ergin, H. 100
estranged students 26, 34n5
ethnicity 2, 60, 203–204, 211–213
ethnic minorities 1, 68, **84–85**
European Convention on Human Rights 88
Evernote (app) 161
expectations 33, 101–103, 105–106, 109
experiences 81, 100, 104–105, 108–110, 113–114

fairness 40
family 4, 43, 150, 162–167, 169, 171, 195, 197
family face 69
Fataar, A. 158
fate control 151
federal financial assistance (US) 37
Federal Law for Support of Education (BAföG, Germany) 108, 115n1, 115n4
Federal Minister for Aboriginal HE 198n2
feminism 50, 71, 89
Ferry, M. 228
Feststellungsprüfung (assessment test) 98
figured worlds 159–160, 164, 171
Fillies, H. 158
financial circumstances 52–53–54, 56, 60–61, 108, 163–164, 171, 194–195
financial difficulties 6, 17, 30
financial management 25–27, 32
Finland: Sámi peoples' educational challenges in HE 139–151
Finnegan, F. viii, 7–8, 119
flexibility 102, 107, 112, 195–196
foetal alcohol syndrome 29
formal rural (category) 161, 172n2
foster care 15–16
Frawley, J. 183, 185
Fredericks, B. 181, 185–186
freedom of conscience 82, 88
freedom of expression 88
freedom of religion 88
freedom of thought 88

Freire, P. 51
friendship networks 30
functional differentiation (Luhmann) 102
functional limitations 50
functionings (Sen) 81–83, 90–91, 233, 235
Further and HE Act (UK, 1992) **85**
further education colleges 21, 33n3, 126

Gale, T. 4–5, 238
Garda Síochána 120
gender 2, 61
genderism: definition 64; trans students (HK) 6–7, 64–74
gender minority stress 67, 71–72
gender parity index (GPI) 222–223
geographical disadvantages 223
German Academic Exchange Service (DAAD) 99
German universities: first contacts for refugees 97, 103–104, 106–111, 113; international offices 97, 103, 105–110, 112
Germany: government policy 7; refugee students 4, 7, 97–118, 234; support systems 7; three forms of protection (for refugees) 98
Germany (Federal Ministry of Education and Research, BMBF) 99
GI Bill (US) 1
Giellagas Institute (2001–) 143
goal programmes (Luhmann) 102
Goldberg, A. 64, 68
Google 83, 161
Gorton Government 179
Graham, D. 87
Gröndahl, S. 142
gross enrolment ratios (GERs, India) 220, **221–222**, 225
Guest, M. 86
Gunstone, A. 184
Guttorm, J. 143

Halsey, J.: *Independent Review into Regional, Rural and Remote Education* (2018) 196
Harrison, N. vii, viii, 1–10, 15–35, 232–242
Hauari, H. 32, 34
health 204
healthcare students in caring roles 49

Henry, O. 228
higher degrees 39, 42
higher education access for Indigenous peoples (Australia) 9, 179–198; discussion 194–198; enablers and barriers 190–197; interviews 190–194; language issue 193–194, 196; perspectives from Indigenous students 190–192; source material 180; staff perspectives 192–194
Higher Education Authority (Ireland) 124, **125**, 126–127, 132, 135n7
higher education for refugees research 99–101
higher education (HE): disadvantaged groups (India) 9, 216–230; genderism and trans students (HK) 6–7, 64–74; Ireland 123–124; Irish Traveller community 7–8, 119–134; marginalised communities 1–10; new entrants (Ireland) **125**; refugees in Germany (overview) 98–99; Sámi peoples (Finland) 8, 139–151; technological barriers 8, 167–170, 172; widening access (21st century) 2
higher education (India): basic statistics 220, **220–221**; gross enrolment ratios (GERs) 220, **220–221**
higher education institutions (HEIs) 7, 19–20, 32–33, 79, 83, 126, 132–133
higher education organisations (HEOs) 97, 99–100, 103–104, 106–114, 115n3, 115n5; research projects 106, 115n3
higher education policies, towards Sámi peoples 143–144
Hill, D. 64, 67
Hirshberg, D. 151
Hirvonen, V. 142
Holland, D. 159–160
Holley, D. viii, 6, 48–61
Hollingworth, K. 32, 34
homelessness 41, 57
Hong Kong (HK) 3; cultural forces 69–70; genderism and trans students 6–7, 64–74
Hong Kong Hospital Authority 70
hostel accommodation 27, 68, 219, 222
Household Income Survey (HIS, Malaysia) 205
Huisman, J. vii
human capital 132, 151
human rights 66, 72, 204–205

Identity and Agency in Cultural Worlds (Holland et al., 1998) 159–160
Inari (traditional Sámi area) 144
Index of Censorship 88
India 211; disadvantaged groups and HE 9, 216–230; economic reforms (1990s) 224; inequalities, education and inclusive development 216–218; subjects studied at university (according to social group, 2014) **224**
Indian Institutes of Management (IIMs) 221, 224, 227
Indian Institutes of Technology (IITs) 221, 224, 227–228
Indian Malaysians 204
indigeneity 234, 242; disadvantaged groups (India) 216–230; Indigenous peoples (Australia) 179–198; Orang Asli (Malaysia) 202–213
Indigenous Advancement Strategy (Australia) 183
Indigenous Advisory Council 182
Indigenous Education Units (IEUs) 182–183, 189–190
Indigenous HE research projects 185–186
Indigenous knowledge 181, 184–185, 187, 189
Indigenous New Career Academics (INCAs) 188
Indigenous peoples (Australia) 9, 179–198
indigenous peoples, definition 139
Indigenous student services 182–183
Indigenous Student Success Programme (ISSP) 183, 195
Indigenous Tutorial Assistance Scheme (ITAS) 183, 195
Indigenous, usage 198n1
Indira Gandhi National Tribal University (Amarkantak) 219
individuals 4; marginalisation 159
inequalities 17–18, 48, 120, 216; barrier to inclusive development 216–218; India 216–218
Institute for Jewish Policy Research 87
institutes of technology (IoTs, Ireland) 123–124, 135n5
institutional racism 187, 238, 242
Integra programme (Germany) 99
Integration Courses (Germany) 98
integrationism 121, 129

internal differentiation (Luhmann) 102
internationalisation 97–114 *passim*, 115n3
internationalisation strategies 107
international students 106–109, 111–113, 115n5
internet access 7–8, 191, 232, 234, **235**, 238
internet cafés 168–169
intersectionality 2; narratives of care and HE 52–61; student carers 50–52
interviews 9, 38–39, 45n1, 45n2, 97–98, 103–105, 114, 115n2, 190; student carers 52–60
Ireland 3, 17; access and participation 124–126; financial crash (2008) 124, 130, 135n4; HE system 123–124; new entrants to HE **125**; Traveller community and HE 7–8, 119–134
Ireland, Department of Education 131
Ireland, Department of Education and Science (DES) 132, 135n8
Ireland, Department of Local Government 120, 135n3
Irish Traveller Movement 122
irritations 102–105, 109–111
Islam 7, 81, 83, 86–91 *passim*

Jackson, S. 17, 32, 35
Jadavpur University 227, 230
Jalvi, P. 143
James Cook University 190
Jawaharlal Nehru University 227, 230
Jensen, S. 241
Jews 80, 86–87
Johnston, C. 32, 34
Joint Entrance Examination (JEE) 224
Joyce, Sindy 134
Jyväskylä Teachers' College 143

Karnataka 225
Keller, R. 103
Kemijärvi Seminar (1950–1970) 144
Keskitalo, P. viii, 8, 139–151
key performance indicators (KPIs) 181
kindergartens 144, 146, 150
Klugman, S. 67–68
Kneale, P. 18, 34
knowledge and imagination (capability) 234, **235**
Kola Peninsula (Russian Federation) 139
Korell, S. 66

kwa-sing-bit (跨性別) (across gender boundaries) 66
Kwok, D. K. viii, 6–7
Kylmäkoski 143

labour market: Germany 99–100, 105–106, 112; India 224, 228–230, 240; Ireland 126
labour market income 158
Land Acts (SA, 1913, 1936) 172n2
language nests 142
language proficiency 7, 98–100, 108, 113, 234, **235**
Lapland College (1979–) 144
Larkin, S. viii, 9, 179–198
Latomaa, S. 141
Learning and Teaching Plans (Australia) 184
learning disposition (capability) 234, **235**
Leaving Certificate examination (Ireland) 127
Leibowitz, B. 158
Lenette, C. 100
Lesotho 160
Lewis, E. 18, 35
life expectancy 121, 204
Limerick, Mary Immaculate College 132
Lindgren, A.-R. 139, 141
local authorities 18–19, 24, 28–29, 32
London, religious hate crimes 81, 87, 91n2
Lorah, P. 66
low expectations 6, 237
low income 2, 48, 115n1, 212, 223, 226, 234
Loxley, A. viii, 7–8, 119–134
Lucas, L. viii, 8, 156–172
Luhmann, N. 101–103

Maila, P. 158, 164
Malays 9, 204
Malaysia: education versus poverty (2004–2014) **205**; ethnic identity 203–204, 211–212–213; HE system 207–208; Orang Asli and HE access 9, 202–213
Malaysia, Ministry of Education 209
Malaysian HE Blueprint (2015–2025) 209
Malaysian Higher School Certificate (STPM) 208, 213n2

Malish, C. 228
marginalisation vii, 159–160, 172, 217, 223, 234, 236–241; definition 4, 80; by relevance *236*, 240, 242; by society *236*, 237–238, 242; by systems *236*, 238–239, 242; by time and space *236*, 239–242
marginalisation concept 80–81
marginalisation processes 232–233
marginalised communities 1–10, 232–242; book purpose 10, 232, 241; book structure 5–9
Marginson, S. 1–2
Marine, S. 70
Masron, T. 203
Mathebula, M. 158
MAXQDA coding 104
meaning-making 232–242
media 100, 112, 142, 165–166
media of communication (Luhmann) 102
mental health 6, 16, 26, 28–30, 32, 49–50, 53, 61–73 *passim*, 234, 238
mentoring 167, 170–171, 188
Messiou, K. 3–4
Metropolitan Police Service 81, 91n2
Mgqwashu, E. 156
microaggressions 67, 237
middle class 1–2, 227
migration: Sámi peoples (Finland) 8, 139–151; studying 140
Mills, C. 4–5, 238
minority stress model 70
Mkwananzi, F. 4–5
mobility 7–8, 95–172, 242; refugee students (Germany) 7, 97–114; rural students (SA) 156–172; Sámi peoples (Finland) 139–151; Traveller community (Ireland) 119–134
modernisation 121, 143, 145
Moreton-Robinson, A. et al.: *On Stony Ground* (2011) 197
Mowat, J. 3–5, 81, 159
Muhuro, P. 162
Mukwanbo, P. 5
Murdoch University 188

Naidoo, K. viii, 8, 156–172
narrative interviews 6, 8, 52, 144–145
Nash, T. 18, 34
National Aboriginal and Torres Strait Islander Higher Education Consortium (NATSIHEC) 180–181, 184–185, 187–189, 197, 198n2
National Access Office (Ireland, 2003–) 132
National Centre for Cultural Competence (NCCC, 2014–) 189
National Centre for Student Equity in HE (NCSEHE) 185–186
National Federation of Atheist Student Societies (2009–) 86
National Indigenous Research Network 185
National Network for Education of Care Leavers (England) 21, 34
National Office for Equity and Access (Ireland) 126
National Plan for Equity of Access to HE 2015–19 (HEA, 2015) 133, 135n10, 135n11
National Sample Survey (NSS, India) 225, 227
National Tertiary Education Union (NTEU, Australia) 187
National Testing Services (India) 224
National Transgender Discrimination Survey (US) 68
National Union of Students 49, 87
National University of Ireland Galway 132, 135n9
National University of Ireland Maynooth 132, 134, 135n9
National University of Malaysia (UKM) 211
Neenan, J. 88
Negrito Orang Asli 202–203, *203*
New Economic Policy (Malaysia) 204, 208
Nicholas, C. 210
Nicolazzo, Z. 70
non-EU international students (Germany) 98
Nordic Council of Ministers 143
Northern Ireland **84–85**
Northern Territory 196
Norway 123, 139, 144
nursing 31
Nussbaum, M. 82–83, 232–233, 242; *New Religious Intolerance* (2012) 83

O'Donnell, V. 50
OECD 123–124
offender reform, indicators 36

Office for Fair Access (UK) 19, 33n2, 35
Office for National Statistics (UK) 49, 79
Office for Students 21, 33n2, 87
Office of UN High Commissioner for Human Rights (2019) 204–205
O'Neill, L. ix, 6, 15–35
online applications 168–169
online learning 193, 232; *see also* distance learning
Orang Asli: background 202–203; cultural distance 212; data deficiencies 209; diversity 203; education 206–207; enabling progression to HE 210–211; HE access 9, 202–213, 234; HE system 211–212; moving forward 212–213; parents 207; residential secondary schools 206; socio-economic life 204–205; special lanes 209, 212; subsistence lifestyle 9; three main groups 202, *203*
organisational semantics (systems theoretical analysis) 7, 97–114
organisational systems 101
Other Backward Classes (OBCs, India) 216, 218–219, 221, 223, 225–226, 228; unemployment rates (2014) **229**; women 222
otherness 147, 237
outreach 19, 21, 126, 132, 183, 197, 238

Palestine Societies 88
parental contribution assumption 26
parole 4, 6, 36, 39–40, 234
parole officers 40–45
pastoral care 191, 195
Pavee Point 119, 122, 130
peer-support networks 196
Perkins, Charles 179
personal relationships 16–17
Petrou, A. 3, 5
Petrov, A. 151
photodiaries 51, 54–55, 58–59
photo-elicited biographical narrative interviews 6, 52–60
physical health 50
police-citizen encounters 36–37
postcode lottery 19
post-prison supervision: collateral impact on college experiences (US) 6, 36–45, 234, 239; data and methods 38–40; discussion 40–45; inductive techniques 40; policy implications 43–44; selection bias (risk) 40; under community supervision and in college 37–38
post-traumatic stress disorder 16, 29–30
poverty 7, 82, 156, 158, 163, 204–205, 209, 217–218, 223, 239
poverty line 205
power differentials 160
practical reason (capability) **235**
previously advantaged 160, 172n1
previously disadvantaged 160, 172n1
Priego-Hernández, J. ix, 6, 48–61
prison officials 37
Private HE Institutions Act (Malaysia, 1996) 207–208
private HE institutions (India) 220
private-sector universities (Malaysia) 207–208, 211–212
probation sentences 39–40
procedural justice (concept) 36–37, 40, 44
professional bodies 241
Professional Counselling Association (HK), Code of Ethics 72
professionals 106, 112, 151
professional training 72–73
Programme for Access to HE (PATH, Ireland, 2017–) 133
Proto-Malay Orang Asli *203*, 203
psychological distress 108, 113
public spending 218
public transportation 115n5
public universities (Malaysia) 207–208, 211–212

qualitative data 26, 38, 144–145, 161, 186, 190
quality of life 81, 90, 150
quantitative research 22, 50
questionnaires 39–40
quotas: India 9, 211, 216–230; Orang Asli 211

Rabahi, M. 207
race 39, 71, 157
racial discrimination 60–61; in workplace 187
racism 8, 119, 184, 187, 196, 237–238
radio 164–166, 168
reconciliation 183–184

Reconciliation Action Plans (RAPs) 183–184
Reconciliation Australia (RA, 2001–) 183–184, 198n3
refugee students (Germany): additional differentiation 108; anticipated benefits of supporting 105–107, 111–112, 114; challenges and needs (different set) 108; expectations, experiences, anticipated outcomes 7, 97–114, 234, 238; formal classification as 'international students' (organisational consequences) 108; impact on discourse 113; methods 103–104; overview 98–99; public funding 110, 113–114; research on HE for refugees 99–101; research questions 104, 111; support structures 97–106 *passim*, 108–111, 114, 115n3; theoretical framework 101–103
refugee students (research findings) 104–114; insecurities and prospects 109–111; international students 106–109, 112–113; irritations and adjustments 109–111; organisational rationales 111–112; reasons for supporting refugee students 105–106
reindeer herding 8, 139–140, 145, 149, 240
Religion and Belief policies (HEIs) 79, 83–91, 91n7; institutional characteristics **84–85**
religious hate crimes 81, 83, 87, 91n2
religious intolerance 87, 91n6
religious students (UK) 3; capabilities approach 7, 79, 81–85, 90–91; definition 81; institutional characteristics **84–85**; marginalisation concept 80–81; marginalisation (UK) 7, 79–91, 233, 237; qualitative data 83; Religion and Belief policies 83–91, 91n7; Russell Group 85–90; terminology 79–81
religious studies 86
Report of Task Force on Travelling Community (GoI 1995) 120, **122**, 123, 129–131
follow-up reports (2000, 2005) 130–131
research (sensitive and ethical) 4
residence status 98, 108, 112

residential coaching academies (India) 219
residential facilities 15, 229
resilience 31, 34, 49, 66, 195
resistance 50
Resource Teachers for Travellers (Ireland) 130
respect, dignity, recognition (capability) 234, **235**
rights-based approaches 121
Right to Education Act (India, 2009) 218
Rigney, L. 185–186
Robertson, K. ix, 9, 179–198
Robeyns, I. 82
Ross, E. 158, 164
Runell, L. L. 6, 36–45
rural areas 9, 195, 205, 212, 218–219, 223; definition 161
rural elders 163
rurality: barrier to accessing HE 8, 156–157; inequities of access to HE 157–159; spatial and non-spatial 157–158, 161
rural students (research findings) 162–172; community cultures 162–164; experiences of applying to university 167–171; getting to know about university 164–167; transitions from rural contexts to university 162; value of HE 162–164
rural students (SA) 3, 8, 156–172, 234; challenging marginalisation 159–160; data deficiencies 158; discussion 170–172; figured worlds, transition, agency 159–160; limited access to broadband technology 164; methodology 160; qualitative data 161; research study 160–162
rural-urban migration 139, 141, 143, 158–159; issues that worried interviewees 147–148; reasons for 145–146
Russell Group **84–85**, 85–90

Sabharwal, N. 228
Safe Space Allies 71
safe spaces 191–193, 195, 238
Sámi diaspora 142, 148
Sámi migration (research findings) 145–151; children's bond to Sámihood 150; connection to Sámi culture and Sámi community 149–151; family

and relatives 150; further measures 150–151; issues that worried interviewees 147–148; life after relocation 148–149; plans to return 148; problems settling down 149; reasons for relocating 145–146; types of people who relocate 146–147
Sámi Parliament viii, 141
Sámi peoples 3; data deficiencies 139–140, 148; demography 139–141; HE and migration (Finland) 139–151; intersectionality 142, 144; language issues 139–150 *passim*; migration (background) 140–143; political action 145–146; research findings 145–151; research methods 144–145; Scandinavian HE policies 143–144; travelling 147
Sámi University of Applied Sciences (Norway) 144
Sanders, D. 139
Sápmi (area inhabited by Sámi) 139, 150
Scheduled Castes (SCs) 9, 216, 218–219, 223, 225–228; GERs (2011, 2019) 211, **221**; unemployment rates (2014) **229**; women 222
Scheduled Tribes (STs) 9, 216, 218–219, 223, 225–228; GERs (2011, 2019) 211, **221**; unemployment rates (2014) **229**; women 222
scholarships 183, 195, 222, 229
schooling 18, 131, 156, 188, 210–211, 237; disrupted 234; English as medium of instruction (India) 227; opportunity cost for disadvantaged groups 223
schools 4, 8, 66, 72, 99, 141–142, 192, 194, 206–207; India 219, 222, 229; Ireland 120, 127, 129–130, 133–134; SA 157, 161, 164–171 *passim*; UK 16–17, 19, 23, 31, 52–53, 56
Schweitzer, P. et al., *Arctic Human Development Report* (2014) 143
Scotland 6, **84–85**; care-experienced students 6, 15–35; care-experienced students (policy context) 19–21; further education colleges 33n3, 34n4; higher-education entrants with care experience (2013–18) **20**
Scottish Funding Council (SFC) 20, 35; national ambition for care-experienced students 21
Scottish Government data 17, 35

Sebba, J. 17, 35
secularism 7, 79, 91
secularity 85–86, 89–90
secular space (UK universities) 85–86
Seelman, K. 68
selective majors 228
self-censorship 88
self-descriptions 101, 103, 107, 112, 114
self-identity 160
semantics 101–114 *passim*
Sempik, J. 49
Sen, A.: capabilities approach 7, 79, 81–85, 232–233, 242
Senior Traveller Training Centres 130
Senoi Orang Asli 202–203, *203*
Shah, N. 203
Silver, Dame Ruth 20
Simler, K. 205
Sinn (generalised meaning) 102
Smith, J. ix, 9, 179–196
Smyth, E. 130
snowball sampling 144
social distancing (Covid-19 pandemic) 232
social exclusion 219
social justice 90, 124, 132
social marketing 190
social media 21
social mobility 60, 217–218
social partnership model 123
social relations and social networks 234, **235**
social responsibility 105–106, 112
social systems 101–103
Social Workers' Registration Board (HK) 72
society 101
Society for Research into HE vii
socioeconomic groups (SEGs) 2, 124, 127–128
socioeconomic model 240
solutions 10, 27, 121, 126, 159, 170, 198, 232, 241
South African General Household Survey (2017) 168
South African Statistics Agency 161
South Africa (SA) 3–5; democratisation (1994–) 158; rural students (getting to university) 8, 156–172
Southeast Asia 52, 56, 202, 211
Southern African Rurality in HE (SARiHE) project 156–157, 172

spatial marginalisation 218, 225
special education centres 167
spirituality 80
staff support 31
state governments: Australia 179; India 219
statistical tests 22
STEM subjects 223, 230n1
Stevenson, J. ix, 7, 79–91, 233
Stichweh, R. 102–103
stigma 6, 39, 66, 70, 73, 109, 112
stigmatisation 4–5, 30, 237, 239
Streitwieser, B. 100
stress 29–30, 58, 67–68, 147
structural differentiation 111
structures 81, 102–103, 110–111, 140, 181
strukturelle Kopplung (structural coupling) 103
student carers (UK) 6, 48–61, 238–239; context 48–49; discussion 60–61; intersectionality 48, 50–52; intersectionality (narratives of care and HE) 52–61; participatory study 51; policy recommendations 61; research methods 51–52; sampling strategy 51; theoretical underpinnings 50–51; transitions 50–51
student engagement 111
student motivation 193
students, care-experienced (England and Scotland) 6, 15–35
student services departments 21
Studienkollegs (preparatory colleges) 98
Suen, Y. T. 71
suicide 70–71
Sulla, V. 158
support networks 23, 34n5
support services 24–25; relational approach (importance) 25
support structures, refugee students (Germany) 97–114
surveillance 37–38, 40
Sweden 16, 139
Swinburne University 184
Syria 99–100
systems theory 7, 101–103, 111
Szymanski, D. 71

tacit assumptions 238–239
teachers 17, 33, 68, 130, 133, 143, 157, 162, 166–171 *passim*, 206, 220, 228

Teaching (OLT, Australia) 180
technological universities (Ireland) 124, 135n5
Telengana 225
television 164–166
Tenth Malaysian Plan (2011–2015) 209
Teranishi, R. 5
Testa, R. 67, 77
time 6, 41, 43
time and space 239–242
Timmis, S. ix, 8, 156–172
Torres Strait Islanders 9, 179–198; *see also* Aboriginal Australians
transgender students (HK) 3, 6–7, 64–74, 237; coming out process 66–67; cultural forces 69–70; definition 64; discussion 70–74; identity development, campus context and 66–67; language and terms 65–66; literature review 65–70; recommendations 72–73; stigma 66; transition 159–160; student carers 50–51
transparency 36, 44, 238
transphobia 72–73
trauma 108, 234
Traveller community (TC, Ireland) 3, 7–8, 119–134; access and participation 126–133; age profile 121; becoming visible 121–123; demographics 120–121; educational attainment (2002–2016) **128**; educational attainment versus settled community (2016) **129**; further research 134; HE access 130–133; inequalities 120–123; life expectancy 121; missing voices 134; policy imperatives 120–123; reports, policy documents, legislation, committees (1960–2019) **122**; school completion rates 127, 130, 135n8; state funding 131; state giveth and state taketh away 130; teacher guidelines (1994) 129; (2002) 131; trajectories and trends across education system 126–133; unemployment 121
Traveller Education Survey (DES, 2005) 127, 132
Traveller People Review Body (GoI, 1983) 120, 129
tribal area (category) 161, 172n2
tribal universities (India) 219
trickle-down effect 217

trust 41–42, 237
trusted individuals 25, 33
tuition fees 19, 108, 113, 115n5, 124
tutors 191–193, 195

Umeå University (Sweden) 144
unfreedoms (Sen) 82, 232–236, 242
unintended consequences 238
United Kingdom 4, 99, 113, 156, 160, 208, 233–234; expansion of HE participation 1; marginalisation of religious students 3, 7, 79–91; number of children in care 15; 'Prevent' strategy 87–88; student carers' narratives 6, 48–61
United Kingdom: Department for Education and Skills (DfES) 18, 34
United Kingdom: Department of Health and Social Care 48–49
United Kingdom, Department for Work and Pensions (DWP): *Family Resources Survey* (2019) 49
United Nations: UN Development Programme 3; UN Malaysia 206; UN Millennium Development Goals 205
United States 4–5, 71, 99, 208; post-prison supervision, collateral impact on college experiences 6, 36–45
universities: preparation programmes 186; rules and regulations 66
Universities and Colleges Admissions Service (UCAS) 49
Universities Australia 184, 189
Universities Scotland 20
Universiti Kebangsaan Malaysia (UKM National University of Malaysia) 211
Universiti Teknologi MARA (UiTM) 209
University College Dublin: *All Ireland Traveller Health Study* (2010) 120, **122**
University Grants Commission (UGC, India) 219
University of Adelaide: Indigenous Education Strategy (2012–2014) 185–186
University of Cambridge 85
University of Dublin (Trinity College) 123, 132

University of Helsinki 143
University of Hyderabad 227, 230
University of Lapland 144
University of Malaya (1949–) 207
University of Melbourne 179
University of Newcastle (Australia) 188
University of Oulu 143–144
University of Oxford 85
University of Saskatchewan 190
University of Sydney 179, 181, 189; Leadership Programme 188
urban areas 161, 205, 225

Varghese, N. V. ix, 9, 216–230
Visiting Teacher Service for Travellers (VTST) 130
Vlasova, T. 151

Wales **84–85**
Walker, M. 4–5, 90, 158
Walsh, J. 123
Wan, C. D. 207
Watson, D. et al.: *Social Portrait of Travellers in Ireland* (2017) 120, **122**, 128
Weir, M. 179
Welcome programme (Germany) 99, 111
widening participation and access 119, 124, 126, 134, 135n6; WPA action plans (2004–) 132
Willoughby, B. 64, 67
Wilson-Strydom, M. 233–234
women 1, 39, 45n1, 45n2, 81, 151, 219, 222, 227
women's seminar in Tornio (1921–1970) 144
working class 2, 158
workshops 161
World Bank 158, 205

xiao (filial piety) 69

YiPPEE project 17–18
yo-yo transitions 18
Yu, Y. 69

Zikhali, P. 158